DATE DUE

NEW ENGLAND INSTITUTE
OF TECHNOLOGY
LEARNING RESOURCES CENTER

SO-AIE-455

Studies in Emotion and Social Interaction

Paul Ekman
University of California, San Francisco

Klaus R. Scherer
Université de Genève and Justus-Liebig-Universität, Giessen

General Editors

Language and the politics of emotion

Studies in Emotion and Social Interaction

This series is jointly published by the Cambridge University Press and the Editions de la Maison des Sciences de l'Homme, as part of the joint publishing agreement established in 1977 between the Fondation de la Maison des Sciences de l'Homme and the Syndics of the Cambridge University Press.

Cette collection est publiée co-édition par Cambridge University Press et les Editions de la Maison des Sciences de l'Homme. Elle s'intègre dans le programme de co-édition établi en 1977 par la Fondation de la Maison des Sciences de l'Homme et les Syndics de Cambridge University Press.

Language and the politics of emotion

Edited by

Catherine A. Lutz
State University of New York at Binghamton

Lila Abu-Lughod
Princeton University

NEW ENGLAND INSTITUTE
OF TECHNOLOGY
LEARNING RESOURCES CENTER

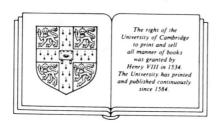

The right of the
University of Cambridge
to print and sell
all manner of books
was granted by
Henry VIII in 1534.
The University has printed
and published continuously
since 1584.

Cambridge University Press
Cambridge
New York   Port Chester   *Melbourne*   *Sydney*

Editions de la Maison des Sciences de l'Homme
Paris

Published by the Press Syndicate of the University of Cambridge
The Pitt Building, Trumpington Street, Cambridge CB2 1RP
40 West 20th Street, New York, NY 10011, USA
10 Stamford Road, Oakleigh, Melbourne 3166, Australia
and
Editions de la Maison des Sciences de l'Homme
54 Boulevard Raspail, 75270 Paris, Cedex 06

Library of Congress Cataloging-in-Publication Data

Language and the politics of emotion.

(Studies in emotion and social interaction)
"Grew out of a session of the 1987 Annual Meeting
of the American Anthropological Association called
'Emotion and Discourse' "—Pref.

1. Sociolinguistics.   2. Emotions.   3. Discourse
analysis.   I. Lutz, Catherine A.   II. Abu-Lughod, Lila.
III. Series.
P40.L284   1990   306.4'4   90-1374
ISBN 0-521-38204-1 hardback
ISBN 0-521-38868-6 paperback

British Library Cataloguing in Publication Data

Language and the politics of emotion.
— (Studies in emotion and social interaction)

1. Man. Social interactions. Role of emotions
I. Lutz, Catherine A.   II. Abu-Lughod, Lila   III. Series
302

ISBN 0-521-38204-1 hardback
ISBN 0-521-38868-6 paperback
ISBN 2-7351-0367-6 hardback France only
ISBN 2-7351-0368-4 paperback France only

Contents

Contributors

Lila Abu-Lughod
Departments of Religion and
   Anthropology
Princeton University
Princeton, NJ 08544

Arjun Appadurai
Department of Anthropology
University of Pennsylvania
Philadelphia, PA 19104

Donald Brenneis
Department of Anthropology
Pitzer College
Claremont, CA 91711

Judith T. Irvine
Department of Anthropology
Brandeis University
Waltham, MA 02254

Catherine A. Lutz
Department of Anthropology
State University of New York
Binghamton, NY 13901

Daniel V. Rosenberg
Department of Anthropology
Harvard University
Cambridge, MA 02138

Margaret Trawick
Department of Anthropology
Hobart and William Smith
   College
Geneva, NY 14456

Geoffrey M. White
Institute of Culture and
   Communication
East-West Center
1777 East-West Road
Honolulu, HI 96848

Preface

Out of anthropological fieldwork in India, Fiji, the United States, Egypt, Senegal, and the Solomon Islands, and out of close critical readings of earlier work in the anthropology of emotion, linguistics, and semiotics, the authors in this volume have explored the interplay of emotion talk and the politics of everyday social life. The contributors share a sense of the beauty and intricacies of conversation, as well as its involvement in power – whether the power to move others or the power that shapes discursive forms and the social relations in which they participate. They show the many ways discourse becomes emotional and emotion becomes discourse, and they treat narratives, conversation, performances, poetry, and song not as texts for cultural analysis but as social practices with serious effects. For this reason, we are happy to have the Cambridge series on emotion and social interaction as the home for this book. We would like to thank Paul Ekman and Klaus R. Scherer, the series editors, for their enthusiastic support for a project that is so wholeheartedly cross-cultural and suspicious of psychology's essentialisms.

We would like to thank a number of other people who helped bring this project to fruition. The anthropological study of emotion and discourse is an exciting and growing field; our work is enriched by being in conversation with that of many others who do not have essays in this volume. That is a matter of history. This particular book grew out of a session at the 1987 annual meeting of the American Anthropological Association called "Emotion and Discourse." We are grateful to Geoffrey M. White for helping to formulate the theme of the session and for soliciting many of the papers in connection with it. John Sabini and Fitz John Porter Poole contributed generously to the lively dialogue at the conference and to our thinking about the issues. Arjun Appadurai, Timothy Mitchell, Margaret Trawick, and Geoffrey M. White gave us helpful critical readings of the introductory chapter. Steven Feld and Stephen

Foster gave us invaluable suggestions for improving each of the chapters and the manuscript as a whole. Lila Abu-Lughod is grateful to the Institute for Advanced Study in Princeton and to the National Endowment for the Humanities for support to work on this project and for the extraordinary opportunity to participate in the Gender Seminar (1987–8), two of whose members, Donna Haraway and Judith Butler, provided clues for developing the arguments about discourse. For help with typing for the volume, we thank Lucille Allsen and Margaret Roe. We are grateful to Hugh M. Lewis for his careful and intelligent indexing. The publication process has been made pleasant and productive by Susan Milmoe, Helen Wheeler, Laura Dobbins, and Sophia Prybylski.

Our work on this book is for Jonathan and Lianna, and for Tim.

1. Introduction: emotion, discourse, and the politics of everyday life

LILA ABU-LUGHOD AND CATHERINE A. LUTZ

Emotions are one of those taken-for-granted objects of both specialized knowledge and everyday discourse now becoming part of the domain of anthropological inquiry. Although still primarily the preserve of philosophy and psychology within the academic disciplines, emotions are also ordinary concerns of a popular American cultural discourse whose relationship to such professional discourses is complex and only partially charted. Tied to tropes of interiority and granted ultimate facticity by being located in the natural body, emotions stubbornly retain their place, even in all but the most recent anthropological discussions, as the aspect of human experience least subject to control, least constructed or learned (hence most universal), least public, and therefore least amenable to sociocultural analysis. The essays in this collection seek to demonstrate, on the contrary, that the sociocultural analysis of emotion is both feasible and important and to suggest new ways of going about it.

In this introductory chapter, we begin by setting out four strategies that have been or could be used to develop the anthropology of emotion: essentializing, relativizing, historicizing, and contextualizing emotion discourse. We then consider the field of meanings and diverse deployments of the key term "discourse," without which, we argue, "emotion" cannot properly be understood. Paying special attention to the theoretical terms "discourse" is meant to replace, we argue that the most productive analytical approach to the cross-cultural study of emotion is to examine discourses on emotion and emotional discourses as social practices within diverse ethnographic contexts. Finally, we review the common themes and specific arguments of the essays in this collection, drawing out their contributions to a new approach to emotion, an approach distinguished by its focus on the constitution of emotion, and even the domain of emotion itself, in discourse or situated speech practices, by its construal of emotion as about social life rather than internal

1

states, and its exploration of the close involvement of emotion talk with issues of sociability and power – in short, with the politics of everyday life.

This book enters a dynamic and growing field of debate on questions about the relationship between the emotions, society, and cultural meaning.[1] Most anthropological works in this field prior to 1980 simply accepted psychological orthodoxy on emotions: Emotions are psychobiological processes that respond to cross-cultural environmental differences but retain a robust essence untouched by the social or cultural. The diverse approaches within the anthropology of emotions may have reflected the heterodoxies of psychology, insofar as there developed various Freudian approaches (e.g., Hiatt 1984), analyses based on learning theory (e.g., Robarchek 1979), and ethological and attachment perspectives (e.g., Lindholm 1982). But only recently has the *doxa* itself – that emotions are things internal, irrational, and natural – been exposed and questioned.

Much work done in the fields of psychiatric and psychological anthropology can be characterized as essentialist in its approach to emotion (even when other aspects of the person are viewed as more fundamentally social in origin or character). From early culture and personality work between World Wars I and II through much contemporary work in psychological anthropology, the amount and kinds of emotion that people experience are assumed to be predictable outcomes of universal psychobiological processes. A particular experience is assumed to stimulate identical emotions in all nonpathological humans, as when mothers are assumed to become attached to their newborns naturally and independently of social context (Scheper-Hughes 1985). In some of this work, for example, it is taken for granted that individuals have a limited and/or necessary amount of affection or love to distribute across persons to whom they become attached; hence the not infrequent concern with the effect on a child of having multiple caretakers, and the question of whether such children have less intense feelings for the mother and/or for other adults. In a related vein, Lindholm (1982) has argued that Swat Pukhtun (Pakistan) social organization promotes fragmented and agonistic social relations, thwarting the need for love in most contexts, but particularly in adult males. The result is that the institution of friendship must bear, virtually alone, the heavy burden of fulfilling that need; because love cannot be expressed in other arenas, friendships become intense and voracious.

Elsewhere (e.g., Hiatt 1984, Scheff 1977), emotions are viewed as "things" with which social systems must "deal" in a functional sense. Ritual frequently has been seen as a device that allows for the expression of preexisting emotions that would create problems if not expressed. Adolescent initiation ceremonies, for example, are presented as means for containing the affective turbulence of young boys. In a somewhat different vein, emotions are sometimes treated as psychic "energies" implicitly marshaled in the service of constructing a social order. Spiro (1965) presents a version of this view when he argues that the emotional conflicts of Burmese men, which include, in his view, their homosexual feelings, are channeled into and defused by entrance into the monkhood.

The strategy of essentializing emotions has several unfortunate consequences. First, if feelings are considered the essence of emotion, then the most reliable way to explore emotions would be through introspective reports. This approach deflects attention from social life and its possible implication in the very language of emotion. It also prevents us from looking at the role of emotional discourses in social interactions. Second, it reinforces the assumption of universality in the forms of distinct emotions (e.g., shame and guilt are each central and separate feelings), in their meaning (e.g., anger in one culture feels/means the same as anger in another), and in emotional processes (e.g., emotions are primarily intrapsychic and subject to masking, repression, and channeling). Finally, hand in hand with essentialism goes a strange invisibility of emotion itself as a problem, since positing emotion universals allows us more easily to take emotion for granted.

For those both committed to some sort of cross-cultural analysis and suspicious of the certainties and unexamined cultural assumptions about that which we most take for granted, three alternative strategies of questioning appear to be fruitful. The first strategy is to do what anthropologists have always to some extent done: to bring into question the certainty and universality of ways we think about and talk about things such as emotions by investigating whether it is so elsewhere.[2] A good deal of (often implicitly) comparative work exists, from the fertile early work by H. Geertz (1959) on the vocabulary of emotion in Java, by C. Geertz (1973) on the person in Bali, and by Briggs (1970) on Utku emotion expression, to Levy's (1973) explication of Tahitian ideas and silences on the subject of emotion.

The most important recent examples of the relativizing strategy are found in the seminal work of Myers (1979, 1986) and Rosaldo (1980).

Unlike much of the earlier ethnopsychological work on emotion, their interpretive approach to emotions stresses not what culturally variable ideas about emotion can tell us about other "deeper" psychological processes, but rather what implications these ideas have for social behavior and social relations. These analysts helped place emotions squarely in the realm of culture by pointing to the ways local cultural concepts of emotion such as the Ilongot *liget* (anger) and the Pintupi *ngaltu* (compassion) borrow from broader cultural themes and reflect, in their ideological shape, the forms of indigenous social relationships. If these works did not always or consistently deessentialize emotions (see Rosenberg, this volume), they certainly began the important process of suspending concern with the psychological paradigm. For both, furthermore, differences observed in talk about emotion had to be traced to social structure rather than to a pure realm of autonomous ideology.

While some of the work of relativizing has been done by examining specific concepts of emotion used in different cultures, many studies of emotion even show how fragile the category itself is. For example, Howell (1981) argues that for the Chewong (Malaysia), what we call "affect" is seen as a minor phenomenon; talk about emotion is replaced by talk about normative rules that provide, she argues, "an idiom for . . . organizing the individual's relationship to himself, to his fellow[s] . . . , and to nature and supernature" (142). Obeyesekere (1985) shows that in Sri Lanka emotion is likely to be taken as a sign of Buddhist religious prescription achieved or unachieved. For the Ifaluk (Micronesia), emotion is often construed as moral judgment and has a similar pragmatic force (Lutz 1988).

In Riesman's work on the Fulani of West Africa, a subtle transition from the analysis of particular emotion concepts and their role in social relations to the questioning of the very cultural meaning and social structural effects of emotionality itself illustrates the direction we think the anthropology of emotion ought to take. In his earlier work, Riesman (1977) was especially concerned to lay out the dimensions of Fulani notions of *pulaaku* (translated as 'Fulaniness' but something others might have called 'honor') and *semteende*, or 'shame'. In his later work (1983), he began to make a suggestive argument linking social hierarchy to emotionality itself (see also Irvine, this volume), arguing that self-control or relative lack of emotional expressiveness is simultaneously taken as a badge of, justification for, and realization of the social superiority of nobles over their ex-slaves. If the meaning of emotionality differs cross-culturally and the applications to social organization of emotional practice are variable, then any certainties about universals are undermined.

A second strategy for those interested in emotions as sociocultural phenomena is to historicize them. That means subjecting discourses on emotion, subjectivity, and the self to scrutiny over time, looking at them in particular social locations and historical moments, and seeing whether and how they have changed. Although a host of potential studies remain to be done, a few works have attempted this sort of investigation. Some have been concerned with the history of formal and informal theories of emotions in the West, and others have examined the fate of particular emotions (Cancian 1987; Gardiner, Metcalf, and Beebe-Center 1970; MacFarlane 1987; Stearns and Stearns 1986). Norbert Elias (1978) has argued, mostly from a reading of etiquette manuals, that vast transformations of affective life in Europe took place concomitant with the development of the absolutist state. Among these he includes an expansion of the contexts in which disgust occurs and a diminution of aggressive affect or behavior. That he calls this the "civilizing process" is symptomatic of his uncritical interpretation of these changes as involving a refinement of a somehow preexisting affectivity, a position that many anthropologists would regard with skepticism. Still, his work opens up an argument about the kinds of changes that have taken place in one geographical, historical setting.

Other scholars have examined these changes in terms of the disappearance of or shift in the social locus of various emotions, as well as the manipulation of emotional discourses for state purposes. The problem of sadness has received an impressive number of historical treatments. Jackson (1985), like Harré and Finlay-Jones (1986), takes on the focused task of tracing the extinction of an emotion called "accidie" and the significance of the obsolescence of "melancholy," both so important during medieval times, in the contemporary period. Sontag (1977) argues that the nineteenth-century Romantic movement came to celebrate individuality in part by viewing sadness as a mark of refinement, as a quality that made the person suffering from it "interesting." The rise of individualism brought with it the celebration of difference; one of the routes by which the new individuals could distinguish themselves was through a focus on feelings defined as aspects of unique personalities. Radden (1987) takes these views further by noting that melancholy was primarily a male complaint, one that was at least in part socially valor-ized. She argues that the related modern discourse on depression differs in pinpointing women as its bearers and in portraying the syndrome as more unequivocally deviant, deficient, and medical in nature.[3] In a different vein and in a non-Western setting, Good and Good (1988) explore the ways in which the Islamic Republic of Iran now organizes, to an unprecedented degree, both public and private emotional discourses. It has transformed the public discourse of sadness and grief, which before the revolution was central to religious ritual, self-definition, and social understanding, into a sign of political loyalty to the state.

What might be most productive, however, would be to begin by tracing the genealogy of "emotion" itself so that, in an enterprise analogous to Foucault's (1978) critical investigation of the production of "sexuality" in the modern age, we might consider how emotions came to be constituted in their current form, as physiological forces, located within individuals, that bolster our sense of uniqueness and are taken to provide access to some kind of inner truth about the self (Abu-Lughod, this volume; Lutz 1986). One promising line of questioning might be to build on Foucault's insights about the growing importance of confession (to which a discourse of emotion is often bound both inside and outside psychotherapy) as a locus of social control and discourse production in the eighteenth and nineteenth centuries.

Foucault's description of his own project suggests more directly how emotion discourse might represent a privileged site of the production of the modern self. He writes, in the second volume of *The History of Sexuality*, that he wishes "to analyze the practices by which individuals were led to focus their attention on themselves, to decipher, recognize, and acknowledge themselves as subjects of desire, bringing into play between themselves and themselves a certain relationship that allows them to discover, in desire, the truth of their being" (Foucault 1985:5–6).[4] He also notes that in each historical period it is "not always the same part of ourselves, or of our behavior, [that] is relevant for ethical judgment," but in contemporary Western society, "the main field of morality, the part of ourselves which is most relevant for morality, is our feelings" (1983:238). Feelings can play this role because they are currently constituted as the core of the self, the seat of our individuality.[5]

The third strategy is to focus on social discourse, building less on anthropology's comparative bent or the broad historical framing of the problem than on a commitment to careful analysis of the richness of specific social situations, whether here or there, as Geertz (1987) puts it.

It is a strategy followed by the authors of the chapters in this volume, all of whom share a concern with emotion and begin with the assumption that it is a sociocultural construct. They go on to explore, through close attention to ethnographic cases, the many ways emotion gets its meaning and force from its location and performance in the public realm of discourse. They also ask how social life is affected by emotion discourse. To assess the nature and value of this strategy first requires attention to the term at its center: the word "discourse."

"Discourse" has become, in recent years, one of the most popular and least defined terms in the vocabulary of Anglo-American academics. It pervades the humanities and now haunts many of the social sciences. Rather than being alarmed by its spread, however, it might be better to ask why so many have adopted it. The best way to pursue that question is to consider what theoretical work they want the term to do.

As everyone readily admits, defining discourse precisely is impossible because of the wide variety of ways it is used. To get a sense of why people use it, and why we have found it useful in thinking about emotion, it might be helpful to consider what terms it replaces. What is discourse not? To what is discourse counterposed? This varies by discipline, but we will be concerned only with anthropology because its peculiar appropriation of the term from the French poststructuralist vocabulary is inflected by the prior and concurrent usage of the term by anthropological linguists.

First, particularly for those whose concerns are linguistic, the term discourse marks an approach to language as spoken and used rather than as a static code analyzable apart from social practice. In Saussure's *langue/parole* distinction, discourse would fall on the side of *parole*. What those who invoke discourse in this context might want to add, however, is that *langue* either does not exist (e.g., Hopper 1987) or at least is always embodied in particular utterances by particular individuals. In privileging speech, those who use the term discourse generally also want to assert the importance of pragmatics versus semantics. The "code," whether it be grammar, structure, model, or, in this case, some purported underlying presocial emotional matrix, is taken as emergent in a social context, even if it is not analyzed as a peculiar Western cultural construct.

Although in some senses associated with speech, discourse is also commonly used instead to suggest a concern with verbal productions more formal, elaborate, or artistic than everyday conversation. Examples of classic forms of discourse in this sense are poems, songs, laments, prayers, myths, and verbal dueling forms such as sounding (Labov 1972). Discourse is also used by some who identify with postmodernism in its literary incarnation to stress the spoken quality of language (Tedlock 1983, 1987) and to evoke its dialogic aspect, allegedly ignored by those of us who live in literate societies. Yet others use the term discourse as a way of including even the nonverbal, like music, crying, or the "unsaid" of past utterances and present unarticulated imagination (Tyler 1978) in our consideration of the meanings humans make.

Sherzer's (1987) recent article advocating a discourse-centered approach to language and culture demonstrates the wide range of uses and resulting ambiguity of the term. Blending many of these senses of discourse together in his "purposely vague" definition, he writes that discourse is

> a level or component of language use . . . [which] can be oral or written and can be approached in textual or sociocultural and social-interactional terms. And it can be brief like a greeting and thus smaller than a single sentence or lengthy like a novel or narration of personal experience and thus larger than a sentence and constructed out of sentences or sentence-like utterances. . . . Discourse is an elusive area, an imprecise and constantly emerging and emergent interface between language and culture, created by actual instances of language in use. (296)

The unfortunate vagueness of this definition is the product of a failure to grasp that terms are used to signal perspectives and to carve out academic domains, not just to refer to definable entities. The kinds of usages we have described thus far for the increasingly employed term discourse could be characterized as largely sociolinguistic or literary. All that is being keyed is an interest in language in context, texts, and the public and social character of what we study. And for the most part, the term as used in this volume stays well within this range of meanings.

Hovering around the edges of many of the chapters and informing the project of the volume as a whole is another way of using discourse, one with more ambitious theoretical goals and different disciplinary roots. Discourse in this other sense is a word that has been taken up by those who find the critique of social theory associated with French poststructuralists like Michel Foucault persuasive, or at least those who have begun to borrow its vocabulary. With this move, the semantic field and pragmatic deployment of the term have begun to shift.

Although only beginning to find its way into anthropological writing, discourse in this much wider Foucaultian sense is being adopted to do the theoretical work of refiguring two terms that it replaces: culture and ideology. For many, the no less definable term "culture" has become problematic for several reasons. First, built into it is a distinction between a realm of ideas, even if public rather than in people's heads, and material realities and social practices, a distinction some users of discourse would like to problematize. Second, the term seems to connote a certain coherence, uniformity, and timelessness in the meaning systems of a given group, and to operate rather like the earlier concept of "race" in identifying fundamentally different, essentialized, and homogeneous social units (as when we speak about "a culture"). Because of these associations, invoking culture tends to divert us from looking for contests for meaning and at rhetoric and power, contradictions, and multiple discourses, or what some now refer to as "heteroglossia" (see Irvine, this volume).[6] It also falsely fixes the boundaries between groups in an absolute and artificial way.[7]

"Ideology" too has come to carry with it meanings that some social theorists want to shed. The Marxist alternative to culture, it has the virtues of seeming less unifying than culture. It can be pluralized even within one society, and is always linked to historically specific social groups assumed from the start to be engaged in struggles of domination and resistance. However, it retains, perhaps even more strongly than the notion of culture, the radical distinction between a realm of ideas and a material or social reality because of its historical association with a distinction between base and superstructure.[8] And even more problematically, it sets up an implicit opposition between itself, denoting a mystifying or at least motivated and interested vision of the world, and some sort of uninterested, unmotivated, and objective truth available either to a class or, perhaps more commonly, to the critical social scientist. Foucault uses discourse to suggest his rejection of these dualisms that are easily and sometimes unconsciously evoked by the notion of ideology.[9]

Although the chapters in this volume do not explore many of the implications of Foucault's work, they do remain faithful to his premise that "discourses . . . [are] . . . practices that systematically form the objects of which they speak" (Foucault 1972:49). For the final work discourse is meant to do, as social theory, is to suggest a concern not so much with meaning as with a kind of large-scale pragmatics. Taking texts and talk and all sorts of other social practices as productive of experience and constitutive of the realities in which we live and the truths with which we work, this approach also considers how power might produce discourses as well.[10] In suggesting that we attend to the efficacy of discourse, this newer and wider usage still resembles the more limited sociolinguistic uses outlined earlier. Yet it goes further by looking at more than speech, by recognizing the local, contradictory, and fragmented character of discourses, and by insisting that discourses be understood in relation not just to social life but to power.

Thus, although each of the authors in this volume uses discourse differently, the term, resonating with its many current uses, stands as a token of our common wariness of mentalist models, our refusal to treat language as simply reflecting thought or experience, and our insistence that all those productions in a community that could be considered cultural or ideological be analyzed as social practices, tied to relations of power as well as to sociability.

The chapters in this collection takes discourse, often as the situated social practices of people speaking, singing, orating, or writing to and about each other, as a point of entry for the study of emotion. They address one or both of two issues: the discourse *on* emotions – scientific or everyday, Western or non-Western – and emotional discourses, that is, discourses that seem to have some affective content or effect. Differing in the extent to which they bring the category of emotion itself into question and in the degree to which they speak as if emotions are internal things or not (and whether it even matters), the authors also differ in the aspects and forms of language they explore. Nevertheless, they all approach emotion through language and understand language as inescapably and fundamentally social.

The turn here to discourse is a turn to detailed, empirical studies of conversation, poetics, rhetoric, and argument about and with emotional content. Building on the work of others who have explored facets of emotion in performance and language (Basso 1985; Brenneis 1987; Crapanzano 1989; Feld 1983; Good, Good, and Fischer 1988; Irvine 1982; Ochs and Schieffelin 1989; Sabini and Silver 1987 and 1988; B. Schieffelin and Ochs 1986; E. Schieffelin 1976; Urban 1988; White and Kirkpatrick 1985), we argue for a view of emotion as discursive practice. What advantages does this have for our understanding of emotion? What can those interested in emotion learn from considering its relation to discourse?

In contrast to other approaches, the emphasis on discourse in studying emotion keeps us fixed on the fact that emotions are phenomena that can be seen in social interaction, much of which is verbal. As the sociolinguist Gumperz has also said of discourse studies, "mere talk to produce sentences . . . does not by itself constitute communication. Only when a move has elicited a response can we say communication is taking place" (1982:1). Attention to discourse leads us therefore to study new problems, such as how an audience's response to emotional performances can be unpredictable given the former's ability to attend to only some parts of the performance and to make idiosyncratic sense of those parts. Attention to discourse also leads us to a more complex view of the multiple, shifting, and contested meanings possible in emotional utterances and interchanges, and from there to a less monolithic concept of emotion. The focus on discourse allows not only for insight into how emotion, like the discourse in which it participates, is informed by cultural themes and values, but also how it serves as an operator in a contentious field of social activity, how it affects a social field, and how it can serve as an idiom for communicating, not even necessarily about feelings but about such diverse matters as social conflict (White, this volume), gender roles (Lutz, this volume), or the nature of the ideal or deviant person (Fajans 1985).

The study of emotion as discourse allows us to explore how speech provides the means by which local views of emotion have their effects and take their significance. If earlier scholars who rejected the notion that emotion was sensation preferred the notion of emotion as judgment (Solomon 1976), their view has since been supplemented by the insight that judgments might better be viewed as socially contested evaluations of the world phrased in an emotional idiom and evident in everyday speech behavior. Rather than seeing them as expressive vehicles, we must understand emotional discourses as pragmatic acts and communicative performances. The more general interest in the social sciences in how language implements social reality coincides with the interest in how emotions are sociocultural facts. If emotions are social phenomena, discourse is crucial to understanding how they are so constituted.

The most important theme running through the chapters is that emotion and discourse should not be treated as separate variables, the one pertaining to the private world of individual consciousness and the other to the public social world. Taking seriously Wittgenstein's (1966) insights about the relationship between emotion and language, articulated first in his description of what kind of "language-game" talk of joy and anger is, we argue that emotion talk must be interpreted as *in* and *about* social life rather than as veridically referential to some internal state.

Emotion should not be viewed, as our quotidian perspective might suggest, as a substance carried by the vehicle of discourse, expressed by means of discourse, or "squeezed through," and thereby perhaps distorted in, the shapes of language or speech. Rather, we should view emotional discourse as a form of social action that creates effects in the world, effects that are read in a culturally informed way by the audience for emotion talk. Emotion can be said to be *created in,* rather than shaped by, speech in the sense that it is postulated as an entity in language where its meaning to social actors is also elaborated. To say this is not to reduce the concept of emotion to the concept of speech, even though a discourse-centered approach might be construed as a rejection or obscuring of the body.

Although in this volume we focus on emotion as discourse, working to pry emotion loose from psychobiology, that does not mean that we do not recognize the possibility that emotions are also framed in most contexts as experiences that involve the whole person, including the body (see Appadurai, this volume). Here Bourdieu's thoughts on "body hexis" are suggestive, providing ways of thinking about the fact that emotion is embodied without being forced to concede that it must be "natural" and not shaped by social interaction. He defines body hexis as a set of body techniques or postures that are learned habits or deeply ingrained dispositions that both reflect and reproduce the social relations that surround and constitute them. The child, for instance, learns these habits by reading, via the body rather than the mind's eye, the cultural texts of spaces and of other bodies (Bourdieu 1977:90).

Extending this definition to the emotions enables us to grasp how they, as cultural products, are reproduced in individuals in the form of embodied experience. To learn how, when, where, and by whom emotions ought to be enacted is to learn a set of body techniques including facial expressions, postures, and gestures. For example, rather than thinking or speaking the respect (*gabarog*) that helps reproduce a gender hierarchy on Ifaluk atoll in Micronesia, girls follow the curve of their mothers' backs in embodying the bent-over posture of respect. Similarly, emotions such as love or friendship that are thought to emanate from ineffable positive feelings between two people might be cued, Bourdieu notes (1977:82), by a sensed similarity of body hexis produced by being reared under similar physical and social conditions. We might eventually develop an analysis of the kinds of bodily discourse on emotion that includes emotional postures that are simultaneously (1) phenomenologically experienced, (2) vehicles for symbolizing and affecting social relations (e.g., when angry glaring represents the imposition of moral obligation), and (3) practices that reveal the effects of power (as in gestures of respect and shame in many cultures).[11]

The move to ensure that emotions remain embodied, however, should be seen as more than an attempt to position them in the human body. Embodying the emotions also involves theoretically situating them in the social body such that one can examine how emotional discourses are formed by and in the shapes of the ecologies and political economies in which they arise.

Emotion can be studied as embodied discourse only after its social and cultural – its discursive – character has been fully accepted. To take language as more than a transparent medium for the communication of inner thoughts or experience, and to view speech as something essentially bound up with local power relations that is capable of socially constructing and contesting realities, even subjectivity, is not to deny non-linguistic "realities." It is simply to assert that things that are social, political, historically contingent, emergent, or constructed are both real and can have force in the world.

This volume goes a long way toward establishing the pragmatic force of emotion discourse and the social character of emotion by showing how centrally bound up discourses on emotion (local theories about emotions) and emotional discourses (situated deployments of emotional linguistic forms) tend to be with social issues. Because we think that it will be more theoretically productive, we have made central, in organizing this volume, questions about the ways emotion discourse can be related to the social. We have not been particularly concerned with cross-cultural differences or regional/cultural issues, although nearly all the chapters make sensitive contributions to the ethnography of societies in India, Fiji, the Solomon Islands, Egypt, Senegal, and the United States. Also, despite their intrinsic interest, we have not stressed the *types* of discourse subjected to analysis because of a link with the emotional. The range, however, is impressive. The chapters analyze poetry, song, and other aesthetic performances, narratives, actual conversations, interviews, regulated modalities of verbal interaction, linguistic registers, and scientific discourse.

Two aspects of social relations emerge as crucially tied to emotion discourse: sociability and power relations. The links to sociability can be seen in the salience of emotion language in settings where solidarity is being encouraged, challenged, or negotiated, or in the essentially interactional nature of discourse as it engages performers or speakers and audiences or interlocutors. Fajans (1985) had earlier shown that the core of Baining (New Britain) emotional discourse was concerned with threats to social cohesion; a central emotion term, translated as "hunger," was used to talk about the importance of ties to others and their mediation through food exchange. In this volume, the chapters by White and Brenneis describe ethnographic contexts in which a relatively formalized emotional discourse is used to promote social harmony. The A'ara practice a quasi-therapeutic discussion to talk about and contain recent social conflicts that threaten a valued community or kin group sociability, and Indian Fijians enact performances whose emotional gestures draw in their audiences rather than alienate them.

Recent work has begun to show that power seems even more thoroughly bound up with such discourses. We look particularly for the ways power relations determine what can, cannot, or must be said about self and emotion, what is taken to be true or false about them, and what only some individuals can say about them. The real innovation is in showing how emotion discourses establish, assert, challenge, or reinforce power or status differences. Discourses on fear have been singled out in a number of studies of colonial violence as crucial aspects of the discursive practices of dominant groups (Stoler 1985; Taussig 1987). Talk of fear of the dominated other in colonial contexts can be interpreted as a means by which powerful groups accomplish several purposes. They justify their suppression of those their rhetoric of fear implicitly paints as powerful and threatening to erupt, as Taussig (1987) argues occurred among rubber collectors in Columbia in the early part of this century. As Stoler (1985) demonstrates in the case of Dutch planters in Indonesia, they also thereby bargain with other elites for the resources and support needed to face down the purported threat.[12]

Scheper-Hughes's fieldwork in a Brazilian underclass community traces the relationship between emotional discourse and political economy. In one analysis (1985), she shows how a purportedly universal mother love is replaced by an emotional rhetoric of detached waiting regarding young infants because of the high infant mortality rate. In another (1988), she discusses how the syndrome *nervios* is part of discursive practice that transforms the symptoms of hunger into the less politically charged terms of emotional anxiety and "nerves" and of individual pathology, whose therapy is tranquilizers rather than a redistribution of food, wealth, and power.[13]

Authors in this volume have explored instead how discourses on emotion and emotional discourses can serve, in other instances, for the relatively powerless as loci of resistance and idioms of rebellion (Abu-Lughod, Lutz, Trawick), as means of establishing relationships and coercing gifts (Appadurai), or even as means of establishing complementarity with status superiors (Irvine). More broadly, the chapters tend to concentrate on the politics of emotion discourse by looking either at the pragmatics of emotion talk, the social deployment of particular emotional discourses, or the politics of ideologies of emotion.

Criticizing the referential models of language used by many anthropologists and the assumptions about human nature that animate much work, particularly that on cultural meaning and cognition, Abu-Lughod argues that we must ask not just what the cultural meanings of various emotions are and how emotional configurations might be related to social life, but how emotional discourses are implicated in the play of power and the operation of a historically changing system of social hierarchy.[14] Building on earlier arguments about what she calls the "politics of sentiment," she analyzes how Egyptian Bedouin love poetry, believed to have a certain force in the world, is now being deployed to challenge male elders. She also shows how this emotional discourse comes to have new social meaning and a different social basis as the Bedouin political economy is being transformed. Taking as her central case the love poems (on cassette) of a young man whose marriage was thwarted by an uncle, she explores the ways in which the introduction of semicommercial cassette recordings combines with the erosion of the tribal ideology concomitant with the economic transformations of Bedouin life to exclude women from this discourse of defiance. That poetry, as an emotional discourse, is seen by the Awlad 'Ali Bedouins as having pragmatic force, as suggested by the effects and intentions of playing these cassettes in particular social contexts.

Defending the importance of constructing models of indigenous conceptual models in anthropological analyses of emotion, White argues that the ethnography of emotion actually offers an opportunity to explore points of convergence between situated practices and interpretive models. In his chapter he tries to reconcile analytically, and show the interaction of, conceptual models and social institutions in a practice called 'disentangling' found on one of the Solomon Islands. The core of his chapter is a fascinating analysis of a narrative from one disentangling meeting that shows how this discourse, whose overt purpose is to make bad feeling public, works through the narrative reconstruction of problematic events to emphasize reconciliation instead of retribution by means of emotion language. The discursive practice of disentangling works to create social harmony by re-creating and valorizing social relations. Yet power is not absent; through attention to both ideology and pragmatics, White reveals that the same narrative performance using the rhetoric of reconciliation can simultaneously work to establish the moral advantage of the speaker over those with whom he or she is in conflict. This alerts us to the crucial importance of analyzing emotional discourses for multiple meanings, intentions, and effects.

In exploring the many ways that ordinary Americans' discourses on emotion are related to gender ideology, Lutz makes a strong case for the argument that this emotion discourse is only apparently about internal state but in fact about social life, power relations in particular. She presents examples of talk about emotions in a group of American women and men, and argues that this discourse on affect is also a discourse on the nature of women, their subordination, and their potential for rebellion in American society. A "rhetoric of control" (of emotion) found more frequently in women's than men's conversations is one of the primary ways people tell a narrative of women's weakness. She also traces the deep resonance of this lay discourse on the relation between gender and emotion with scientific discourse on the same topic. But finally, her chapter presents a finding that demonstrates the importance of distinguishing carefully between multiple levels of discourse. Her analysis of the organization of emotion discourse on a syntactic level shows how it actually fails to differentiate female and male speech. This suggests that ideas about links between emotion and the female, however pervasive at the ideological and narrative levels, do not organize discourse at the more microscopic or unconscious levels.

Taking a different strategy for the exploration of the complex relationship between discourse and emotion, Appadurai begins with a culturally inflected discursive form: praise in Hindu India. He then proceeds to show that understanding the meaning and pragmatic force of such a form in Indian life requries attention to several things: the multiple and mutually relevant contexts (praise of the divine, of kings, of patrons, and assessment of people and goods) that give it a particular meaning; the social uses to which this form is put in a variety of different social relationships (from flattery of politicians to coercion by beggars); and the indigenous theories of emotion and the local topography of the self, which render our own Western judgments of its excesses and emotional inauthenticity inapplicable. Arguing that praise is a public, regulated discourse and an embodied strategy of interaction that does not assume anything about the "inner" states of those involved, he shows how the practices of praise nevertheless create sentimental bonds with social consequences.

Like White and Appadurai, Brenneis begins with the argument that we have to take indigenous theories of emotion seriously because they inform emotional performances. Noting a tendency in the new literature on language and emotion to focus on speakers, he warns us not to overlook the audiences who actively interpret and respond to emotional communications and may become interlocutors. He suggests that local "social aesthetics" among a group of Hindi-speaking Indians in Fiji inform audience responses to communicative events. Here sociability and emotion discourse appear to be closely associated in two ways. First, villagers distinguish between social and individual emotions but only positively value the former. Second, socially recognized emotions like amity and friendship are the only emotions to be indexed and enacted in performances that are social and sociable. One implication of understanding how emotions are generated in particular types of events is that we can begin to see how groups excluded from participation in particular events may thereby also be precluded from having certain emotional experiences. Brenneis hypothesizes that women in that community may be prevented from realizing the socially valued emotions of sociability because they do not join men in certain performances and social settings.

Turning to another dimension of the relationship between social performance and emotion, Irvine explores one important way that linguistic structure is tied to emotion. She argues for the copresence in many languages of registers, that is, situational variations in language use, many of which have an affective dimension. Proposing the term "affective registers" to suggest a culturally defined set of complementary representations of emotion linked to conceptions of the person as well as the situation, Irvine analyzes the differences between two Wolof (Senegal) styles of speaking in these terms. She shows how a variety of features – prosody, phonology, morphology and syntax, lexicon, discourse management and interactional devices – distinguishes the speech of two social castes, nobles and griots (a hereditary caste of bards) and how, furthermore, the contrasts in speech styles are rooted in images of the person. Even more important than her argument that conventional linguistic displays of affectivity index social divisions is Irvine's suggestion that the essential complementarity of this heteroglossia also helps the Wolof define relationships of power difference as nevertheless sociable.

Stepping back from the emergent field defined by this volume, Rosenberg offers a critical overview of the first wave of anthropological work on emotion and personhood done by cultural anthropologists claiming an interest in language. With a linguist's eye, he reads some representative texts for the thorny problems raised when language is invoked as a locus of meaning and as a methodological key. He argues that despite an avowed interest in situated discourse and rejection of ethnographic semantics, most earlier studies make a number of problematic theoretical moves. For example, they abstract individual words, mostly nouns, from their discursive contexts and then recontextualize them into a social matrix; they use these key terms as master metaphors for a culture; they expand the references of nouns to include mental models or schemas and misattribute to others the ideas we have about language and meaning; and through inadequate attention to the way actual conversation proceeds, they mistake grammatical or indexical features of language for nontrivial cultural facts. The problem with these moves, he argues, is that they smuggle back into studies of emotion and personhood our ethnopsychology and our metalinguistic habits, making it difficult to distinguish methodological differences from cultural differences. He sorts out a number of distinct ways emotion and language might be related and suggests that future work attend carefully to the distinctions between semantics, reference, pragmatics, and ideology.

Bringing together issues of the language of power, the power of language, and the entanglement of emotion and power, Trawick closes this volume with a lyrical and itself quite moving meditation on caste pollution, the fear of death, and a song sung into a tape recorder for her by an untouchable Tamil woman from South India. Building on some of Julia Kristeva's thoughts on abjection and language, she tries to answer the question of "how it feels to be beyond the pale." Through a close textual and stylistic analysis of this hymn, Trawick reveals the singer's concern with the problems of inclusion and exclusion so crucial to caste and with the issues of separation and remainders so critical to a sense of personal wholeness. She argues that the singer's artistic technique, which involves deviating from the code of grammar as well as the social code, is a strategy for challenging that which has cast her out.

In suggesting in their many ways that we consider not emotions but the discourses of emotion, the chapters in this book do not deny the force of emotion and subjective experience. They do advocate a shift in focus that may be illuminating. Arguing that the reality of emotion is social, cultural, political, and historical, just as is its current location in the psyche or the natural body, they show clearly how discourses on emotion and emotional discourses are commentaries on the practices essential to social relations. As part of the politics of everyday life, these discourses are not, therefore, just the stuff of psychological anthropology but of sociocultural and linguistic theory as well. The chapters to follow offer positive ways of developing both a nonindividualized and a nonreductionist approach to emotion and a more dynamic socially and politically grounded analysis of all discursive practice.

Notes

1. For recent reviews, see Heelas (1986), Levy and Wellenkamp (1987), and Lutz and White (1986).
2. For a recent consideration of anthropology's (with the exception of feminist anthropology's) role in developing cultural critiques, see Marcus and Fischer (1986).
3. This shift may have corresponded to the general process of medicalization and normalization that, for Foucault (1978), characterize the modern age.
4. See also Foucault (1983) for a clear discussion of his views on the relationship between subjectivity and subjection or the creation of the individual through disciplinary power.
5. Foucault's assertion, of course, calls for ethnographic evidence, the beginnings of which Lutz (1988:53–80) provides. It would be worth speculating further whether the proliferation of emotion discourse in American life, combined with the construal of emotion as a private and subjective state, might not both confirm a sense of self as separate (in giving the individual "experiences" of his or her own – as Lutz (1986:299), Riesman (1983:123), and Foucault (1985:5) have argued in linking the construction of "experience" and the sense of individuality) – and provide an idiom for asserting the existence of bonds between people in the face of the actual attenuation of such bonds by mobility, distance, and the social fragmentation of class, gender, and race.
6. Heteroglossia is a term that seems to have filtered into anthropology, both in the narrow linguistic sense of many languages and in the larger sense of many discourses, through Bakhtin (1981). For a critical discussion of the absence of social theory in and the conservative implications of most of the work on culture done under the rubric of cognitive anthropology, see Keesing (1987). The notion of culture promoted by interpretive anthropology has many critics, but Asad's (1983) consideration of the problems as related to the study of religion is particularly intelligent.
7. See Appadurai (1988) for a persuasive argument that "natives," people from certain faraway places who belong to those places and are somehow incarcerated in those places and especially in their "mode of thought," are "creatures of the anthropological imagination" – that is, produced by anthropological discourse. For a discussion of the similarity of the concepts of culture and race, see Mitchell (1988:105).
8. See Williams (1973, 1977) and Comaroff (1985) for attempts to mediate this divide.

9.   For an elaboration of the problems with ideology, see Foucault (1980:117–18).
10. Foucault himself substituted the term 'apparatus' (*dispositif*) for discourse in some of his later work on sexuality in order to emphasize that he was concerned with "a thoroughly heterogeneous ensemble" of nondiscursive elements – statements, writings, architectural forms, rules, institutions, etc. – that are related to one another in varying ways and have, as a formation, "a dominant strategic function" (1980:194–5).
11. See Scheper-Hughes and Lock (1987) for a view of the "three bodies" that can be applied to the three bodies of emotion just described.
12. She also shows the power of the denial of fear by those same planters. Denial or negation both posits a fear and a threat and claims to have conquered them (cf. Kress and Hodge 1978).
13. See also Hochschild (1983) on the relationship between power and the emotional practices of service workers, such as stewardesses, in the United States.
14. Other strong critiques of the referential view of language have been made by Crapanzano (1981) and Good and Good (1982).

References

Abu-Lughod, Lila. 1986. *Veiled Sentiments: Honor and Poetry in a Bedouin Society.* Berkeley: University of California Press.
Appadurai, Arjun. 1988. Putting Hierarchy in Its Place. *Cultural Anthropology* 3:36–49.
Asad, Talal. 1983. Anthropological Conceptions of Religion: Reflections on Geertz. *Man* (n.s.) 18:237–59.
Bakhtin, Mikhail M. 1981. *The Dialogic Imagination.* M. Holquist, ed. Austin: University of Texas Press.
Basso, Ellen. 1985. *A Musical View of the Universe.* Philadelphia: University of Pennsylvania Press.
Bourdieu, Pierre. 1977. *Outline of a Theory of Practice.* Cambridge: Cambridge University Press.
Brenneis, Donald. 1987. Performing Passions: Aesthetics and Politics in an Occasionally Egalitarian Community. *American Ethnologist* 14:236–50.
Briggs, Jean. 1970. *Never in Anger.* Cambridge, MA: Harvard University Press.
Cancian, Francesca. 1987. *Love in America: Gender and Self-Development.* Cambridge: Cambridge University Press.
Comaroff, Jean. 1985. *Body of Power, Spirit of Resistance: The Culture and History of a South African People.* Chicago: University of Chicago Press.
Crapanzano, Vincent. 1981. Text, Transference, and Indexicality. *Ethos* 9:122–48.
    1989. Preliminary Notes on the Glossing of Emotions. *Kroeber Anthropological Society Papers* Nos. 69–70:78–85.
Elias, Norbert. 1978 (1939). *The History of Manners,* trans. E. Jephcott. New York: Pantheon Books.
Fajans, Jane. 1985. The Person in Social Context: The Social Character of Baining "Psychology." In G. White and J. Kirkpatrick, eds., *Person, Self, and Experience: Exploring Pacific Ethnopsychologies.* Berkeley: University of California Press, pp. 367–97.
Feld, Steven. 1983. *Sound and Sentiment: Birds, Weeping, Poetics and Song in Kaluli Expression.* Philadelphia: University of Pennsylvania Press.

Foucault, Michel. 1972. *The Archaeology of Knowledge and the Discourse on Language*. New York: Pantheon.

    1978. *The History of Sexuality*, Vol. 1. New York: Pantheon.

    1980. *Power/Knowledge*. Colin Gordon, ed. New York: Pantheon.

    1983. On the Genealogy of Ethics: An Overview of Work in Progress. In H. Dreyfus and P. Rabinow, *Beyond Structuralism and Hermeneutics*, 2nd ed. Chicago: University of Chicago Press, pp. 229–52.

    1985. *The Use of Pleasure*. Vol. 2 of *The History of Sexuality*. New York: Random House.

Gardiner, H. M., Ruth C. Metcalf, and John Beebe-Center. 1970 (1937). *Feeling and Emotion: A History of Theories*. Westport, CT: Greenwood Press.

Geertz, Clifford. 1973. Person, Time, and Conduct in Bali. In *The Interpretation of Cultures*. New York: Basic Books, pp. 360–411.

    1987. *Works and Lives*. Stanford: Stanford University Press.

Geertz, Hildred. 1959. The Vocabulary of Emotion: A Study of Javanese Socialization Processes. *Psychiatry* 22:225–37.

Good, Mary-Jo Delvecchio, and Byron Good. 1982. Toward a Meaning-Centered Analysis of Popular Illness Categories: 'Fright Illness' and 'Heart Distress' in Iran. In A. Marsella and G. White, eds., *Cultural Conceptions of Mental Health and Therapy*. Dordrecht: D. Reidel, pp. 141–66.

    1988. Ritual, the State, and the Transformation of Emotional Discourse in Iranian Society. *Culture, Medicine, and Psychiatry* 12(1):43–63.

Good, Mary-Jo Delvecchio, Byron Good, and Michael M. J. Fischer. 1988. *Emotion, Illness and Healing in Middle Eastern Societies*. (Special Issue). *Culture, Medicine and Psychiatry* 12(1).

Gumperz, John. 1982. *Discourse Strategies*. Cambridge: Cambridge University Press.

Harré, Rom, and Robert Finlay-Jones. 1986. Emotion Talk Across Times. In Rom Harré, ed., *The Social Construction of Emotions*. Oxford: Basil Blackwell, pp. 220–33.

Heelas, Paul. 1986. Emotion Talk Across Cultures. In Rom Harré, ed., *The Social Construction of Emotions*. Oxford: Basil Blackwell, pp. 234–66.

Hiatt, L. R. 1984. Your Mother-in-Law Is Poison. *Man* 19:183–98.

Hill, Jane. 1987. Weeping and Coherence in Narrative and Selfhood: The Sorrows of Dona Maria. Paper presented at the annual meetings of the American Anthropological Association, Chicago.

Hochschild, Arlie. 1983. *The Managed Heart*. Berkeley: University of California Press.

Hopper, Paul. 1987. Emergent Grammar. *Proceedings of the 13th Annual Meeting of the Berkeley Linguistics Society*. Berkeley, CA: Berkeley Linguistics Society, pp. 139–57.

Howell, Signe. 1981. Rules Not Words. In P. Heelas and A. Lock, eds., *Indigenous Psychologies*. London: Academic Press, pp. 133–43.

Irvine, Judith. 1982. Language and Affect: Some Cross-Cultural Issues. In H. Byrnes, ed., *Contemporary Perceptions of Language: Interdisciplinary Dimensions*. Washington, DC: Georgetown University Press, pp. 31–47.

Jackson, S. W. 1985. Acedia the Sin and Its Relationship to Sorrow and Melancholia. In A. Kleinman and B. Good, eds., *Culture and Depression: Studies in the Anthropology and Cross-Cultural Psychiatry of Affect and Disorder*. Berkeley: University of California Press, pp. 43–62.

Keesing, Roger. 1987. Models, "Folk" and "Cultural": Paradigms Regained? In D. Holland and N. Quinn, eds., *Cultural Models in Language and Thought*. Cambridge: Cambridge University Press, pp. 369–93.

Kress, Gunther, and Robert Hodge. 1979. *Language as Ideology*. London: Routledge & Kegan Paul.

Labov, William. 1972. Rules for Ritual Insults. In *Language in the Inner City*. Philadelphia: University of Pennsylvania Press.

Levy, Robert. 1973. *Tahitians: Mind and Experience in the Society Islands*. Chicago: University of Chicago Press.

Levy, Robert, and Jane Wellenkamp. 1987. Methodology in the Anthropological Study of Emotion. In R. Plutchik and H. Kellerman, eds., *The Measurement of Emotions*. New York: Academic Press.

Lindholm, Charles. 1982. *Generosity and Jealousy: The Swat Pukhtun of Northern Pakistan*. New York: Columbia University Press.

Lutz, Catherine. 1986. Emotion, Thought, and Estrangement: Emotion as a Cultural Category. *Cultural Anthropology* 1:405–36.

  1988. *Unnatural Emotions: Everyday Sentiments on a Micronesian Atoll and Their Challenge to Western Theory*. Chicago: University of Chicago Press.

Lutz, Catherine, and Geoffrey White. 1986. The Anthropology of Emotions. *Annual Review of Anthropology* 15:405–36.

MacFarlane, Alan. 1987. *The Culture of Capitalism*. Oxford: Basil Blackwell.

Marcus, George, and Michael M. J. Fischer. 1986. *Anthropology as Cultural Critique*. Chicago: University of Chicago Press.

Mitchell, Timothy. 1988. *Colonising Egypt*. Cambridge: Cambridge University Press.

Myers, Fred. 1979. Emotions and the Self: A Theory of Personhood and Political Order Among Pintupi Aborigines. *Ethos* 7:343–70.

  1986. *Pintupi Country, Pintupi Self: Sentiment, Place, and Politics Among Western Desert Aborigines*. Washington, DC: Smithsonian Institution Press.

Obeyesekere, Gananath. 1985. Depression, Buddhism and the Work of Culture in Sri Lanka. In A. Kleinman and B. Good, eds., *Culture and Depression: Studies in the Anthropology and Cross-Cultural Psychiatry of Affect and Disorder*. Berkeley: University of California Press, pp. 134–52.

Ochs, Elinor, and Bambi Schieffelin. 1989. Language Has a Heart. *Text* 9:7–25.

Radden, Jennifer. 1987. Melancholy and Melancholia. In David Levin, ed., *Pathologies of the Modern Self*. New York: New York University Press, pp. 231–50.

Riesman, Paul. 1977. *Freedom in Fulani Social Life*. Chicago: University of Chicago Press.

  1983. On the Irrelevance of Child Rearing Practices for the Formation of Personality. *Culture, Medicine and Psychiatry* 7:103–29.

Robarchek, Clayton. 1979. Learning to Fear: A Case Study of Emotional Conditioning. *American Ethnologist* 6:555–67.

Rosaldo, Michelle Z. 1980. *Knowledge and Passion: Ilongot Notions of Self and Social Life*. Cambridge: Cambridge University Press.

  1983. The Shame of Headhunters and the Autonomy of Self. *Ethos* 11:135–51.

  1984. Toward an Anthropology of Self and Feeling. In R. Shweder and R. LeVine, eds., *Culture Theory: Essays on Mind, Self, and Emotion*. Cambridge: Cambridge University Press, pp. 137–57.

Sabini, John, and Maury Silver. 1987. Character: The Moral and the Aesthetic. *International Journal of Moral and Social Studies* 2:189–201.

  1988. Emotion, Character, and Responsibility. In F. Schoemann, ed., *Responsibility, Character, and the Emotions*. New York: Cambridge University Press.

Saussure, Ferdinand de. 1966. *Course in General Linguistics*. New York: McGraw-Hill.

Scheff, Thomas. 1977. The Distancing of Emotion in Ritual. *Current Anthropology* 18:483–505.

Scheper-Hughes, Nancy. 1985. Culture, Scarcity and Maternal Thinking: Maternal Detachment and Infant Survival in a Brazilian Shantytown. *Ethos* 13:291–317.

1987. The Madness of Hunger: Sickness, Delirium and Human Needs. Paper presented at the annual meetings of the American Anthropological Association, Chicago.

Scheper-Hughes, Nancy, and Margaret Lock. 1987. The Mindful Body: A Prolegomenon to Future Work in Medical Anthropology. *Medical Anthropology Quarterly* 1:6–41.

Schieffelin, Bambi, and Elinor Ochs, eds. 1986. *Language Socialization Across Cultures.* Cambridge: Cambridge University Press.

Schieffelin, Edward L. 1976. *The Sorrow of the Lonely and the Burning of the Dancers.* New York: St. Martin's Press.

Sherzer, Joel. 1987. A Discourse-Centered Approach to Language and Culture. *American Anthropologist* 89:295–309.

Solomon, Robert. 1976. *The Passions.* New York: Anchor Press/Doubleday.

Sontag, Susan. 1977. *Illness as Metaphor.* New York: Farrar, Straus.

Spiro, Melford. 1965. Religious Systems as Culturally Constituted Defense Mechanisms. In M. Spiro, ed., *Context and Meaning in Cultural Anthropology.* New York: Free Press, pp. 100–13.

Stearns, Carol, and Peter Stearns. 1986. *Anger: The Struggle for Emotional Control in America's History.* Chicago: University of Chicago Press.

Stoler, Ann. 1985. *Capitalism and Confrontation in Sumatra's Plantation Belt, 1870–1979.* New Haven, CT: Yale University Press.

Taussig, Michael. 1987. *Shamanism, Colonialism, and the Wild Man: A Study in Terror and Healing.* Chicago: University of Chicago Press.

Tedlock, Dennis. 1983. *The Spoken Word and the Work of Interpretation.* Philadelphia: University of Pennsylvania Press.

1987. Questions Concerning Dialogical Anthropology. *Journal of Anthropological Research* 43(4):325–37.

1987. On the Representation of Discourse in Discourse. *Journal of Anthropological Research* 43(4):343–4.

Tyler, Steven. 1978. *The Said and the Unsaid.* New York: Academic Press.

Urban, Greg. 1988. Ritual Wailing in Amerindian Brazil. *American Anthropologist* 90:385–400.

White, Geoffrey, and John Kirkpatrick, eds. 1985. *Person, Self and Experience: Exploring Pacific Ethnopsychologies.* Berkeley: University of California Press.

Williams, Raymond. 1973. Base and Superstructure in Marxist Cultural Theory. *New Left Review* 82:3–16.

1977. *Marxism and Literature.* Oxford: Oxford University Press.

Wittgenstein, Ludwig. 1966. *Zettel.* G. Anscombe, trans. London: Basil Blackwell.

2. Shifting politics in Bedouin love poetry

LILA ABU-LUGHOD

One morning in New York, I turned on the radio and happened to catch a call-in therapy show in which listeners telephoned the station and spoke to a psychologist about their problems. The first caller was an older housewife who presented her predicament as an inability to stick to a diet. She was distressed that she kept binging. The psychologist skill-fully questioned her until it emerged that she did this eating at night, after her husband had gone to sleep, and that she was "really" angry with him because he always came home late and tired from the office and never wanted to do anything with her in the evenings.

What struck me most about what I heard was that the psychologist kept asking over and over, "How did you feel?" – How do you feel when this happens, what did you feel when he said that, what did you feel when he did that? She took for granted this mode of getting at the truth, this focus on emotions as touchstones of personal reality. And I suspect that the poor caller, had she later gone into therapy, would have learned to populate her narratives about herself and her relationships with a legion of emotions too. She would have learned to practice on herself and on others, to adapt a notion from Foucault (1985:5), a her-meneutics of feeling.

The Bedouins I lived and worked with in Egypt would find the com-mand to confess one's feelings strange – on the one hand improper and undignified, and on the other, as will become clear, nonsensical. Non-sensical not just because they never ask each other the question "How did you feel?" and because I cannot think of how it could be said in their dialect. And not just because they are more likely to ask each other "What did she do?" or "What did you say?" It is nonsensical, first, because it implies that there is a satisfying explanation to be had by resorting to the inspection of emotions and, second, because it presumes that the sentiments one would talk about in this publicly broadcast confessional would be the same as those in other social contexts and in other forms or media. In short this question assumes that emotions could be detached in meaning and consequence from the flow of social life.

In anthropology, the last decade or so of work on emotion, associated as it has been with a growing interest in such notions as the person, the self, and experience, has radically questioned such assumptions.[1] Many anthropologists have become skeptical of Western academic and popular ideas about emotions – about their naturalness and thus universality, their internal location, and their personal or individual quality. Lutz (1986) has brilliantly mapped the shared cultural terrain of philosophical, psychological/psychiatric, and lay Euro-American middle-class discourse on emotions, showing how "emotion" plays into a double-edged system of signification as the opposite of both reason (or thought) and estrangement. One important contribution of her analysis is, as she puts it (Lutz 1986:304), that "by demonstrating the nature and extent of the Western cultural construction of emotion, it is possible to contrast these conceptions to the ethnopsychological premises upon which the emotional lives of people of other cultures are based, premises which we might now only gingerly term 'emotional'." By beginning to deconstruct the concept of emotion itself through showing its specific cultural meaning, she undermines the certainties that guided traditional psychological anthropology, as it borrowed from psychology and philosophy, and articulates a position that is implicit in much of the work on emotion that falls under the rubric of interpretive anthropology.

Nevertheless, exposing the ethnocentrism[2] of our scientific and ordinary discourse on emotion does not guarantee that basic and pervasive cultural notions about emotion cannot slip back into our work or that we may not draw instead on other cultural notions in our reformulations. That emotions are somehow already there or that they have some ontological being is slipped back in by their very designation as the object of disciplinary study: "the anthropology of emotions."

There are also more serious problems that arise in precisely that work that offers the most sustained critique of psychological, psychobiological, or psychoanalytic conceptualizations of emotions and their human carriers. Interpretive and cognitive anthropologists argue that emotions are embedded in cultural contexts that give them meaning and thus have explored the cultural variability of emotional configurations and vocabulary. In work on what could be labeled the "cultural construction of emotion," they have set themselves the tasks of cultural translation, mapping the conceptual domains of emotion words in various cultures, tracing the cultural systems in which these related concepts participate, and considering the situations to which these emotion constructs are tied.[3]

Although I am sympathetic to the intent of this work, have contributed to it myself (Abu-Lughod 1985, 1986), and believe it begins the important task of relativizing, there are at least three aspects of it that I find problematic. I will take up the first two here and the third later in my discussion of discourse. First, for many involved in this work of demonstrating the emotions to be cultural rather than natural, the Western thought–feeling dualism has been seen as a key to our mistakes. As a solution, however, the stress on the inherently cultural character of emotions risks assimilating emotion to thought. Myers (1986:106) makes the point that "emotions are not simply reactions to what happens, but interpretations of an event, judgments [about situations]." Lutz and White (1986:428) conclude that in the new work on emotions, "emphasis is shifted away from the question of whether a somehow decontextualized emotional experience is 'the same' or 'different' across cultures to that of how people make sense of life's events." Rosaldo (1984:137–8) argues that "thought is always culturally patterned and infused with feelings, which themselves reflect a culturally ordered past," and suggests that feelings must be understood as "embodied thoughts" (1984:138). In privileging in their theories of emotion activities such as understanding, making sense of, judging, and interpreting, these theorists may be inadvertently replicating that bias toward the mental, idealist, or cognitive that Lutz (1986) points out is such a central cultural value for us.

A second and related problem with the cultural approach is that it assumes that all humans are primarily engaged, like social scientists or philosophers, in the project of interpretation and understanding rather than other practices. Rosaldo (1984:139) outlines a trend in the social sciences that has at its center the desire to grasp "how human beings understand themselves and [how] to see their actions and behaviors as in some ways the creations of those understandings." It strikes me that, without in any way denigrating their philosophical inclinations or consciousness, the people we study are just as likely to be interested in other aspects of living as in interpreting or undertstanding. Thus, rather than relativizing Western psychology by calling it "ethnopsychology," thereby attributing the essentially contemplative project of psychologizing, or for that matter anthropologizing, to everyone, we might want to bring into question, as Foucault (1970) does, the very peculiar and historically specific developments of which the enterprises known as the human sciences and what he calls, following Nietzsche, our modern Western "will to truth" are part.

As Lutz and White (1986:420) point out, more attention is now beginning to be paid to the relationship between emotions and social structure.[4] In many cases, this turn to the social is found within the interpretive paradigm. Myers (1986:107), for instance, who argues for a concern with emotional constructs' "place within a larger cultural system of meanings," adds that "if the emotions are relational, the relationships they constitute are given meaning and value by the social process in which they are embedded." Rosaldo too, in the latter part of her article, begins exploring the notion, with regard to shame, guilt, and egalitarian versus hierarchical societies, that "notions of the person, affective processes and forms of society itself are interlinked" (1984:148). She concludes by arguing that we are "social persons" (1984:151) and that what is needed is to relate "lives of feeling to conceptions of the self, as both of these are aspects of particular forms of polities and social relations" (1984:150). In suggesting, as do many whose work on emotions considers the realm of the social, that there might be some correlation between emotion constructs and forms of society, she raises the somewhat troubling possibility of a new brand of national character studies.[5] This can be avoided only if society is not conceptualized as a unitary body but rather as composed of individuals and groups with competing interests involved in relations of power, and if politics is not reified in the notion of a polity.

I prefer to follow out a more dynamic strand of Rosaldo's argument, one that carries more sociolinguistic assumptions, as a promising direction for the anthropological study of emotion. She writes that "what individuals *can* think and feel is overwhelmingly a product of socially organized modes of action and of talk" (1984:147). I would use this aspect of her argument against her interpretive bent to argue that instead of enriching our concept of culture (1984:138), we need to break with it by pressing harder on the question of social action and talk. In other words, we need to examine emotion as discursive practice (see Abu-Lughod and Lutz, this volume, for a critique of the culture concept). This brings up the third problem with much cultural analysis, a problem that has received a good deal of attention in this volume and elsewhere: It generally models itself on theories of language as referential and communicative. This promotes a lingering concern with meaning, which always implies that it is the referents that are the object of study rather than the speakers (see also Rosenberg, this volume). I would argue that the first step must be to ask how emotion discourses are deployed in social contexts. This would shift the concern from what Foucault has argued is characteristic of and widespread in the modern West – a focus on what is *said* in discourse – to the more interesting and political questions of what discourse is, what it does, and what forms it.[6] What we need to know is how discourses on emotion, or emotional discourses for that matter (see Abu-Lughod and Lutz, this volume), are implicated in the play of power and the operation of historically changing systems of social hierarchy (see also Trawick, this volume).

One can look at the relationship between emotion, social life, and power as Lutz (1986) does by noting the ideological functions of emotion attribution (e.g., the labeling of women, children, primitives, and lower classes as emotional "to justify the exclusion of these individuals from positions of power and responsibility" [Lutz 1986:294]) or by looking at the actual social contexts in which emotion discourses are deployed. To study the ways emotion discourses are used, to focus on practice rather than meaning, and to examine discourses rather than their putative referents are, it seems to me, the projects shared by the contributors to this volume.[7]

I focus, in this chapter, on the emotions or sentiments associated with relations between men and women in a Bedouin community in Egypt's Western Desert, especially the discourses of "love." My argument proceeds by way of a Bedouin love story. The community of Bedouins about which I write are part of a group known as the Awlad 'Ali who inhabit the area along the Mediterranean coast of Egypt west of Alexandria into Libya.[8] I lived in this community from 1978 to 1980, visited once for a month five years later, and went back for five months of fieldwork in 1987. Until about thirty-five years ago, those still living in the Western Desert made a living mostly by herding sheep, growing barley, and organizing camel caravans to transport dates from the oases to the Nile Valley. Now they are involved in all sorts of activities, from the old one of raising sheep to the newer ones of tending orchards, smuggling, supplying construction materials, and speculating in real estate. They used to live in tents. Now most of them live in houses, although they still pitch their tents next to their houses and prefer sitting in the tents at least during the day. They used to ride on horses, camels, and donkeys; now they prefer Toyota trucks. Although sedentarizing, they still proudly distinguish themselves from the settled peasant and urban groups of the Nile Valley – the Egyptians – by their tribal organization and what they see as their superior morality. But, as I will discuss, even this is beginning to change.

Here is the love story. I was back in Egypt in 1985, visiting for the first time since my initial fieldwork the families I had lived with for almost two years. It was early in the morning of the last day I was there. My host, the head of the family, with whom I had lived as a sort of adopted daughter, was getting ready to drive me to Cairo to catch my plane. He rummaged around in the pockets of his various robes and vests, looked in his briefcase, and finally in exasperation asked his children, who were all standing around, if they knew what had happened to the cassette of Fathalla Aj-jbēhi. His eldest daughter sheepishly went and got it from the cassette player she and her sisters often secretly listened to when he was away. The kids put my suitcases in the trunk of his new Mercedes, I said my goodbyes, and we set off. As soon as we were on the desert highway, he turned on the tape deck and said that I had to listen to this tape. We listened. A man chanted, in a moving and pained voice, poem after poem of the type called the *ghinnāwa*.

My host listened raptly, interjected exclamations of sympathy at the end of some of the poems, and elaborated, with intense and obvious admiration, on some of the references in the poems. Among the poems were the following two:

> Patience is hard
> for my heart, so freshly wounded . . .
>
> wa'r 'alēh iṣ-ṣabr
> jarḥā jdīd māzāl khāṭrī . . .
>
> I'd figured, oh beloved, that distance
> would be a cure but it only made it worse . . .
>
> niḥsāb yā 'azīz il-mōḥ
> yabgā lī dwā nādh zādni . . .

My host explained that Fathalla, the young man reciting the poems (whose kinship relation to one of our neighbors he identified) had been in love with his paternal cousin and wanted to marry her. Their fathers had first agreed to it but then got into an argument with each other. The young woman's father decided to refuse to give his daughter to the young man. In despair and thinking that he might get over this more easily if he put distance between them, the man set off for Libya (where until recently many Bedouin men went looking for work). Some time afterward, the girl's father arranged to marry his daughter to someone else. When Fathalla heard the news, he composed and recorded these poems and sent the tape to the girl's brother, a cousin with whom he had grown up. Fifteen days after the wedding, when the bride came back to her family's household for the ritual postmarital visit, her brother played her the tape. She listened to it and when it was over, she gasped for air, fainted, and then fell over, dead.

This story tells us a great deal about the politics of emotion discourse in Bedouin society. I will take up four aspects of it. First, there is the matter of the poignant love poems and their relationship to other Bedouin discourses on "love." Second, there is the import of the reactions to the young man's poetry and its apparent power. Third, there is the fact of the cassette. In the conclusion, I will consider a fourth issue: the context of the particular telling of this story to the anthropologist.

When Fathalla wanted to express the sentiments of love, he did so in the traditional and formulaic medium of poetry. The way he expressed these feelings and the medium in which he expressed them could be said to be distinctively Bedouin. One could easily say that they were shaped by the culture in which he lived. Fathalla expressed his painful feelings in a genre of oral lyric poetry that is so much a part of everyday life and so cherished by the Bedouins that on my first field trip I had ended up studying it. Reminiscent of Japanese haiku in its length and condensation of imagery, but more like the blues in emotional tone, this is the poetry of personal life. It is by no means the only kind of poetry the Bedouins recite. They have many distinct genres of long rhyming verse, usually composed by men, often specialists, and recited at formal gatherings. They also have special types of wedding poems and songs. But poems of this genre, the *ghinnāwa*, can be composed and recited by anyone, male or female. Although the poems can be changed or sung, sometimes at weddings, and as you could tell from my story, now even into cassettes passed from person to person, most often as I heard them they were just recited in the middle of ordinary conversations with intimates.

The poetry is rich in sentiment, so one might be tempted to explore the language of poetry in order to get at the cultural construction of Bedouin sentiment. But there would be a problem with this project. As I began to pay attention to the way people used this form of poetry, I discovered an intriguing pattern: There was a discrepancy between the feelings individuals expressed in their poems and the ones they expressed in their ordinary language communications about the same situations.[9] This is not apparent from Fathalla's case, because his poems were out of context. But it is obvious from a more typical case I have written about, that of a middle-aged woman I called Safiyya.

When she told me about her divorce from the man she'd been married to for almost twenty years, she showed the aggressive nonchalance I'd come to expect as the typical attitude toward love and marriage. She explained that she had never liked him and didn't care when he divorced her. But two days later, when a conversation between Safiyya and several other women in her household turned to the whereabouts of her ex-husband, away on a trip at the time, she suddenly recited a poem that everyone knew was about her husband. In it she expressed a very different set of sentiments, especially her sadness at losing him. This and several other poems she recited suggested a feeling of attachment to her husband and were recognized as doing so by all the women who heard them.

Like Fathalla, Safiyya expressed the sentiments of love in poetry – but she denied those sentiments in her ordinary conversation. There she expressed the more characteristic sentiments of everyday male–female relations in this society – which involved the denial of concern about the husband. In general, male–female relations among the Bedouins are marked by distance. Sexual segregation characterizes daily life. People deny interest in love or sexual matters and avoid members of the opposite sex except close relatives. An important goal of the socialization process is to teach children, especially girls, to do this. I heard a girl confide in her uncle's new wife. "To tell you the truth, I don't even know what this love is. I hear about it in songs and hear about this one giving some guy her necklace, that one her ring, but I don't know what they are talking about." The older woman responded approvingly, "That's my girl." Even married women deny any interest in their husbands, not to mention other men. Women rarely use their husbands' names, referring to them as 'that one' or, if affectionate, 'the old man'; if they are being formal, they refer to him politely as 'the master of my household.' At least in front of others, they are formal and distant with husbands, showing no public affection.

By the same token, men do not spend much time with their wives and rarely talk about them. They are ridiculed if they show too much concern. When one man's new bride ran away and he sulked and seemed miserable, his relatives all teased or scolded him. His mother said, "What, you worry about a woman? You're an idiot." Fathalla, the man who recorded the poetry on the cassette, had probably rarely spoken to his beloved, and there is little doubt that he had been unable to broach the subject of love or marriage with his own father. For the marriage arrangement he had probably relied on an intermediary. The extremity of the avoidance of the subject, especially in front of elders, is well illustrated by an incident described by Peters (1952), who worked with a related group of Bedouins in Cyrenaica. She was sitting in a tent with a group of Bedouin men and brought up the topic of marriage or women. She suddenly noticed that all the young men had fled the tent, in their haste leaving their shoes behind.

This avoidance is said to be motivated by a sentiment, called *hasham*, which can be translated as "modesty," "embarrassment," or "shame." *Hasham* refers both to what we might think of as an internal state of shyness, embarrassment, or shame and to a set of behaviors associated with these "feelings," although the Awlad 'Ali do not make that distinction. The cultural repertoire of such behaviors includes dressing modestly for both sexes (which means covering the hair, arms to the wrists, and legs to the ankles) and aspects of demeanor such as downcast eyes, formal posture, and refraining from eating, smoking, talking, laughing, and joking. It is also marked, for married women, by veiling in certain circumstances. Very importantly, as I have described, it involves sexual propriety. What is clear is the *hasham* is *the* moral sentiment. The person with social sense, the good person – *tahashshams* – feels shy and acts modestly in the appropriate situations. Children, idiots, and the insane don't. Nor do bad people.

The question that comes up at this point is what one should make of this disjunction between the two sorts of sentiments Bedouins express about "love." As I have argued elsewhere (1986), several obvious types of explanation do not seem satisfactory. The first, that people are being hypocritical or engaging in acts of self-presentation, underestimates the commitment to morality among the Awlad 'Ali, attributing to them Euro-American ideological notions about the opposition between individual freedom and social restraint. A weaker version of this argument, but one no less steeped in our cultural assumptions, is that we are dealing with moral (i.e., social) constraint versus personal expression. Related to these interpretations is the safety-valve argument that sees the poetry as providing release from the pressures of moral conformity, a theory that has the added drawback of conceiving of society as a machine. All of these theories about the contradictions between the two discourses on sentiment privilege the poetic sentiments as in some sense the truer ones. Is this because, as Foucault (1985:5) has argued and the radio therapist demonstrated, in the modern West we have come to search for the truth of our being in desire, or more broadly, in feelings?

I prefer a different argument, one that does not mistake discourses on sentiment for emotion and one that pays close attention to the place in social and political life of what is said. Going back to the issue of modesty, I want to show how, if modesty is tied up with morality, morality, in turn, is tied up with power in a specific way. Modesty has two aspects, which are easier to grasp if we look at the negative case – the bad person, the immoral person who lacks *hasham*. Where women are concerned, such persons are described as either 'willful' (*gāwya*) or 'slutty' (*qhaba*). The first term describes someone who talks back or disobeys her elders. The word itself comes from the root meaning to be strong or powerful but in this form suggests excessive assertiveness. Such assertiveness is inappropriate for those in positions of dependence or social inferiority. This suggests that modesty is about deference to others. *Hasham* can refer to a general attitude of propriety, but most often it is thought of as operating in the context of particular relationships. *Hasham* is such a good index of hierarchy that when a young woman married into the community in which I was living, one of the first questions she asked her husband's young kinswomen was who was modest in front of whom. The girls responded by telling her which women veiled for which men and which men did not smoke in front of other men. Through this outline of deference patterns, the bride determined the hierarchy in her new marital community.

The second term for someone without *hasham* – slut – refers to sexual propriety. I have already described the elements of sexual modesty as they play themselves out in daily life. Here I want to show how sexual modesty as the denial of love interests is actually another form of deference. To make this argument, I will talk not about Islam – that totalizing concept to which everything that happens in Middle Eastern society tends to be reduced – but about the Bedouin social order.

The Awlad 'Ali are tribally organized. For them, common descent through the male line and shared blood provide the primary and the only legitimate basis for binding people together. Paternal kin live together, share some property, pass it on, and go to social functions together. They are also expected to feel close. If blood bonds between paternal relatives, male or female, are privileged as the only basis of social relationships, then heterosexual or romantic love, even in its legitimate guise of marriage, although necessary for the reproduction of society and the perpetuation of lineages, is hard to deal with. It does not rest easily within this framework for social relations and is in fact a threat.

Love and the bonds it might establish between individuals are not just threats to the framework that orders social relations, but are also talked about as threats to the solidarity of the paternal kin group, something often noted in the literature on patricentered societies from traditional China to Zinacantan (Collier 1974; Wolf 1972). The Awlad 'Ali view sexual bonds and the bonds of agnation as competing. Even more importantly, sexual bonds are seen as threats to the authority and control of elder male relatives who represent the interests of the agnatic family group, control its resources, and make its decisions. At marriage, sons begin to have a small domain of authority of their own, and daughters leave the domain of authority of their father and kin.

The threat marriage represents is counteracted at every point by social and ideological strategies. The marital bond is undermined in numerous ways: Women retain close ties to their paternal relatives, senior male relatives control the choice of marriage partners, and sexual segregation ensures that husbands and wives spend little time together. Divorce is easy and polygyny possible. And the married couple is rarely economically independent. Love matches are actively discouraged. One man told me that the only way people who loved each other would be allowed to marry was if their elder male relatives or the girl's paternal cousins did not know. Women often told me that love matches always ended badly for the woman because she would not have the support of her male kin if her husband mistreated her.

I have argued that the cultural preference for patrilateral parallel cousin marriage is another such strategy (Abu-Lughod 1986). The Awlad 'Ali frequently marry first cousins or other cousins on the father's side, and the male even has a legal claim to his paternal uncle's daughter. This type of marriage may be upheld as the cultural ideal, because it provides a means of defusing the threat of the sexual bond in this social system; it *subsumes* the marital bond under the prior and more legitimate bond of kinship.

The moral code that prescribes modesty is the most effective means of undermining the sexual bond. If the threat to the social order can be made to seem a threat to the respectability or moral worth of the individual, then that order will be reproduced by the actions of individuals in everyday life. The modesty code ensures that even individuals who do not have as much stake in the system – like young men and especially women – will help perpetuate it, because their virtue or their standing as moral beings, as good persons, depends on denying their sexuality. As I hinted earlier, these sentiments of sexual modesty are situational. They are important to display only in front of certain people – the elder male agnates. So, sexual modesty must be seen as a form of deference to them. The moral sentiments of modesty are part of a discourse that sustains and perpetuates the particular social system and the power of certain groups within it.

Conversely, then, the immodest sentiments of "love" are subversive. To express them is subversive of the social order and defiant of those whose interests are served by this order. This element of defiance is made concrete in the story of Fathalla. In singing about his feelings of love, he was, in a sense, defying the authority of his paternal uncle, who had thwarted his desires and prevented him from marrying his cousin.

Because it carries subversive sentiments of love, one could consider the *ghinnāwa* the Bedouin discourse of defiance. There is plenty of evidence that poetry is in general associated with opposition to the ideals of normal social life. This type of poetry is considered un-Islamic. The pious shouldn't recite it or show any interest in it. It is also considered unrespectable. Even the term "to sing" can't be said in mixed-sex company without causing all-around embarrassment. People say that they are ashamed or embarrassed about singing in front of nonintimates, especially elders. Women told me never to share their poems with the men. And in the past, older men avoided public settings like weddings and sheep-shearing parties where young men usually recited this type of poetry. The most persuasive evidence of the oppositional character of poetry is who recites poetry and who avoids it. Although older men occasionally recite them, *ghinnāwas* are most closely associated with youths and women. These are the disadvantaged dependents who have least to gain in the system as structured.

Dialectics of deference and defiance

The existence of defiant or subversive discourses by those not in power is probably fairly common in the world. We must take care not to romanticize this rebellion by taking it out of the context of social and political relations in particular societies. This brings me back to my second general point: We need to consider Bedouin reactions to this poetry. What may be specific to the Awlad 'Ali Bedouins is that even though this resistant emotional discourse goes against the system and makes the groups with power nervous, it is both culturally elaborated and positively sanctioned. Poetry is a highly developed art and the Awlad 'Ali cherish and privilege it, in certain contexts listening intently to poems, memorizing, repeating, and being moved by them. Most of the adults I lived with suggested that poetry was the best thing they had to offer as a cultural group. They thought of poetry as distinctively Bedouin, associated with their noble past when they were politically autonomous, tough, and independent.

Similarly, those who recite poetry, expressing those sentiments that challenge the social system and the authority of elders, are not just tolerated or *not* disapproved of but actually admired. This is apparent in my host's reactions to Fathalla. He and the many who wanted to hear this tape over and over clearly admired this young man for his passion and for his ability to express it in poetry. They were moved by his poems and awed by the power of his words.

I have argued that this ambivalence about love poetry – the discomfort surrounding it on the one hand, and its glorification on the other – reflects a fundamental tension in the organization of Bedouin social and political life. It may be related to an uneasy recognition of the way that the system of hierarchy within the lineage and family, the one to which the sentiments of deference apply, violates the tenets of tribal politics, where the paramount ideals are autonomy and equality. Day-to-day politics, however, puts in the hands of elder male agnates control over resources and power over dependents. This domination contravenes the ideals that sustain the wider tribal system. It may be rationalized through the elaboration of a moral code that justifies the privilege of elders and dignifies the deference of dependents. But it is a contradiction.

Love poetry, as a discourse of defiance, is seen as a discourse of autonomy and freedom. Recited mostly by those slighted in the system – that is, women and young men – it is exalted because a refusal to be dominated is key to their tribal political ideology and so a key value, even for these individuals. To love, or to express the sentiments of love, then, also signifies one's freedom. But to talk about sentiments or the discourses on sentiments as signifying something – in this example, freedom – is misleading in that it suggests something too static and too idealist. Love poetry as a discourse of rebellion is used to assert this freedom and is credited by others with tremendous power.

This is the other sense in which sentiments should be seen as political and reciting love poetry as a political act.[10] Fathalla's poems challenged his uncle's authority and ended up undermining the old man's control over the lives of his daughter and nephew and thwarting his attempt to deny them what they wanted. Others, including my host, who was an older head of a lineage and a paternal uncle to many, were awed by the fatal power of this poetry. Partly this was because they recognized that the uncle had abused his authority, but partly it was because, in Bedouin eyes, the legitimacy of authority is always in question. Resistance has positive valence, and Fathalla's love poetry was a kind of resistance.

Of course, it is sadly telling that all Fathalla could do with his poems was to thwart his uncle. He was not able to get what he wanted. The story's tragic end – the death of the woman Fathalla loved – suggests the ultimate power of the system and the futility of resistance. Perhaps that is what made the tale so compelling and poignant. It may have captured people's imaginations because it so vividly portrayed the complex relationship between love poetry and power in Bedouin society.

The cassette

The third aspect of Fathalla's story I want to take up is the somewhat surprising fact that his love songs were on a cassette. I had thought, when I left Egypt after my first period of fieldwork in 1980, that the Bedouin *ghinnāwa* was dying out. The adolescents I knew did not sing or recite this type of poetry, nor did they seem particularly interested in it. They were beginning to listen to Egyptian radio, and it was from their mothers, aunts, and grandmothers, and sometimes from their fathers and a few young men, that I collected poetry. These adults offered one explanation for why poetry was dying out: They said that there were no longer any occasions for singing. There is a certain truth to their deceptively straightforward explanation to which I will return.

If, however, it was the ideology of the political system, with its value of autonomy, that lent positive valence to expressions of love as defiance, even when they came from below, then one would not be surprised to find such discourses dying as the Awlad 'Ali Bedouins' political autonomy was undermined. This has been going on for quite a while as the Egyptian state has sought, over the last 35 years, to introduce its authority into the Western Desert, a process that has been underway in Bedouin areas closer to the Nile Valley for 150 years or more. The Awlad 'Ali have developed an impressive array of strategies to resist, subvert, and circumvent the authority of the state, which they consider illegitimate. Since they are not fazed by guns, and prison sentences carry no stigma, it is even hard to intimidate them into good citizenship.

There is, however, one process that began in their region in the 1970s that, more effectively than government efforts to disarm them, school them, put them in the military, license and register them, is progressively undermining their resistance to the state: the gradual shift in their economic life from herding and commercial activities, including smuggling, to investment in land. Land reclamation efforts by the government are transforming some of their desert into agricultural land, which they are increasingly buying and relying on for a livelihood, if not actually farming themselves. Land along the coast, on the other hand, has become valuable for tourist development, and many of them are doing quite well selling beachfront property. They are also fighting with each other over this land, which was formerly tribally held rather than individually owned. With this involvement in land, the Bedouins have become enmeshed in the state's legal system, since they need to get titles and make claims through it.[11]

This shift in the Bedouin political economy can be connected with what I see as a shift in the dialectic of deference and defiance in which love songs are deployed. As the economic basis of the tribal system erodes, and with it the political underpinnings of the value of autonomy, the older reality of mutual responsibility within the family and lineage is changing. There used to be a complex division of labor, with resources managed by elders but not owned. Now private ownership puts tremendous control in the hands of patriarchs. Young men suffer, as I will discuss, but those most dramatically affected are women. They are now economically dependent on men, having little access to money, and their work is increasingly confined to housework. With the moral value of modesty still in force, these women who live in the new circumstances of sedentarized communities, where they are surrounded by neighbors most of whom are nonkin, must be *more* secluded, more often veiled, and less free to move around.

Older women comment on these changes, reminiscing about things they used to do that young women today cannot get away with – like having rendezvous with sweethearts and exchanging songs with men at weddings and sheep shearings.[12] But they are also convinced that they were more modest, a perception that I think relates to a sense that it was more self-imposed. They often complain that their sons, husbands, nephews, and grandsons harshly restrict the girls, not letting them go anywhere. Girls, for their part, are beginning to complain that they feel imprisoned. The domestic political divide now runs along gender lines, whereas it used to be between elders on one side and women and young men on the other. All men have access to the market and increasing freedom of movement; all women do not.

This shift in the political economy has implications for traditional love poems, which, as I have discovered, are not, after all, dying out. Bedouin love songs are taking on different meaning and force, having been given new life by the advent of the cassette. The Bedouins had said that songs were dying out because there were no occasions for singing. In a sense, they were right. By the time I first met them, in 1978, they were reciting love poems only in intimate social situations. As I later learned, however, the most important forum for love songs had been weddings, at which young men and women had sung within earshot of and sometimes to each other.[13] Those kinds of celebrations had stopped by then, and the weddings I attended were sexually segregated. The women sang only songs of blessing, congratulation, and praise, and the men did nothing but sit around. Today, locally made cassettes – copied, re-copied, and sometimes sold for money – provide a new occasion for song, as does a new kind of wedding celebration coming into fashion. At this new wedding, attended by invited guests but also attracting a growing group of somewhat rowdy young men, the small-time stars of these low-budget commercial cassettes perform. Because of the public nature of these occasions, where, unlike in the past, "public" includes a wide range of nonkin and complete strangers, women are absent. They are also, out of modesty, absent from the recording sessions where tapes are made. They make no tapes and no longer sing in public. No longer having as much social and political support for defiance, the women also seem to be losing one of the means for it – love poetry.

The poems sung on cassettes and at *mīkrofōn* weddings seem now to be part of a discourse of defiance by young men against the more absolute authority and economic control of their fathers and paternal uncles. This is a period when, at the same time, young men are beginning to have more possibilities for independence from the kin group through wage labor and more knowledge than their fathers about the ways of the state through their experiences in the army and school. A new sort of generational conflict produced by these transitional circumstances is being played out partly in the language of love.

I had unexpected confirmation of the new use of "love" on my visit in January 1987, when I was listening with friends to one of the latest cassettes of popular Bedouin songs of a different genre. There was a

long and somewhat humorous song about the tribulations of a young
man whose father and uncle had arranged three terrible marriages for
him with women he'd never met. The first woman turned out to be bald,
the second dumb, and the third insane and violent to boot. In the final
verse of his song the poet, speaking on behalf of all young men who
have suffered the tyranny of such fathers and uncles, sings:[14]

> My warnings are to the old man
> who imprisons the freedom of youths
> who's forgotten a thing called love
> affection, desire, and burning flames
> who's forgotten how strong is the fire of lovers
> how strong the fire of lovers who long for one another
> What's exquisite is that they're afraid
> they say, any minute my prying guard will turn up
> oh my father's about to catch us

The relationship between love and freedom in this song is complex –
because, although he does not want the elders to force loveless marriages on their children, the poet recognizes that what makes love ex-
quisite is that it is stolen – it is against the authority of elder agnates. In
other words, he wants the freedom to defy the elders a bit, a freedom
he reminds them they used to want, but he does not reject the system
as a whole or want to have love easy or open.

The continuity of form in love songs is consistent with this attitude.
Unlike rock and roll, which some would argue played and plays a similar role in our society, the protests occur in an idiom that the elders can
appreciate: the poetry they themselves love and must respect, given their
own values. This is true even though they disapprove of the young men's
bare heads, occasional long hair, experimentation with drugs and li-
quor, and general loss of _hasham_. Everyone comments on this now – the
new brand of young men aren't modest in front of their fathers. According to the girls I talk with, in front of their fathers these young men not
only smoke cigarettes but, worse, they shamelessly play love songs on
their cassette recorders.

This is only a partial analysis of the shifting politics of Bedouin discourses on love, a complex subject on which I do not want to impose a
false coherence. Yet it should be sufficient to make clear my larger analytical point regarding the anthropology of emotion. As long as emotions remain the object of study, we can break with neither the idealism
and mentalism of the interpretive approach nor the assumptions that

animated our radio therapist's project.[15] These assumptions keep making it difficult to see how, for us, emotions serve as tokens in the construction of our subjectivity, how they bolster our belief in the truth of our individuality, and how all of this might also be political and specific to our place and time – that is, something worth analyzing critically rather than universalizing.[16]

If instead we take discourses as the object of analysis, we can get at something more interesting. I am not making a narrow plea for sociolinguistics or the ethnography of communication, although they are also involved. "Discourse" is a concept that recognizes that what people say, generously defined (which is, after all, what anyone is dealing with in the anthropological study of emotions), is inseparable from and interpenetrated with changing power relations in social life. There is a double movement implied in this notion. First, social and political life is to be seen as the product of interactions among individuals whose practices are informed by available discourses; second, language and culture are understood pragmatically rather than referentially. They are understood as part of social and political life. Analyzing emotion discourses as discourses rather than as data for our own "scientific" discourses on emotion provides us with a technique for avoiding the false attribution of the project of psychologizing to others as it reminds us relentlessly of the social nature of emotional expression.[17]

A discourse redeployed

If any further evidence need be offered for the critical importance of retaining a sense of the always social character of emotion discourse, consider the fourth and final aspect of this Bedouin love story: the context in which it was told. Fathalla's story was told to me, as I recounted, by my host, the man whose household I had lived in for two years. He played me the tape of those poignant love songs as I was about to depart again for the United States. I had been absent for five years the first time, and they did not know when I would next return. I promised it would be soon.[18] Although my host and his family had begged me to stay, and my host had gone as far as to offer to set up a job for me directing a private school he would finance, I insisted that my life was in *amrīka* and that it was not likely that I would come to live permanently in Egypt. When he played this tape for me and told me its sad tale, he was not interested in explicating Bedouin emotion concepts or in understanding himself, but rather in impressing on me the force of poetry.

Wasn't he, in a way, using the force of poetry on me? Of course, he knew I was writing a book about poetry, and we often discussed poems. Was there more? Did he wish to move me, to resist my departure by these songs and by telling me what effect they had had on another woman?

I sensed that this may have been part of his intent when, two years later, as I went over Fathalla's love poems with my host's wife, a woman I always talked with about poetry and who was good at explaining poems, I heard something surprising. She knew the poems and knew Fathalla's story, but said she had not heard that the girl had died. In fact, she was fairly certain that she was alive and living with the husband of her arranged marriage.

This incident can serve as a reminder that the emotional discourses we might want to use for our anthropological discourse on emotion are hardly inert. They may indeed have a cultural context, but the more important thing about them is that they participate in social projects – whether the larger ones of generational contests over power in an eroding tribal system or the local and particular ones of a conversation between a Bedouin man and a youngish female anthropologist driving to Cairo in a Mercedes.

Notes

This paper was completed while I was a member of the Institute for Advanced Study, a unique institution to which I am grateful for many things, including support, through the National Endowment for the Humanities, for writing. Earlier versions were presented at the Anthropology Department Colloquia at New York University and the City University of New York Graduate Center, where questions from the audience helped sharpen my arguments. Several people, including Timothy Mitchell, Catherine Lutz, and Buck Schieffelin, carefully read and commented on drafts, and their suggestions, sometimes taken, sometimes not, are gratefully acknowledged. As always, my greatest debt is to the Bedouin families in Egypt who let me participate in their lives and learn from them. Funding from NEH, Williams College, and the Fulbright Commission enabled me to spend more time with them in Egypt in 1985, 1986, and 1987.

1. For a comprehensive review of this literature, see Lutz and White (1986).
2. This ethnocentrism is expressed beautifully in the title of one of Lutz's (1985) articles, "Ethnopsychology Compared to What?"
3. For extensive references to this work, see Lutz and White (1986:417–20). Also, for a wonderfully insightful and playful reflection on some of the thorny problems shared by philosophers and anthropologists engaged in the cultural translation of feelings, see Rorty's (1979:70–127) discussion of the Antipodeans (persons without minds).
4. They cite my work, that of Myers (1979, 1986), Appadurai (1985), Keeler

(1983), Riesman (1977), Lindholm (1982), and others as examples of this type of work.
5. Both Buck Schieffelin and Ward Keeler, in personal communications, have voiced these sorts of worries even about their own exemplary work.
6. I am paraphrasing Foucault on discourse (1972:218, 229).
7. I am using "discourse," that admittedly slippery and overused term, not just as linguists do, to refer to the speech of individuals, but also in the Foucaultian sense of a range of culturally available and historically specific statements. See our introduction to this volume.
8. For a fuller discussion of the Awlad 'Ali, see Abu-Lughod (1986).
9. Much of the argument in this section was developed in Abu-Lughod (1986).
10. In other words, to have certain feelings or at least to express particular sentiments becomes a political statement, if not a political act. Although in the story of Fathalla the poems seem to have the power to kill, Bedouins usually just say that it moves people or causes them to change their actions. That is, they see it as persuasive.
11. When I was there doing fieldwork most recently (in 1987), every Bedouin I knew seemed to have a lawyer. They still tried to resolve disputes through their own tribal mediation system, and my host, who is a mediator, was strained to the limit with the number of tense cases he was asked to help resolve. What was happening, however, was that they had to work both through their own system and through the courts.
12. They talk about an institution called the *mijlās*, in which a young unmarried woman would entertain all the eligible young men in a tent, challenging them to respond to her songs.
13. Like the dissolution of the discourse of women's weaving in North Africa, argued by Messick (1987) to be related to the capitalist transformation of domestic weaving, with the disappearance of one occasion for song have died the songs appropriate to it among the Awlad 'Ali. Sheep shearings, which used to be occasions for groups of young men to go from household to household shearing the sheep, no longer occur, as professionals, mostly from Sinai, have taken over this work. The songs that accompanied sheep shearing were more explicitly sexual than the *ghinnāwa*, couching in innuendo their references to relations between men and women. These are no longer heard, and I heard of no equivalently sexual genres.
14. The Arabic original, as sung by 'Awadh al-Mālkī, is as follows:
nṣūḥa minnī lish-shāyib
illī ḥābis ḥurrīt ish-shab
wnāsī ḥāja ismhā ḥub
w'aṭf wshōg wnār thib
yā magwā nār il-ghāwī
yā magwā nār il-'ajgīn
illī ba'dhun mishtāgīn
simāḥithā yagbō khāyfīn
ygūl in-nāgir sā'a yjī
ygūl in-nāgir sā'a ytūg
15. For a critique of the idealism implicit in interpretive anthropology, see Asad (1983).
16. Lutz (1986) makes some of these points, but I think that three further sets of questions about the Euro-American emotion concepts she outlines need to be researched. First, which cultural concepts are most salient, and does this pattern differ by subcultures? Second, when do certain ways of think-

ing about emotion historically come into view, and what institutions and practices are they tied to? Third, when do ways of conceptualizing emotion come into play rhetorically in conversation?
17.   See also LeVine (1984:82–3) for a discussion of the relative absence of psychologizing among the Gusii in East Africa.
18.   I returned a year and a half later.

References

Abu-Lughod, Lila. 1985. Honor and the Sentiments of Loss in a Bedouin Society. *American Ethnologist* 12:245–61.
   1986. *Veiled Sentiments: Honor and Poetry in a Bedouin Society.* Berkeley: University of California Press.
Appadurai, Arjun. 1985. Gratitude as a Social Mode in South India. *Ethos* 13:236–45.
Asad, Talal. 1983. Anthropological Conceptions of Religion: Reflections on Geertz. *Man* (n.s.) 18:237–59.
Collier, Jane. 1974. Women in Politics. In M. Z. Rosaldo and L. Lamphere, eds., *Women, Culture, and Society.* Stanford: Stanford University Press, pp.89–96.
Foucault, Michel. 1970. *The Order of Things: An Archaeology of the Human Sciences.* New York: Pantheon.
   1972. *The Archaeology of Knowledge and the Discourse on Language.* New York: Pantheon.
   1985. *The Use of Pleasure.* Vol. 2 of *The History of Sexuality.* New York: Pantheon.
Keeler, Ward. 1983. Shame and Stage Fright in Java. *Ethos* 11:152–65.
LeVine, Robert. 1984. Properties of Culture: An Ethnographic View. In R. Shweder and R. A. LeVine, eds., *Culture Theory.* New York: Cambridge University Press, pp. 67–87.
Lindholm, Charles. 1982. *Generosity and Jealousy: The Swat Pukhtun of Northern Pakistan.* New York: Columbia University Press.
Lutz, Catherine. 1985. Ethnopsychology Compared to What?: Explaining Behavior and Consciousness Among the Ifaluk. In G. M. White and J. Kirkpatrick, eds., *Person, Self and Experience.* Berkeley: University of California Press, pp. 35–79.
   1986. Emotion, Thought, and Estrangement: Emotion as a Cultural Category. *Cultural Anthropology* 1:405–36.
Lutz, Catherine, and Geoffrey White. 1986. The Anthropology of Emotions. *Annual Review of Anthropology* 15:405–36.
Messick, Brinkley. 1987. Subordinate Discourse: Women, Weaving, and Gender Relations in North Africa. *American Ethnologist* 14:210–25.
Myers, Fred. 1979. Emotions and the Self: A Theory of Personhood and Political Order Among Pintupi Aborigines. *Ethos* 7:343–70.
   1986. *Pintupi Country, Pintupi Self: Sentiment, Place, and Politics Among Western Desert Aborigines.* Washington, DC: Smithsonian Institution Press.
Peters, Stella. 1952. The Bedouin Bait. Unpublished B.Lit. Thesis, Oxford University.
Riesman, Paul. 1977. *Freedom in Fulani Social Life.* Chicago: University of Chicago Press.
Rorty, Richard. 1979. *Philosophy and the Mirror of Nature.* Princeton: Princeton University Press.

Rosaldo, Michelle Z. 1984. Toward an Anthropology of Self and Feeling. In R. Shweder and R. LeVine, eds., *Culture Theory: Essays on Mind, Self, and Emotion.* Cambridge and New York: Cambridge University Press, pp. 137–57.
Wolf, Margery. 1972. *Women and Family in Rural Taiwan:* Stanford: Stanford University Press.

3. Moral discourse and the rhetoric of emotions

GEOFFREY M. WHITE

Theories of emotion and theories of culture have not always acknowledged their mutual relevance. To the extent that relations have been explored, this has usually come under the rubric of "culture and personality" – with the former regarded as the domain of public symbols and shared cognitions and the latter as that of individual affects and motivations. As Lutz (1985) has noted, this compartmentalization, and the implied division of labor between anthropology and psychology, parallel neatly our folk model of the person, which tends to dichotomize worlds of thinking and feeling, of society and the individual. In this chapter I explore briefly some of the ways in which culture theory and emotion theory (or, more broadly, self theory) may enrich one another. I do this by arguing that discourse occupies a strategic place in the ethnographic study of emotion and culture, and illustrate my argument with an example of emotive discourse from a Solomon Islands society.

Parallel to such familiar dichotomies as competence – performance and language – speech, approaches to discourse and discourse analysis tend to be split between those that emphasize conceptual process (e.g., Holland and Quinn 1987) and those that are largely interactional (e.g., Gumperz 1982).[1] Whereas the former, more textual approaches are concerned with interpretive models, the latter focus to a greater degree on situated practices and institutional structures. This chapter explores points of convergence between these approaches by searching out relations between ideology and praxis in a specific, culturally constituted discourse of emotion referred to as 'disentangling' (*graurutha*). Beginning with a culturally defined and socially situated activity – disentangling – it is possible to ask, "What are people doing with talk of emotion in this context?" and "What are the presuppositions and social conditions necessary for the rhetoric of disentangling to have the pragmatic effects it does?" Noting that emotion talk in this context not only represents but creates social reality, the analysis identifies specific rhetorical moves that work to transform socioemotional reality – specifically, by transmuting emotions of divisiveness into those of solidarity.

Emotion schemas, inference, and ambiguity

Attributions of emotion obtain much of their social meaning from ethnopsychological understandings about the role of emotions in mediating social action (Lutz 1987). Folk models of social process are frequently structured in terms of scenariolike schemata that represent emotions as arising in social situations and compelling certain types of response. At a general level, the chain of reasoning represented in emotion schemas takes the following form (see Lutz 1987:293–4):

SOCIAL EVENT
↓
EMOTION
↓
ACTION RESPONSE

This representational format captures only the broad, simplified outline of a highly generalized structure – a "prototypical scenario" of social and emotional process (Lakoff and Kovecses 1987).[2] But positing this type of structure is useful in directing attention to specific classes of inference likely to obtain in emotive discourse. Although not all emotional understanding adheres to the interpersonal character of the preceding schema, it is hypothesized that such structures occupy the heartland of emotional discourse across cultures.

Culturally defined emotions are embedded in complex understandings about identities and scenarios of action, especially concerning the sorts of event that evoke it, the relations it is appropriate to, and the responses expected to follow from it.[3] To the extent that these understandings are elaborated in a generalized model, talk of a specific emotional response implicitly characterizes an action or event as an instance of a general type. In most cultures, a limited number of key emotions encode such generalized understandings. Applying these conceptions to the great diversity of everyday happenings sets up a dialectic between structure and event in which particular events are assimilated to prior structures of understanding. At the same time, the conceptual models so used may themselves by modified as they are accommodated to the comprehension of ongoing events. Analysis of this type of accommodation, beyond the scope of this chapter, would deal with historical transformations in the institutionalized patterns of emotion.

As an example of the type of emotion schema outlined here, consider the English-language concept of "anger." Commonsense understandings of anger posit that it typically follows from a moral violation that infringes upon the self, leading to a desire for retribution (Lakoff and Kovecses 1987). More than any other English-language emotion term, "anger" has been frequently applied in ethnographic accounts of social and psychological processes across cultures (e.g., Briggs 1970; Harris 1978; Valentine 1963). For the most part, it is only those studies with a stated interest in ethnopsychological meaning that have examined directly issues of translation and cross-cultural relevance (see, e.g., Myers 1988; Poole 1985; Rosaldo 1980; Schieffelin 1983). These studies have much to say about the culturally specific ways in which angerlike emotions adhere to local contours of meaning. And yet, the English word "anger" remains a comparison point for these and other ethnographic studies. Allowing for the inevitable distortions that occur from the cross-cultural application of English-language terms, the reason such "translations" work to the extent that they do is that they rely on cross-cultural convergences in prototype scenarios used to conceptualize emotion. Thus, for example, core elements in the meaning of American English "anger" and Santa Isabel *di'a tagna*, to be discussed, may both be outlined in terms of the following action-emotion-response sequence:[4]

TRANSGRESSION (Other, Self)
↓
[*di'a tagna*, 'anger']
↓
RETRIBUTION (Self, Other)

Even in this simplified form, denuded of social contextual information, the prototype schema gives an indication of the types of inferential paths that make emotion talk a moral idiom (i.e., a mode of evaluating and constituting social reality). As a personal response mediating social action and reaction, specific emotions such as "anger" designate interactive scenarios with known evaluative and behavioral implications. The attribution of emotion brings to bear presupposed knowledge about the desirability or undesirability of generic courses of action on the interpretation of events. For example, prototypic 'anger' represented in the preceding schema would be regarded as problematic because of the implied propensity for retribution and the harm to persons and the social order likely to result. In this manner, an expression of emotion becomes a pronouncement or claim (often implicit) about the way things are or, more significantly, the way they ought to be (Bailey 1983). To continue with the example of 'anger', expressions of 'anger' draw attention to an antecedent event as a moral breach (i.e., as a generic type of social action) while at the same time implying the need for corrective action. Some examples from the discourse of disentangling, which is centrally concerned with problems of conflict, transgression, and 'anger', will illustrate.

In one disentangling meeting, where people are encouraged to 'talk out' their bad feelings about conflicted events, an older man, a village catechist, recounted an incident in which he chastised one of his neighbors, Edi (also a catechist), for hitting several misbehaving children. The alleged hitting runs counter to a strong proscription on the physical punishment of children and against the generalized ethos of nonaggression (White 1985b). Reporting his own speech on the occasion when he confronted his neighbor, the old man quoted himself:

> Catechists shouldn't hit, shouldn't be angry towards children and people, man. [They] should take care of them, just like chiefs, in order to be good. But you were hitting children. . . . I was very angry with you, Edi. Because you are a catechist, you should be teaching people, not hitting.

Here the speaker's 'anger' is attributed to a clear-cut violation of moral strictures – a widely shared proscription against physical punishment of children. As he began his narrative of this event, the speaker threatened to report his neighbor, implying that his own felt 'anger' was inclined toward some kind of retribution. In this way, the speaker's 'anger' mediated an antecedent event (hitting) with his own impulse toward a corrective response (reporting).

It may seem ironic that the speaker says that he got 'angry' at Edi for getting 'angry.' The difference, and it is an important one, is that the two angers are differently contextualized: between adult catechist and child on the one hand, and between mature men on the other. In the A'ara view, sharp 'anger' should not be expressed in relations marked by asymmetries of power; hence the speaker's analogy between Edi's relation to the children and a chief's relation to his followers. Talk of 'anger', then, is not only an idiom of moral claims. It also indexes social relations. Another example illustrates the relational rhetoric of emotion even more clearly.

In one of the recorded meetings, a man claimed to be 'angry' with his sister's son for stealing betel nut from one of his trees. But because he simply expressed 'anger', without acknowledging either the asymmetry or the close relation of kinship between himself and his nephew, others saw his talk of anger as inappropriate. Two other participants responded not to the act of stealing but to the uncle's stated 'anger' toward his maternal nephew. One of the listeners spoke to the uncle, saying:

> This kind of talk that you are making is as if you are all separate [*soasopa*] people. It is better to speak to your nephew to teach him, like I do with my nephew. . . . That kind of ['angry'] talk can be aimed at other people, but to our own nephews, our own children, it is very bad.

The speaker's reprimand mirrors that of the first example. Both focus on the social context of expressed 'anger': one between adult and child, the other between mother's brother and sister's son. This second example is more explicit about the primacy of the social component ("['anger'] can be aimed at other people"). Given these assumptions about emotion and morality, it can be seen that the experience of anger poses a dilemma here: 'Anger' expressed in the context of community relations is likely to be regarded as contrary to the ideals of solidarity, whereas suppressed 'anger,' according to the folk theory of misfortune, poses a danger to the self and others (see White 1985a for more on this).

As an arena for the sanctioned expression of emotion, disentangling would appear to be a culturally constituted solution to the dilemma of suppressed 'anger'. Yet, as the preceding examples indicate, this is not as straightforward as it might seem. In disentangling as in other contexts, talk of 'anger' in close relations is likely to be disapproved. The disentangling context does not legitimate expressions of hostility that are not tempered by ideals of solidarity and the goal of repairing damaged relations. What it does provide is an opportunity for the creation of a social reality in which 'angry' events are rhetorically transformed and damaged relations symbolically repaired.

Talk of 'anger' is somewhat out of place in disentangling sessions, defined as they are as occasions for reestablishing community solidarity rather than uncovering transgressions or imposing sanctions. The examples cited account for most of the 'anger' attributions in the recorded meetings. Instead, one finds numerous examples of talk about 'sadness' (*di'a nagnafa*) and 'shame' (*mamaja*). The following analysis suggests that these attributions are particularly well suited to the work of transform-

ing 'angry' events to fit the avowed aims of disentangling while at the
same time promoting a particular point of view about those events. The
effectiveness of emotion talk in accomplishing the pragmatic work of
disentangling is enhanced by the fact that it is both indirect and ambiguous.

As a moral idiom, emotion talk is indirect because it relies on presup-
position and implication to state interpretations and evaluations of contested events. The quality of indirection is particularly important in small-
scale, face-to-face communities such as that considered here, where overt
public statements about others' behavior are often proscribed. The rhetoric of emotions offers a remedy. Relying on shared models of socioemotional process, speakers may pose and counterpose statements about
their own actions and emotions, leaving moral assertions about others
unstated. The availability of an idiom with which to assert moral claims
indirectly while simultaneously acknowledging the overt agenda of reestablishing solidarity is essential to successful disentangling.

Related to the indirect quality of emotion talk is the fact that emotions
are susceptible to multiple moral readings. The potential for ambiguity
arises from the complexity of conceptual and situational factors contributing to emotional meaning. A specific emotion attribution may have
a range of potential entailments, and just which implications are brought
to bear in a given interpretation may remain ambiguous. The following
analysis pursues this point by examining the use of a particular emotion
term, *di'a nagnafa* ('sad'), in disentangling discourse.[5] This concept is
central to the disentangling activity because it is seen to follow from
transgressions that threaten interpersonal relations, but at the same time
gives rise to attempts to repair those relations. Represented schemati-
cally, basic elements of the *di'a nagnafa* scenario may be sketched as follows:

DAMAGE CLOSE RELATIONS (Other, Self)
↓
di'a nagnafa ('sad')
↓
REPAIR (Self, Other)

An important source of moral ambiguity in talk of 'sadness' derives from
the potential for focusing variously on the antecedent (transgression) or
the implied response (attempt at repair). The former may constitute a
challenge to the other, whereas the latter emphasizes reconciliation and
relatedness.[6]

The following analysis shows that interpretive ambiguity in talk of emotions facilitates the rhetorical transformation of socioemotional reality – a transformation central to the task of disentangling. Specifically, narrative constructions of past events reformulate those events so as to transmute threatening and conflict-ridden 'anger' rhetorically to solidarity-engendering 'sadness'. Both 'anger' and 'sadness' pertain to the sorts of problematic events in which the transgressions of others impinge on the self. Disentangling institutionalizes a speech event in which speakers reframe 'angry' responses in terms of 'sadness', 'shame', and related emotions. In doing so, conflict events are narrated so as to highlight valued interpersonal relations and community solidarity. The analysis also raises questions about the experiential basis of rhetorical transformations accomplished in discourse.

The conceptualization of 'disentangling'

Santa Isabel is one of five major islands in the Solomon Islands, with a present population of more than 14,000. Half of the population speak an Austronesian language known variously as A'ara or Cheke Holo (White, Kokhonigita, and Pulomana 1988). People engage primarily in subsistence gardening while pursuing various agricultural schemes to produce cash crops. Prior to changes at the turn of the century, sociopolitical activity was organized largely by relations of descent and regional alignments in which local big men or 'chiefs' (*funei*) were the focal point for intergroup feasting and raiding. The idiom of descent is distinctly matrilineal. In former times, the territorial locus of descent group identity was marked by shrines where propitiatory offerings were made to ancestral spirits.

Although economic changes have been slow in coming, cultural transformations associated with Western influence, especially Christianity, have been more dramatic (White 1988). Historically, the most significant agent of change was the Anglican Melanesian Mission (now the Church of Melanesia), which completed its work of converting the island population just after the turn of the century. The Isabel people, who had been severely victimized by marauding headhunters from the western Solomon Islands, eagerly received the mission at the end of the nineteenth century. Conversion entailed major shifts in residential patterns in which people formerly scattered throughout the mountainous interior migrated to coastal villages of unprecedented size (100–200 people), where ritual life was (and continues to be) centered on the village chapel. More importantly for this chapter, contemporary moral ideals are also cast largely in terms of Christian ideology.

A'ara-speaking people sporadically (and decreasingly; White in press) engage in a practice known as *graurutha*, or 'disentangling' (from *rutha*, 'undo' or 'untie'). Put briefly, disentangling is an activity in which family members or village mates meet together to talk about interpersonal conflicts and 'bad feelings' (*di'a nagnafa*). The point of this talk is to make bad feelings public so as to defuse their destructive potential. The A'ara believe, as do people in many cultures (e.g., Harris 1978; Ito 1985; Strathern 1968) that negative emotions that remain hidden may cause illness and misfortune – ranging from personal injury to a poor catch of fish or failure to locate domestic pigs in the forest. Furthermore, bad feelings are not only potentially damaging to the self, they may harm others as well. It is therefore in the interest of the community as a whole to repair social discord and maintain emotional harmony. Disentangling is an institutionalized means for achieving those ends. It provides an occasion in which people are encouraged to talk about conflicts and resentments that would otherwise be difficult and even proscribed topics of conversation.

The significance of disentangling depends on a presupposed world of understandings about persons and emotions. As already stated, a central tenet of this world is that hidden 'bad feelings' arising from interpersonal conflict may cause illness and misfortune for the self and others. The operative word here is 'hidden'. By implication, if negative emotions can be 'talked out' and made public, they lose their potential for causing harm. But this 'talking out' is not conceived of as catharsis in the sense of reexperiencing or releasing intense emotions "bottled up" (my metaphor) in the person, as would be expected, for example, in the American model of anger (Lakoff and Kovecses 1987). To the contrary, disentangling talk is conducted in a narrative mode of reporting on past events rather than enacting demonstrative displays of felt emotion. For A'ara speakers, public talk about conflict in this context is itself an act of reconciliation. Individuated 'anger', hidden from the restraining moral judgments of the community, may, in the local view, give rise to a broad range of destructive behaviors (White 1985a, 1985b). By engaging in disentangling, speakers tacitly acknowledge the prior value of community solidarity, ritually closing the conflict episode as a source of disruptive thoughts and actions.

This interpretation of the local conceptualization of disentangling is evident in a range of conventional metaphors used to talk about the activity. These metaphors suggest that disentangling is thought about as a process of *revelation*, of moving personal thoughts and emotions into community awareness. By examining a range of interrelated linguistic expressions, it is possible to identify key images used to conceptualize the rationale of disentangling.

Presuming an image of the person as a container, two commonly used metaphorical expressions describe disentangling as either 'talking out' (*cheke fajifla*) bad feelings or as 'opening up' (*tora*) so that thoughts and feelings do not remain hidden. In the former expression, problematic feelings are described as moving from inside to outside the person so that they become visible or known to the community. The directional adverb *fajifla* ('out') signifies physical movement across a boundary, as in leaving a room or removing an object from a container. The second metaphor also builds on a sense of revelation – of becoming known by virtue of coming into view. The verb 'open up', often used to describe opening a door or lifting the lid to a box, describes the sort of talk that 'opens up' persons in the context of disentangling.

Metaphors of sight and visibility are further elaborated in a variety of expressions used in this context. For example, disentangling makes thoughts and feelings public by 'bringing them to the surface', just as a turtle is spotted when it 'surfaces' (*thagra*) for air. And, by removing covering layers, disentangling reveals feelings that have been 'buried' (*fruni*) or 'covered over' (*plohmo*) by problems and reluctance to talk about them.

Metaphors of concealment and revelation represent a local analogue of the opposition of "public" and "private." Disentangling presumes that the person is a bounded locus of experience that may or may not be communicated in discourse. The expressions mentioned previously are indicative of the local view that disentangling transforms personal thoughts and feelings by placing them in a wider field of knowledge circulation. Participants in disentangling invoke images of 'talking out' and 'opening up with talk' to remind one another that *just by talking* in a certain way, one may fulfill the overt agenda of disentangling, of making thoughts and feelings public. Disentangling performances are not only *seen* as efficacious, they *are* efficacious in transforming that which is 'hidden', 'inside', or 'below the surface' to that which is 'visible', 'outside', and 'above the surface'. However, as anyone familiar with the family life of small communities might expect, there is more to disentangling than the overt agenda. A closer analysis of the practice of disentan-

gling gives a more complex picture of the multiple social and emotional
realities created in context.

The practice of disentangling

Local theories of misfortune reflect the indigenous rationale for disentangling as a desired and even necessary activity (White 1985a). These
understandings (among others) constitute an intersubjective basis for its
joint enactment. To some extent, a disentangling session achieves its
purpose simply by taking place. By virtue of their coparticipation, people signal their mutual commitment to repairing community relatedness. However, beyond the simple fact of its performance, a disentangling session creates a communicative environment in which a certain
type of discourse is possible – specifically, narrative reconstructions of
problematic events.

Consider some of the ways in which the social organization of disentangling supports its communicative goals and facilitates the transformation of 'angry' emotions. To begin with, the narrative mode is well
suited to the avoidance of 'anger' in the disentangling session itself. For
an event that has as its goal the alleviation of hostility, it would not do
to provoke further expressions of resentment. And, given that participants are expected to talk about interpersonal conflicts, the avoidance
of hostility is a difficult problem. The organization of disentangling as a
sequence of narratives minimizes or suppresses the kind of quick chal-
lenge-and-riposte that typically leads to confrontation and argumentation. The social genius of disentangling is that the conversational organization of the event is managed through the joint participation of all
present. No designated person or group leads the meeting. Rather, various participants take turns urging one another to speak and, where
necessary, jointly direct conversation away from problematic topics or
formats (White in press).

Even the physical setting of disentangling works to defuse confronta-
tional modes of interaction. The two meetings I attended were both held
at night in a large house with people gathered in the shadows both inside and outside. (The nighttime format may be more characteristic of
larger, village-level meetings than of smaller, family disentangling sessions.) Not only would the protagonists not address their speech to one
another, they would likely not even see one another. Narratives are produced for a largely unseen audience. And yet, the unseen coterie of

listeners is essential to the successful enactment of disentangling (cf. Brenneis, this volume). Furthermore, disentangling participants are not just passive listeners. They actively collaborate to evoke narrative performances from those known to be involved in not-quite-resolved conflicts, and to orchestrate the interaction so as to minimize the potential for antagonistic confrontation.

Each narrative produced in this environment is an opportunity for reforming socioemotional reality. Given the avowed purpose of disentangling to 'talk out' bad feelings, it is not surprising that the narratives are punctuated with overt talk of emotions – talk dense with moral significance. In light of the fact that each emotion concept entails specific interpersonal information (Levy 1984; Myers 1979), what sorts of emotion talk recur in disentangling sessions? In my limited sample of recorded sessions,[7] three emotions emerge as particularly salient: 'sadness', 'shame', and 'anger'.[8] For reasons that should now be apparent, the last term, 'anger', appears less frequently than the former two. This finding is consistent with the hypothesis that disentangling is concerned with rhetorically transforming 'anger' in relations where overt tensions are not easily voiced. The following discussion takes up this hypothesis in more detail.

A review of several conflict narratives recorded in two separate meetings indicates that statements to the effect that "Event x made me *di'a nagnafa* ('sad')" occur frequently as speakers seek to draw attention to the problematic nature of event x. In my analysis talk of 'sadness' in this context, like talk of 'anger', presupposes some sort of morally questionable action – an action that has harmed the speaker or someone identified with the speaker. At a generalized level of understanding, both of these emotions (*di'a nagnafa* 'sad' and *di'a tagna* 'angry') may be seen to derive from forms of transgression. It is at a more specific level of cultural knowledge that they are differentiated in terms of distinctions about particular types of transgression. Although both 'sadness' and 'anger' are evoked by rule violations, 'sadness' pertains to social actions that damage relations, whereas 'anger' is regarded as a response to actions that harm or threaten the self or significant others. These differing degrees of generality in cultural understandings of emotion reflect the hierarchical organization of knowledge such that models are nested within models, with reasoning about specific emotions drawing upon more global understandings about kinship obligations and the social order generally (see Quinn 1987:189). The nesting of cultural models allows speakers to range across varying levels of specificity in their narrative, thus leaving room for differing degrees of ambiguity in their moral assertions.

The possibility of finding both 'sadness' and 'anger' as plausible responses to the same events is the basis for their substitutability – a feature of A'ara understandings that lies at the crux of disentangling discourse. By relying upon generalized understandings about responses to rule violations to talk about 'sadness' rather than 'anger', a speaker may then draw out differing implications for his or her response – interpreted in terms of a scenario of repair rather than retribution. Combining the schemas outlined earlier, one may visualize the potential for attributing 'anger' and 'sadness' to the same eliciting event, with divergent implications for the type of reaction inferred.

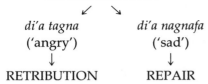

TRANSGRESSION

di'a tagna	*di'a nagnafa*
('angry')	('sad')
↓	↓
RETRIBUTION	REPAIR

A case of disentangling

An example of narrative drawn from a village disentangling meeting illustrates the process by which emotion talk is used to create an emergent social reality (a transcript of the entire meeting is given in White in press). The case summarized here was the second incident taken up in a meeting conducted one evening as people met to clear away possible unresolved conflicts that might interfere with preparations for an upcoming feast. (Hidden resentments might, for example, cause failure or injury to those going out pig hunting or turtle hunting.) The meeting, in fact, served two purposes. With the disentangling portion of the evening finished, villagers turned to a discussion of preparations for the upcoming feast.

Discussion of this case in the meeting consisted primarily of just one long narrative by one of the people principally involved in the incident (whom I refer to as Tom). Tom's narrative is then followed by a series of shorter statements. Several others who figure prominently in the story were not present at the meeting (a fact that was noted prior to Tom's speaking, as participants in the meeting attempted to get all the parties involved to speak before realizing that they were absent).

Tom's account focuses on the way he and others responded to the revealed transgressions of two young people (his younger brother and a young woman) who had been having an endogamous extramarital affair. His discussion is not concerned directly with the illicit relationship, but with the ways people reacted to it and the implications of those reactions for their relations with one another. In other words, his is a narrative of metaconflict – articulating conflicting views of conflict in the community.

When the mother of the young woman learned what was going on, she apparently told the young man to "never set foot" in her village (Paka) again. The young man then went off in a rage and at some point cut himself with his bush knife. Tom later encountered his younger brother in the bush and elicited his story about what had happened. After leading his brother back up to their village (Holo), Tom decided to return to Paka to see the people there and retrieve his brother's bag. Along the way, he encountered the young woman's father, Gata, and talked with him about what had occurred prior to his brother's injury. The father told him that his wife, Fala, had told Tom's brother not to set foot in their village again.

Tom then proceeded to Paka, where he found Fala's mother, Sukhi, and apparently told her that if that was how they were going to talk to his brother, then she and her family should not come up to his village, Holo, either. These mutual rejections had the potential to involve wider circles of people, since the planned Christmas feast was to be held at Holo. Tom's encounter with Sukhi was followed by a period of uncertainty as to who, if anyone, from Paka would participate in preparations for the upcoming feast. As in many such incidents in small communities, an initial transgression reverberated throughout the social order, threatening to ignite a wider conflict between others related to the antagonists.

Tom's narrative chronologically reconstructs his involvement in the events following his brother's self-inflicted injury, making extensive use of reported speech to give the account immediacy and validity. He punctuates his retelling of these events by describing his feelings during the episode. It is the emotions of 'sadness' and 'shame' that emerge most clearly in the account, serving to reinforce and amplify Tom's interpretations.

Tom begins speaking by distancing himself from the illicit affair and his brother's self-inflicted injury. He then proceeds to narrate the sequence of events leading to his first encounter with the young woman's father, Gata. In the course of his narrative, Tom twice emphasizes his younger brother's responsibility for his own injury. However, following this, he shifts attention to Fala's rejection of his brother, twice quoting her utterance "Don't set foot in Paka again!"

It is the moral significance of this rejection that becomes the focus of Tom's narrative. He brings Fala's act into moral scrutiny by placing his relationship with Fala in the foreground of his account. The evaluative implications of Fala's utterance are delineated most clearly by Tom's characterization of their relationship in terms of close kinship. He says that Fala is "like another mother" to him. (Tom and Fala are in fact related as maternal half-cousins. Fala's older age is the basis for Tom referring to her as "mother.") The idioms of kinship and food sharing are invoked to assert close relations among those involved in the entanglement. These images emerge clearly in Tom's narrative as he describes his encounter with Fala's husband, when he first heard about Fala's expulsion of his brother. The narrative establishes the incongruity between that act and the fact of kinlike relations:

> Then he (Fala's husband) told about [the statement] "Don't set foot again in Paka."
> [So I said] "Who said that man?"
> "Fala."
> "Fala! So, alright, [she] is just like another mother to me. You married her, but she was already [just like] my mother. There is water, there is food, there are sweet potatos there [for me to share]. 'Don't set foot in Paka!' [she said to] my younger brother! He did do wrong before they started thinking like this, so alright," I said. But my thoughts became all confused ('knotted') about that.

Note that Tom uses a metaphor of entanglement ('knotted' *haru*) to express his response to the moral conflict created by his brother's transgression and his relatives' subsequent rejection of him. The image of entanglement effectively comments on the fact of a moral dilemma without committing to a specific interpretation pinpointing the agency and the responsibility.

Having established his sonlike relation with the woman Fala, Tom goes on to assert that her banishment of his younger brother made him *mamaja* ('ashamed') with her and, most immediately, with her husband, who reported the act of exclusion to him. Although a thorough account of A'ara 'shame' is not possible here, it typically signifies some kind of mismatch between context and event, usually involving a violation of appropriate social distance. In this instance, Tom's attribution of 'shame' upon hearing of Fala's remarks implies that her act of rejection implicitly misread or undervalued the relations that should have obtained in that context. To underscore this point, Tom characterizes his relations with Fala in terms of potent symbols of food sharing, invoking a commonly used scenario of entering someone's house and helping oneself to their food.[9]

The juxtaposition of this characterization and the attribution of 'shame' induced by Fala's rejection calls attention to her act as one that placed inappropriate distance between kin relations, thereby creating the need to repair the moral damage. This implication is then further reaffirmed by the attribution of 'sadness' – just the emotion that would be expected in response to a transgression that damages close relations.

Each emotion attribution may be seen as a partial "filling in" or instantiation of a general schema such as those discussed previously. Once the emotion portion of a scenario is instantiated, the listener may draw inferences about how the events leading to or following from that emotion are to be interpreted. In other words, the listener fills in other portions of the schema through inference, even though the speaker has not been explicit about those aspects of the events.

Much of the "action" in emotion rhetoric involves the instantiation that results from giving an interpretation to precipitating events. Thus, when Tom asserts that the banishment of his brother made him 'sad', he is implying, in this context, that the rejection is an instance of a certain *kind* of social action – one that damages close relations, that is, the sort of thing that evokes 'sadness'. And, even more importantly for his portrayal of the incident, he implicitly claims that *his* response of telling off the offending parties was an attempt at withdrawal rather than some kind of 'angry' getting even.

The portion of Tom's narrative in which he talks most concertedly about his emotional responses is given subsequently so as to look more closely at the conceptual role of emotion rhetoric in building a desired interpretation. By combining Tom's overt statements about emotion with the hypothesized knowledge structures discussed earlier, the analysis seeks to identify implicit structures of emotional meaning. (For this analysis, only attributions of 'sadness' are expanded in this way, but see White (in press) for a similar treatment of 'shame'.) Certain conventions are useful for depicting interpretation as a process of inference (Hutchins 1973; Quinn 1987). Borrowing from the standard format for representing syllogistic reasoning, the implications of emotion attribution are shown here as an inference drawn from a set of premises. As noted earlier, in many cases these inferences pertain to instantiating a generalized schema. In the conventions adopted here, a specific proposition about emotion is shown in quotation marks and the hypothesized background schema is indicated by capital letters. The proposition implied by instantiating the schema is depicted below a horizontal line as follows:

GENERAL SCHEMA
+
"attributed emotion"
_____
inferred proposition

Following the passage quoted earlier, Tom continues his narrative by recalling his thoughts and feelings at the time he encountered the young woman's father and heard him tell about the expulsion of his younger brother. He characterizes his feelings as a mixture of 'sadness' and 'shame':

> It was the "Don't set foot in Paka" that made me ashamed with him. This man [the young woman's father] is like our father, we two [Tom and his younger brother] would go inside [their] house, these sweet potatoes were our food, these houses, these beds . . . These feelings were probably with him [Tom's younger brother]. Because of this I was *sad*.

DAMAGE CLOSE RELATION → SAD
"Fala's remark → sad"
_____
Fala's remark = damage close relation[10]

> I was just ashamed from those ways, from the way "Don't set foot here." [So] I came to the old woman [Sukhi] up there.

Tom's talk of 'shame' and 'sadness' creates a context for rationalizing his own actions. Most problematic is his telling Fala's group (through a conversation with her mother, Sukhi) not to bother coming up to his village for the Christmas feast. The attribution of 'shame' provides a motive for Tom's hasty words. The prototypical scenario for shame (not detailed here) entails a response of withdrawal. He here implies that his remarks to Sukhi were more of a response of avoidance in the face of the social distance created by Fala's rejection of his brother.

As Tom goes on with his narrative, he focuses more directly on his feelings and motives prior to making those remarks to Fala's mother. His talk of 'shame' is embedded in attributions of 'sadness'. At this point

in the narrative, the emotion rhetoric is oriented more to types of response than to characterization of antecedent events.

The hypothesis that much disentangling discourse is concerned with
the transformation of scenarios of 'anger' to a more desired reality is
examined in the following passage. In this portion of Tom's narrative,
as he continues describing his encounter with Sukhi, the anger-retribution
schema can be seen to be lurking just behind the scenes. In fact, Tom
here applies a tactic unusual to disentangling discourse: He explicitly
poses the anger scenario as a possible alternative interpretation of his
hasty words so that he can reject it from consideration (see Quinn
1987:185–6 for a similar example).[11]

> It's just that when my real father said that [reported Fala's remarks]
> that I was *sad* and came and talked to the old woman [Sukhi] up
> here.
>
> SAD → REPAIR DAMAGED RELATION
> "sad → Tom's remarks to Sukhi"
> _____
> Tom's remarks = repair damaged relation
>
> I was just *ashamed* is all. It was not [I didn't mean], "You all don't
> come back up. Don't set food in my village, you all." I didn't [mean]
> that.
>
> ANGER → RETRIBUTION
> "Tom's remark not retribution"
> _____
> not anger
>
> That was just from my *sadness*, my own *shame*.
>
> SAD → REPAIR DAMAGED RELATION
> "sad → Tom's remarks"
> _____
> Tom's remarks = repair damaged relation
>
> Now I'm in front of my mothers and sisters [in the village Paka].
> These houses should be for coming inside. These houses are for
> me to get a drink. These houses should be for taking a rest, so
> when my [fictive] father said that, I was *sad* about it.
>
> DAMAGE CLOSE RELATION → SAD
> "Fala's remark → sad"
> _____
> Fala's remark = damage close relation

In this passage, the attributions of 'sadness' and 'shame' both contribute
to an emerging interpretation of Tom's response to his brother's rejec-

tion. 'Sadness' is the emotion that links Tom's reaction to the exclusion of his brother with his own confrontation with Fala's group – an emotion that follows from a concern for valued relations and is supposed to lead to efforts at moral repair. Although Tom's statements in the preceding passage emphasize the types of action that follow from 'sadness' (and 'shame'), he also reminds his listeners about the source of those emotions in disrupted social relations by reiterating images of kinship and food sharing. These images emphasize the social ties that are an essential element of the interpretation that replaces a scenario of angry confrontation with an awkward withdrawal motivated by 'shame' and 'sadness'. Whether this strategy works, of course, is uncertain. But it is not so much the truth value of his assertions as their coherence and forcefulness in the disentangling context that constitute a successful performance.

This example, drawn from a single disentangling narrative, illustrates the ethnofunctional beauty of disentangling as a predefined social occasion in which people rhetorically mend minor tears in the social fabric before relations unravel further. In this context, direct talk of 'anger' that leads to retribution seems to surface only in regard to minor incidents, and even then it may be problematic (White in press). Instead, disentangling discourse plays on the inherent moral ambiguities of interpersonal conflict to characterize 'angry' reactions as responses of 'sadness' and 'shame', thereby reframing events that have been problematic for persons and communities alike. In short, disentangling – as ideology and as social institution – works (however imperfectly) to bring conditions of divisiveness and individuated 'anger' more in line with models of solidarity.

Conclusion

Disentangling institutionalizes an activity in which community members ritually realign skewed relations. Talk of emotions such as *di'a nagnafa* is a culturally constituted means of periodically re-creating these alignments while simultaneously advancing more covert agendas of moral argumentation. The consistent attribution of 'sadness' and 'shame' to problematic events (seen by many as having evoked hostile responses) suggests that disentangling discourse rhetorically transmutes 'anger' to 'sadness'. There is enough overlap in the 'anger' and 'sadness' schemas so that they may plausibly be applied to the same events, with the effect of reconstruing conflict situations so as to emphasize reconciliation instead of retribution. And, by implication, the likelihood of suffering any of the broad range of damaging effects seen to follow from unresolved 'anger' is reduced.

Without either the shared model of disentangling or the institutionalized context in which to produce narrative accounts of conflict, neither the rhetoric nor the reality of emotion manifest in disentangling would be what it is. If one construes emotions as sociocultural *institutions* that depend on both the cultural model and the interactive situation for their meaning and effect, then analytic attention is directed more widely than a strictly person-centered approach would suggest.[12] By recognizing that emotions are not simply expressed in social situations, but are in fact constituted by the types of activities and relations in which they are enacted, ethnographic attention may be given to the institutionalized discourse practices that shape emotional meaning and experience (Lutz and White 1986).

Because of its evocative functions, emotion discourse is especially relevant for theories of social action. To talk about or express emotion in context is to expect to evoke a certain type of response in both the self and the listening other. However, analysis of the socioemotional realities so created is complicated by the fact that the analysis is likely to go beyond the conscious awareness of the participants. In the case of disentangling, participants appear not to recognize or acknowledge the transformative effects of disentangling narrative, referring instead to the 'talking out' aspect of disentangling. Even though participants acknowledge the attempts of narrators to replay past events to their moral advantage, the folk theory of disentangling does not encompass the act of re-forming specific emotions. In disentangling, as in many emotive institutions, the nature and degree of participants' awareness of discourse functions are important elements in the institution's ability to achieve its interactive ends.

Perhaps ironically, a discourse-centered approach such as that outlined here holds particular promise as a method for examining significances of emotional meaning unrecognized or unacknowledged by participants. It is usually taken for granted that the analysis of discourse is an avenue to identifying public constructions of socioemotional reality. To this we should add that analysis of patterns of unspoken meaning in emotive discourse may also provide a means of investigating less "visible" transformations of personal experience.

Notes

This chapter is based on fieldwork in Santa Isabel carried out in 1975–6 and on more focused research on disentangling conducted during two months in 1984. Support of the latter project by the Wenner-Gren Foundation (grant no. 4248) is gratefully acknowledged. I am also grateful to Jack Bilmes, Lamont Lindstrom, and Catherine Lutz for helpful comments on this chapter, as well as to numerous others who have offered insightful remarks on a longer analysis of disentangling discourse (White in press).

1. A third major thrust in anthropological approaches to discourse not addressed directly in this chapter is that represented in poststructuralist concerns with the historical and political conditions necessary for statements to obtain truth value and moral force (epitomized in the work of Foucault, e.g., 1981]). I take the sociopolitical preconditions of knowledge and power that make a certain discourse possible to be different from the conceptual and communicative structures through which that discourse takes on cultural and experiential reality. However, approaching emotion as discourse opens up the former vantage point as a way of delineating the historical and institutional determinants of emotions as a culturally constructed political force (see Abu-Lughod, this volume).

2. As a prototype structure, the schema represents a typical or default course for socioemotional process, but not one that is seen as invariant or completely predictable. Ethnopsychological knowledge of persons and action may be elaborated in a great variety of ways and may still be consistent with the basic shape of the event-emotion-response scenario. For example, D'Andrade's (1987) discussion of the American folk model of the mind postulates a more detailed picture of conceptions of feelings and desires related to a range of mental and behavioral processes.

3. This chapter does not examine in detail the more specific sorts of relational information encoded in emotion concepts. Knowledge about the social contexts of emotions applies to the salience of certain emotions for certain relations, as well as to their appropriateness of expression in those relations. For example, 'anger' in Isabel is widely regarded as a problematic response to conflict and transgression. Yet, according to cultural ideals, it is not appropriately expressed in relations that are either close (e.g., among family members) or sharply asymmetrical (e.g., between a 'good' chief and his followers).

4. See Wierzbicka (1986) for a discussion of translation issues in the domain of emotion. She draws attention to the need to decouple the cross-cultural study of emotion from the unexamined semantics of English emotion terms. Although the type of semantics outlined by Wierzbicka is narrowly lexical (and ultimately limited by the absence of contextual and performative information), her suggestion that translation work may be advanced by the use of explicit metalinguistic models is consistent with the search for prototype structures in emotional meaning.

5. The vernacular term *di'a nagnafa* (literally, 'bad heart' or 'bad feeling') is not well translated by the English gloss 'sad.' For a more extended discussion of the local meanings of this emotion, see White (in press). English glosses such as 'sad' and 'angry' used in this chapter for expository purposes should not be read as a claim of cross-cultural equivalence.

6. The 'sadness' schema as sketched centers on the response of the experi-

encing subject. However, as Lutz notes in her discussion of Ifaluk emotion theory (1987:295–8), cultural models of emotion also encompass understandings about the evocative power of emotions to elicit specific feelings and responses from others. Thus, in the case of 'sadness', not only does the self desire repair [REPAIR (Self, Other)], but so, ideally, does the other [REPAIR (Other, Self)]. Here the reciprocal quality of 'sadness' implies a convergence in goals, with both self and other, according to the schema, seeking to reestablish mutual relations. By implication, then, talk of 'sadness' may also assert implicit claims about the appropriate (or inappropriate) response of the other.

7.   My "sample" of disentangling discourse is based on four particular sessions, two of which were tape-recorded.

8.   Concepts of shame have received a great deal of attention in the crosscultural literature on emotion (see, e.g., Epstein 1984, White and Kirkpatrick 1985). Although the A'ara term for 'shame', mamaja, figures importantly in disentangling discourse, limitations of space preclude a detailed discussion here (but see White in press).

9.   In this instance, the entering-a-house-for-food scenario is stated with conditional past tense markers, indicating that the relations signified are contingent on their continuing acknowledgment by participants. Tom implies that Fala's exclusion of his brother constituted a failure of such acknowledgment, thus creating shame in contexts where none would be evoked if conditions for the scenario were in force.

10.   For the sake of simplicity, the relation achieved by instantiating a generalized category with a specific action is indicated by an equals sign ($=$). This notation is intended as shorthand for the phrase "is an instance of" (not "is equivalent to"). It should also be noted that this sort of inference is not one compelled by the canons of propositional logic. The closest syllogism to that represented here would be something like: given $A \rightarrow B$, and B ("sad") is true, therefore A. But, since reasoning from the consequent is not a move compelled by logic (not a "strong" inference), mathematicians and others have legitimized this sort of inference as "plausible" reasoning (see Hutchins 1980:56 for examples and discussion). This is the most common type of inference in the examples discussed here.

11.   I'm grateful to Naomi Quinn for drawing my attention to this example of a discourse strategy in which a proposition is rejected, even as the schema necessary to its interpretation is invoked to do so.

12.   This notion of "emotive institution" is well illustrated in recent work on suicide in Pacific societies. For example, Rubinstein's (1984) study of Trukese amwunumwun shows that the emotions implicated in suicide events are constituted in particular communicative forms and culturally patterned scenarios of conflict. The indigenous conceptualization of these responses appears to bridge categories of affect and action. The study of this and related practices in the Pacific (see, e.g., Freeman 1983:218–22 on Samoan musu) requires an ethnography of situated practices of talk and interaction, as well as an investigation of models of the person (Watson-Gegeo and White in press).

References

Abu-Lughod, Lila. 1986. *Veiled Sentiments: Honor and Poetry in a Bedouin Society.* Berkeley: University of California Press.

Bailey, F. G. 1983. *The Tactical Uses of Passion: An Essay on Power, Reason and Reality.* Ithaca, NY: Cornell University Press.

Briggs, Jean. 1970. *Never in Anger: Portrait of an Eskimo Family.* Cambridge, MA: Harvard University Press.

D'Andrade, Roy. 1987. A Folk Model of the Mind. In D. Holland and N. Quinn, eds., *Cultural Models in Language and Thought.* Cambridge: Cambridge University Press, pp. 112–48.

Epstein, A. L. 1984. *The Experience of Shame in Melanesia: An Essay in the Anthropology of Affect.* London: Royal Anthropological Institute of Great Britain and Ireland, Occasional Paper No. 40.

Foucault, Michel. 1981. The Order of Discourse. In R. Young, ed., *Untying the Text: A Post-Structuralist Reader.* Boston: Routledge & Kegan Paul, pp. 48–78.

Freeman, Derek. 1983. *Margaret Mead and Samoa: The Making and Unmaking of an Anthropological Myth.* Cambridge, MA: Harvard University Press.

Gumperz, John. 1982. *Discourse Strategies.* Cambridge: Cambridge University Press.

Harris, Grave. 1978. *Casting Out Anger: Religion Among the Taita of Kenya.* New York: Cambridge University Press.

Holland, Dorothy, and Naomi Quinn, eds. 1987. *Cultural Models in Language and Thought.* Cambridge: Cambridge University Press.

Hutchins, Edwin. 1973. An Analysis of Interpretations of Ongoing Behavior. Unpublished manuscript, Department of Anthropology, University of California, San Diego.

1980. *Culture and Inference.* Cambridge, MA: Harvard University Press.

Ito, Karen L. 1985. *Ho'oponopono*, "To Make Right": Hawaiian Conflict Resolution and Metaphor in the Construction of a Family Therapy. *Culture, Medicine and Psychiatry* 9:201–17.

Lakoff, George, and Zoltan Kovecses. 1987. The Cognitive Model of Anger Inherent in American English. In D. Holland and N. Quinn, eds., *Cultural Models in Language and Thought.* Cambridge: Cambridge University Press, pp. 195–221.

Levy, Robert. 1984. Emotion, Knowing and Culture. In R. Shweder and R. LeVine, eds., *Cultural Theory: Essays on Mind, Self and Emotion.* Cambridge: Cambridge University Press, pp. 214–37.

Lutz, Catherine. 1985. Ethnopsychology Compared to What? Explaining Behavior and Consciousness Among the Ifaluk. In G. White and J. Kirkpatrick, eds., *Person, Self and Experience: Exploring Pacific Ethnopsychologies.* Berkeley: University of California Press, pp. 35–79.

1987. Goals, Events and Understanding in Ifaluk Emotion Theory. In D. Holland and N. Quinn, eds., *Cultural Models in Language and Thought.* Cambridge: Cambridge University Press, pp. 290–312.

Lutz, Catherine, and Geoffrey M. White. 1986. The Anthropology of Emotions. *Annual Review of Anthropology* 15:405–36.

Myers, Fred. 1979. Emotions and the Self: A Theory of Personhood and Political Order Among Pintupi Aborigines. *Ethos* 7:343–70.

1988. The Logic and Meaning of Anger Among Pintupi Aborigines. *Man* (N.S.) 23:589–610.

Poole, F. J. P. 1985. The Surfaces and Depths of Bimin-Kuskusmin Experiences of "Anger": Toward a Theory of Culture and Emotion in the Constitution of Self. Paper given at the 84th Annual Meeting of the American Anthropological Association, Washington, DC.

Quinn, Naomi. 1987. Convergent Evidence for a Cultural Model of American Marriage. In D. Holland and N. Quinn, eds., *Cultural Models in Language and Thought*. Cambridge: Cambridge University Press, pp. 173–92.

Rosaldo, Michelle. 1980. *Knowledge and Passion: Ilongot Notions of Self and Social Life*. Cambridge: Cambridge University Press.

Rubinstein, Donald. 1984. Self-Righteous Anger, Soft-Talk and *Amwunumwun* Suicides of Young Men. Paper given at the 83rd Annual Meeting of the American Anthropological Association, Denver, CO.

Schieffelin, Edward. 1983. Anger and Shame in the Tropical Forest: On Affect as a Cultural System in Papua New Guinea. *Ethos* 11: 181–91.

Shweder, Richard, and Robert LeVine, eds. 1984. *Culture Theory: Essays on Mind, Self and Emotion*. Cambridge: Cambridge University Press.

Strathern, Marilyn. 1968. Popokl: The Question of Morality. *Mankind* 6:553–62.

Valentine, Charles A. 1963. Men of Anger and Men of Shame: Lakalai Ethnopsychology and Its Implications for Sociopsychological Theory. *Ethnology* 1:441–77.

Watson-Gegeo, Karen, and Geoffrey M. White, eds. In press. *Disentangling: The Discourse of Interpersonal Conflict in Pacific Island Societies*. Stanford: Stanford University Press.

White, Geoffrey M. 1985a. Premises and Purposes in a Solomon Islands Ethnopsychology. In G. White and J. Kirkpatrick, eds., *Person, Self and Experience: Exploring Pacific Ethnopsychologies*. Berkeley: University of California Press, pp. 328–66.

    1985b. 'Bad Ways' and 'Bad Talk': Interpretations of Interpersonal Conflict in a Melanesian Society. In J. Dougherty, ed., *Directions in Cognitive Anthropology*. Urbana: University of Illinois Press, pp. 345–370.

    1988. Symbols of Solidarity in the Christianization of Santa Isabel. In G. Saunders, ed., *Culture and Christianity*. Westport, CT: Greenwood Press, pp. 12–31.

    In press. Emotion Talk and Social Inference: Disentangling in a Solomon Islands Society. In K. Watson-Gegeo and G. White, eds., *Disentangling: The Discourse of Interpersonal Conflict in Pacific Island Societies*. Stanford: Stanford University Press.

White, Geoffrey M., and John Kirkpatrick, eds. 1985. *Person, Self and Experience: Exploring Pacific Ethnopsychologies*. Berkeley: University of California Press.

White, Geoffrey, Francis Kokhonigita, and Hugo Pulomana. 1988. *Cheke Holo Dictionary*. Canberra: Pacific Linguistics.

Wierzbicka, Anna. 1986. Human Emotions: Universal or Culture-Specific? *American Anthropologist* 88:584–94.

4. Engendered emotion: gender, power, and the rhetoric of emotional control in American discourse

CATHERINE A. LUTZ

In Western academic discourse, emotions have begun to move from their culturally assigned place at the center of the dark recesses of inner life and are being depicted as cultural, social, and linguistic operators. In the process, we can ask not only about the cultural foundations of things construed as emotional, but about the organizing category of "emotion" itself. One important aspect of that category is its association with the female, so that qualities that define the emotional also define women. For this reason, any discourse on emotion is also, at least implicitly, a discourse on gender.

As both an analytic and an everyday concept in the West, emotion, like the female, has typically been viewed as something natural rather than cultural, irrational rather than rational, chaotic rather than ordered, subjective rather than universal, physical rather than mental or intellectual, unintended and uncontrollable, and hence often dangerous. This network of associations sets emotion in disadvantaged contrast to more valued personal processes, particularly to cognition or rational thought, and the female in deficient relation to her male other. Another and competing theme in Western cultural renditions of emotion, however, contrasts emotion with cold alienation. Emotion, in this view, is life to its absence's death, is interpersonal connection or relationship to an unemotional estrangement, is a glorified and free nature against a shackling civilization. This latter rendition of emotion echoes some of the fundamental ways the female has also been "redeemed," or alternatively and more positively, construed (Lutz 1988).

In this chapter, I will explore how emotion has been given a gender in some sectors of American culture and, in the process, make two related arguments. First, I will demonstrate that local or everyday lay discourse on emotion explicitly and implicitly draws links among women, subordination, rebellion, and emotion by examining interview conver-

69

sations conducted with a small group of American women and men. In particular, I will explore a "rhetoric of control" that frequently accompanies women's (and, to a lesser extent, men's) talk about emotion, and argue that talk about the control or management of emotion is also a narrative about the double-sided nature – both weak and dangerous – of dominated groups. Talk about emotional control in and by women, in other words, is talk about power and its exercise. Second, I will argue that this and further aspects of local discourse are echoed and reproduced in many areas of social and natural scientific discourse that deal with the "emotional female." Finally, I will present a further, more syntactic analysis of the interview conversations that contradicts at least some of the stereotypical beliefs about the relationship between gender and emotion that these informants, as well as social science, have voiced. This analysis looks at the degree to which women and men might differentially use syntactic patterns that distance, disavow, or depersonalize the experience of emotion. The failure to find systematic differences can be taken as tentative evidence that cultural models that paint women as more emotionally expressive or more comfortable with a discussion of their own emotions remain surface models and do not organize discourse at more microscopic or out-of-awareness levels.

Gender, power, and the rhetoric of emotional control

Western discourse on emotions constitutes them as paradoxical entities that are both a sign of weakness and a powerful force. On the one hand, emotion weakens the person who experiences it. It does this both by serving as a sign of a sort of character defect (e.g., "She couldn't rise above her emotions") and by being a sign of at least temporary intrapsychic disorganization (e.g., "She was in a fragile state" or "She fell apart"). The person who has "fallen apart," needless to say, is unable to function effectively or forcefully. On the other hand, emotions are literally physical forces that push us into vigorous action. "She was charged up," we say; "Waves of emotion shook his body." Women are constructed in a similar contradictory fashion as both strong and weak (e.g., Jordanova 1980), and I will present evidence from the interviews mentioned earlier that when American women and men talk about emotion, they draw on that similarity to comment on the nature of gender and power. This feature of the emotional and of the female produces frequent discussion in the interviews of the problem of controlling one's feelings. Such discussion is found in both men's and women's discourse, but much more frequently in the latter. I will show that this talk about control of emotions is evidence of a widely shared cultural view of the danger of both women and their emotionality. It is also talk that may mean different things to both the speaker and the audience when it is uttered by women and by men, and this factor will be used to help account for differences in the rate of use of this rhetoric of control. Although both women and men draw on a culturally available model of emotion as something in need of control, they can be seen as often making some different kinds of sense and claims from it.

The material I turn to first was collected in four extended interviews on emotion with fifteen American working- and middle-class women and men. All white, they ranged in age from the early twenties to the mid-seventies and included a bank teller, factory worker, college teacher, retiree, housing code inspector, and stockbroker. Most were parents. The interviews were usually conducted in people's homes, and the interviewers included myself and a number of graduate students, most of them women. Each person was interviewed by the same individual for all four sessions, and although a small number of questions organized each session, every attempt was made to have the interviews approximate "natural conversation." Nonetheless, it is clearly important to keep in mind the context of the discourse to be analyzed, as it was produced by a group of people who agreed on letter and phone solicitation "to talk about emotion" for an audience of relative strangers who were also academics and mostly females.

Many people mentioned at one or several points in the interviews that they believe women to be more emotional than men. One example of the variety of ways this was phrased is the account one woman gave to explain her observation that some people seem inherently to be "nervous types." She remembered about her childhood that

> the female teachers had a tendency to really holler at the kids a lot, and when I was in class with the male teacher, it seemed like he just let things pass by and it didn't seem to get his goat as fast, and he didn't shout at the same time the female may have in the same instance. . . . I think emotional people get upset faster. I do. And like with men and women, things that are sort of important or bothering me don't bother my husband. . . . I think that's a difference of male and female.[1]

One theme that frequently arises in the interviews is what can be called the "rhetoric of control" (Rosaldo 1977). When people are asked to talk about emotions, one of the most common set of metaphors used is that in which someone or something controls, handles, copes, deals, disciplines, or manages either or both their emotions or the situation seen as creating the emotion. For example:

> I believe an individual can exercise a great deal of *control* over their emotions by maintaining a more positive outlook, by not dwelling on the negative, by trying to push aside an unpleasant feeling. I'm getting angry and like I said, he's over being angry, more or less dropped it and he expects me to also. Well we don't have the same temper, I just can't *handle* it that way.

And in a more poetic turn, one person mused:

> sadness . . . dipping, dipping into that . . . just the out-of-*controlness* of things.

People typically talk about *controlling* emotions, *handling* emotional situations as well as emotional feelings, and *dealing* with people, situations, and emotions.

The notion of control operates very similarly here to the way it does in Western discourses on sexuality (Foucault 1980). Both emotionality and sexuality are domains whose understanding is dominated by a biomedical model; both are seen as universal, natural impulses; both are talked about as existing in "healthy" and "unhealthy" forms; and both have come under the control of a medical or quasi-medical profession (principally psychiatry and psychology). Foucault has argued that popular views of sexuality – as a drive that was repressed during the Victorian era and gradually liberated during the twentieth century – are misleading because they posit a single essence that is manipulated by social convention. Rather, Foucault postulated, multiple sexualities are constantly produced and changed. A popular discourse on the control of emotion runs functionally parallel to a discourse on the control of sexuality; a rhetoric of control requires a psychophysical essence that is manipulated or wrestled with and directs attention away from the socially constructed nature of the idea of emotion (see Abu-Lughod and Lutz, this volume). In addition, the metaphor of control implies something that would otherwise be out of control, something wild and unruly, a threat to order. To speak about controlling emotions is to replicate the view of emotions as natural, dangerous, irrational, and physical.[2]

What is striking is that women talked about the control of emotion more than twice as often as did men as a proportion of the total speech each produced in the interviews.[3] To help account for this difference, we can ask what the rhetoric of control might accomplish for the speaker and what it might say to several audiences (see Brenneis, this volume). At least three things can be seen to be done via the rhetoric of emotional control: It (1) reproduces an important part of the cultural view of emotion (and then implicitly of women as the more emotional gender) as irrational, weak, and dangerous; (2) minimally elevates the social status of the person who claims the need or ability to self-control emotions; and (3) opposes the view of the feminine self as dangerous when it is reversed, that is, when the speaker denies the need for or possibility of control of emotion. Each of these suggestions can only briefly be examined.

First, this rhetoric can be seen as a reproduction, primarily on the part of women, of the view of themselves as more emotional, of emotion as dangerous, and hence of themselves as in need of control. It does this first by setting up a boundary – that edge over which emotion that is *un*controlled can spill. A number of people have noted that threats to a dominant social order are sometimes articulated in a concern with diverse kinds of boundaries (whether physical or social) and their integrity (e.g., Martin 1987; Scheper-Hughes and Lock 1987). One of the most critical boundaries that is constituted in Western psychological discourse is that between the inside and the outside of persons; individualism as ideology is fundamentally based on the magnification of that particular boundary. When emotion is defined, as it also is in the West, as something inside the individual, it provides an important symbolic vehicle by which the problem of the maintenance of social order can be voiced. A discourse that is concerned with the expression, control, or repression of emotions can be seen as a discourse on the crossing back and forth of that boundary between inside and outside, a discourse we can expect to see in more elaborate form in periods and places where social relations appear to be imminently overturned.

This rhetoric of emotional control goes further than defining and then defending boundaries, however; it also suggests a set of roles – one strong and defensive and the other weak but invasive – that are hierarchized and linked with gender roles. Rosaldo (1984) notes of hierarchical societies that they seem to evince greater concern than do more egalitarian ones with how society controls the inner emotional self and, we can add, with how one part of a bifurcated and hierarchically layered self controls another. The body politic, in other words, is sometimes replicated in the social relations of the various homunculi that populate the human mind, a kind of "mental politic." When cognition outreasons and successfully manages emotion, male–female roles are replicated. When women speak of control, they play the roles of both super- and subordinate, of controller and controllee. They identify their emotions and themselves as undisciplined and discipline both through a discourse on control of feeling. The construction of a feminine self, this material might suggest, includes a process by which women come to control themselves and so obviate the necessity for more coercive outside control.

There is the example of one woman in her late thirties; she talked about the hate she felt for her ex-husband, who began an affair while she was pregnant and left her with the infant, an older child, and no paid employment:

> So I think you try hard not to bring it [the feeling] out 'cause you don't want that type of thing at home with the kids, you know. That's very bad, very unhealthy, that's no way to grow up. So I think now, maybe I've just learned to control it and time has changed the feeling of the hate.

The woman here defines herself as someone with a feeling of hate and portrays it as dangerous, primarily in terms of the threat it poses to her own children, a threat she phrases in biomedical terms (i.e., "unhealthy"). She replicates a view that Shields (1987) found prevalent in a survey of twentieth-century English-language child-rearing manuals; this is the danger that mothers' (and not fathers') emotions are thought to present to children. In addition, this woman's description of her feelings essentializes them as states; as such, they remain passive (see Cancian 1987 on the feminization of love) rather than active motivators, a point to which we will return.

In other cases, people do not talk about themselves, but rather remind others (usually women) of the need to control themselves. These instances also serve to replicate the view of women as dangerously emotional. Another woman spoke about a female friend who still grieved for a son who had died two years previously: "You've got to pick up and go on. You've got to try and get those feelings under control." The "you" in this statement is a complex and multivocal sign (Kirkpatrick 1987), and directs the admonition to control simultaneously to the grieving woman, the female interviewer, the speaker herself, no one in particular, and everyone in a potential audience.

A second pragmatic effect of the rhetoric of emotional control is a claim to have the ability to "rise above" one's emotions or to approve of those who do. Women, more than men, may speak of control because they are concerned about counteracting the cultural denigration of themselves through an association with emotion. "I think it's important to control emotions," they say, and implicitly remind a critical audience that they have the cooler stuff it takes to be considered mature and rational. It is important to note that, as academics, I and the graduate students who conducted the interviews may have been perceived as an audience in special need of such reminders. The speakers would have been doing this, however, by dissociating themselves from emotion rather than by questioning the dominant view both of themselves and of emotion.

Although women may have less access to a view of themselves as masterful individuals, a common aspect of the cultural scheme that *is* available paints them as masterfully effective with others on joint tasks, particularly interpersonal or emotional tasks (social science versions of this include Chodorow 1978, Parsons and Bales 1955). This subtly alters the meaning of the rhetoric of control; knowledge of what the feelings are that "need" control and of what control should be like is perceived and described as a social rather than an individual process. For example, one woman says: "If you're tied in with a family, . . . you have to use it for guidance how you control your emotions." This is the same woman whose central life problem during the interview period was coping with her husband's ex-wife and family, who lived across the street from her. The regular, friendly contact between husband and ex-wife has left her very unhappy but also unsure about what to do. The ambiguity over who ought to control or regulate what is evident in her description of an argument she had with her husband over the issue.

> I was mad. I was mad. And I said, "I don't care whether you think I should [inaudible word] or stay in this at all, it's too, and cause I'm going to say it." And I said, "How dare you tell me how I'm supposed to feel," you know. Bob [her husband] would say, you know, "You got to live with it" or "You got to do this" or "How dare you tell me this, I don't have to put up with anything" or "I don't have to feel this way because you tell me I have to feel this way." You know, it was, in that case Robin is his ex-wife, "and you have to just kind of deal with it," you know, "all the problems that she presents in your own way." And it was almost sort of like saying "You're going to have to like it." Well I don't. I don't, you know. And for a year and a half he kept saying, you know, "You're

going to have to like it, this is the way it's going to be, you're going to have to do this, you're going to have to have, be, act, this certain way," you know, act everything hunky-dory, and it wasn't, you know, and I was beginning to resent a whole lot of things. I, I, I resented him for telling me I had to feel that way when I, I wasn't real fond of the situation. I didn't like it. When I would tell him that I didn't like it, it was "It's your problem, you deal with it." I didn't like that, that made me really angry because I was saying, "Help me out here, I don't know how to deal with this."

This woman is frustrated with her husband for failing to join her in a collaborative project of "dealing with" her feelings of resentment. Here control is given away to or shared with others. This strategy of control is more complex and subtle than the simple self-imposition described in other parts of the transcripts so far; it aims to control both the emotions of the self *and* the attention and assistance of the other. Note also that she speaks of "resenting" or "not liking" (relatively mild terms of displeasure) the overall situation but is most incensed ("mad, mad, mad") about her husband's assumption that she ought not to feel a certain way. She asserts the right to "feel" unhappy about her predicament but is clearly defining that feeling in the standard contemporary sense of a strictly internal and passive event. Nowhere in the interview does she explicitly state or appear to imply that she wants, intends, or ought to act in concert with those feelings. What is being controlled or dealt with, therefore, has already been defined as a relatively innocuous feeling rather than an action tendency.

Finally, the rhetoric of emotional control can also be employed in both idiosyncratic and "reversed" ways that may intend or have the effect of at least minimally resisting the dominant view of emotionality, and thus of women. A few people, for example, spontaneously spoke about the problem of emotional control, thereby evoking the whole schema we have just been looking at. They went on, however, to define "control" in a way that entailed relatively minimal constraints on emotional communication. One woman, a twenty-eight-year-old bank teller, said: "Let me explain control. It's not that you sit there and you take it [some kind of abuse] and, you know, I think controlling them [emotions] is letting them out in the proper time, in the proper place." Perhaps more radically, some women (as well as one of the gay men with whom I spoke) denied that they had the ability to control some or many of their emotions.[4] One man in his twenties critically described a previous tendency he had to over-intellectualize problems and explained that he worked against that tendency because

> It wasn't that I wanted to cut off my emotions, I just didn't, they would get out of control, and I found that the more I tried to suppress them, the more powerful they would become. It was like this big dam that didn't let a little out at a time, it would just explode all of a sudden, and I'd be totally out of control.

The question remains, however, of the validity of seeing these latter seemingly resistant uses of the rhetoric of emotional control as "oppositional" forms (Williams 1977) within that system.[5] This is certainly a dangerous rhetorical strategy, caught as they (we) are within a hegemonic discourse not of our own making. The opposition to self-control will most likely be absorbed into the logic of the existing system and so come to equal not resistance but simple deficiency or lack (of control).[6] A possibly oppositional intent may have collaborative outcomes to the extent that the denial of self-control is taken by most audiences as a deficit and a confirmation of ideas about women's irrationality.

The culturally constructed emotionality of women is rife with contradiction. The emotional female, like the natural world that is the cultural source of both affect and women, is constructed as both pliant (because weak and a resource for use by civilized man) and ultimately tremendously powerful and uncontrollable (Strathern 1980).[7] Emotionality is the source of women's value, their expertise in lieu of rationality, and yet it is the origin of their unsuitability for broader social tasks and even a potential threat to their children.

There are vivid parallels between this and the cultural meanings surrounding colonialism that Taussig (1984) and Stoler (1985) have described. Looking at early-twentieth-century colonists' views of the local Columbian labor force, Taussig describes their alternation between fear and awe of Indians who were perceived as dangerous and powerful figures, on the one hand, and disgust and denigration of their perceived weakness and lack of civilization, on the other. Taussig describes the process as one in which a "colonial mirror" "reflects back onto the colonists the barbarity of their own social relations" (1984:495). In a (certainly less systematic or universally brutal) way, a "patriarchal mirror" can be conceptualized as helping to produce the view of women as emotional – as dangerously "eruptive" and as in the process of weakly "breaking down." A "paradox of will" seems consistently to attend dominating relationships – whether those of gender, race, or class – as the subordinate other is ideologically painted as weak (so as to need protection or discipline) and yet periodically as threatening to break the ideological boundary in riot or hysteria. Emotion talk, as evident in these transcripts, shows the same contradictions of control, weakness, and strength. Given its definition as nature, at least in the West, emotion discourses may be one of the most likely and powerful devices by which domination proceeds.

The engendering of emotion in science

Demonstrations of the political, moral, and cultural bases of Western science have been made convincingly in a number of natural and social fields (e.g., Asad 1973; Fausto-Sterling 1985; Haan, Bellah, Rabinow, and Sullivan 1983; Sampson 1981). In like fashion, it can be argued that the sciences of emotion have been, in a significant sense, a product of their social context. In particular, the academic literature on emotion can be considered a form of political discourse on gender relations because of the marked associations between the two domains. That literature thus arises out of and reenters a field of power struggles for the definition of true womanhood. As Haraway (1986) has said of American primatology, it can be seen as "politics by other means," and in the case of emotions, it is most centrally a politics of gender by other means. By examining several examples of studies of emotion, we will see that much research over the years in biology, psychology, sociology, sociolinguistics, and other fields has been implicitly based on everyday cultural models linking women and emotionality, and that this research moves from the assumption of these cultural premises to their "proof." Most striking about these studies is the number that naturalize the purported gender differences by attributing them to biological or necessary and universal features of the female role in physical and social reproduction. I will briefly examine several areas of research, including the analysis of premenstrual syndrome and mood, sex differences in the recognition of facial expressions of emotion and in aggression, and studies of the affective components and concomitants of motherhood. Feminist critiques of a number of these latter fields have been intensive, and I will draw on them while extending the analysis to the domain of emotion.

Studies of the relationship between mood and hormonal changes have focused on women's (rather than men's) cycles and in the process have discovered the hormonal disease of premenstrual syndrome. This syndrome is characterized by both physical pain and mood disturbances and has been attributed by the biomedical research community to hormonal imbalances in the women who suffer from it. The syndrome has been used to explain a host of emotions ranging from irritability and mood swings to depression, anxiety, and panic attacks. A number of feminist critiques (Archer and Lloyd 1985; Fausto-Sterling 1985; Gottlieb 1987; Whatley 1986) have pointed out the weakness of the evidence for this syndrome. Assessment of women's mood is usually based on retrospective self-report via questionnaires (one popular version being titled the "Menstrual Distress Questionnaire"), which allow women to draw on cultural knowledge about the relation between gender, emotion, and hormones. Conversely, studies that disguise the purposes of the questionnaire show no significant premenstrual mood changes. The putative therapeutic effects of hormone injections are taken as primary evidence of the female hormonal basis for mood changes, but these studies have not been "double-blind." As Whatley argues, this biomedical discourse on emotions and gender may "cause us to ignore the fact that our premenstrual mood changes . . . may also correlate more closely to a monthly cycle of low bank balances than of hormonal fluctuations" (1986:183). Moreover, the emotional symptoms of premenstrual syndrome can be seen as a discourse on both the good and the deviant woman, on the necessity of her emotional suffering and the abnormality of, especially, her anger or irritability (Gottlieb 1987), both common symptoms attached to the syndrome. Normative academic and clinical work on premenstrual syndrome focuses on the emotionality of women as both common and yet as a "symptom" in need of a cure. This research draws on the entrenched cultural view of emotions as sited in females, as natural in essence (like but independent of the "naturalness" of females), and as irrational or pathological when they occur.

This line of research follows from and reinvigorates the cultural model in which women are more emotional than men because they are more tied to the biological processes that produce emotion. Wombs, menstruation, and hormones "predict" emotion. A more tacit part of the cultural logic connecting women and emotion may arise from the view of women as biologically inferior both because they menstruate and because they are smaller, weaker, and lack a penis. When viewed as a form of physical chaos or "breakdown," emotion is one other form of biological weakness suffered by women.[8]

A number of people in the interview study just described spontaneously articulated related ideas about the relationship between women, hormones, emotion, and pathology. In several cases, they referred to research as the authoritative source of their assertions, although my argument is that the relationship between everyday and scientific ideas about women and emotion is dialectical rather than an idea system imposed hegemonically on a previously blank or very different lay model. According to one woman, a forty-eight-year-old telephone operator, "women have been known to have different reactions to the same situation at different times of the month. And that's been a study. I've seen where some women can be downright dangerous, they could be potential killers."

Another field in which some attention has been paid to sex differences is the study of facial expression of emotion. In one sociobiological account, female emotionality is a product of evolution. Babchuk, Hames, and Thompson (1985) interpret studies showing that women are better able than men to read facial expressions of emotions in infants. In their view, this is the result of women's long history of being the primary caretakers of infants and the reproductive value of using these facial cues to detect infant distress. This argument is implausible on many grounds, not the least of which are the redundancy in infants of facial expression and other cues to discomfort, and the theoretically at least equal value of facial expression recognition skills for the prehistoric males, who, in many evolutionary accounts, were engaged primarily in defending the female and infant against threatening and dissembling outsiders. In addition, one of the central studies that demonstrates female superiority in decoding facial expressions of emotion (Hall 1978) has been reanalyzed and shown to account for less than 4 percent of the variance between individuals in facial expression recognition skills (Deaux 1984, cited in Shields 1987).

Despite its obvious problems, this account of the evolution of facial expression identification is a story with some power, as it draws on entrenched cultural narratives about women, motherhood, children, and love. Here, the first premise is that women are more attuned to emotion in themselves and others. Unlike the premenstrual syndrome studies, however, female emotionality is celebrated here, with emotions taking on their positive sense of the interpersonally engaged, the unalienated. Women's emotionality becomes a skill and an asset. It is significant that the sociobiological account focuses on the use of that asset to detect distress (rather than, for example, threat). Distress, of course, calls for nurturance, whereas other facial expressions (in either infants or adults) might call for flight or defense, but only the former behavior is normative for women and mothers.

Another line of research, on sex differences in aggression, also draws on cultural views of emotion and women. This happens, first, because aggression, at least in the Western cultural view, is seen as retrospectively predictive of anger (Montague 1978). Anger is the one emotion that is exempted in everyday discourse from the expectation that women feel and express more emotion than men. It is in fact every emotion *but* anger that is disapproved in men and, conversely, expected in women (Hochschild 1983). This gender stereotype has been shown to have been thoroughly learned by American children as early as the preschool period (Birnbaum, Nosanchuck, and Croll 1980, cited in Shields 1987). A recent, widely accepted, and often cited set of studies makes the parallel claim to have demonstrated a relationship between levels of the "male" hormone testosterone and aggression. Fausto-Sterling (1985) demonstrates the weakness of the evidence for this claim and questions why it has been taken up so enthusiastically by so many.

The echoes of the lay view in the scientific are followed by the echoes of the scientific view in the lay on this point as well. A professional woman in her forties in the interview study commented on the association between aggression and gender: "So far the research shows that, yes, little boys are inherently more aggressive than little girls. . . . I think it bothers me that there's a sex link with aggression. There are a couple of sex-linked ones that bother me but . . . but I can't do anything about it."

A number of studies that use the cultural logic of engendered emotion focus less on physiological differences to account for emotional ones than on universal functions and roles. In particular, they draw on the notion of women's reproductive role and the nurturing role and emotions that supposedly naturally accompany it. From ethological bonding theory (Bowlby 1969) to some schools of feminism (e.g., Ruddick 1980), focus is placed on the natural or inevitable emotional concomitants of motherhood (rather than fatherhood), including particularly the positive emotions of love, caring, and attachment. Bowlby follows the prevailing cultural emphasis on women's emotional qualities when he focuses on the emotions of women and their children. He wants to explain the intensity of the bond between mother and infant, and roots that explanation in an instinctual need for attachment in the infant and fear of separation. Feelings of love for the child on the part of the mother are naturalized (cf. Scheper-Hughes 1985), and disastrous consequences are chronicled should the infant fail to receive sufficient quantities of mother love. These two facets of Bowlby's approach provide the carrot and stick of natural instinct and psychological harm to the child as reasons for continued emphasis on the need for emotionality in women.

Ruddick (1980), on the other hand, identifies "resilient good humor and cheerfulness," "attentive love," and "humility" as among the central features of maternal virtue that follow from (rather than precede) the task of parenting and, by frequent correlation, the task of being female. From these perspectives, women are more deeply embedded in relationships with others (with the mother–infant bond as the primary example and the primary cause). This interpersonal engagement with others is what produces emotion, which is here defined as responses to others with whom one is involved. From the perspective of feminism, male individualism is antithetical to the experience of emotion (see also Chodorow 1978).

The differences between these two perspectives on mothering and emotion are, of course, crucial. Bowlby-style bonding theory naturalizes the connection between women and affect through evolutionary theory and is continuous with earlier theorizing about the elevated moral status of women achieved through their divinely assigned and naturally embedded mothering skills. Feminist theory most often identifies the social division of labor rather than nature as the ultimate source of such emotional differences. Interestingly, however, both kinds of discourse on emotion elevate women (the first to a domestic pedestal, the second to self-esteem and/or the ability to resist patriarchy) by focusing on positive emotions such as love and by using "emotion" in its positive Romantic sense of connection and disalienation.

Yet another version of the cultural view of women as emotional is found in the Parsonian normative construction of family roles, in which women are the "expressive expert" and men the "instrumental expert" (Parsons and Bales 1955). These competencies are seen as an outcome of the domestic–market spheres in which the genders differentially participate. Compare this notion, however, with the contradictory view of women's emotional impact on the family noted in the interview example and the child-rearing manual themes described earlier. The point may be that women are expected to be experts in noticing and attending to the emotional needs of others (also per Bowlby), not their own, which are rather objects of control or suppression because they, unlike the emotions of other family members, are defined as dangerous.

Hochschild's (1983) important feminist revision of Parsons and Bales's scheme paints emotion less as a skill than as a form of labor. Women are socially assigned a much heavier burden of emotional labor than are men. Hochschild's ideas contribute to a breaking down of the dichotomy of emotion and thought; they can also extend the notion of women's double day of domestic and wage labor as women are required to contribute both emotional and cognitive labor in both paid and unpaid spheres. In this and other feminist analyses, gender and emotion are related through the relations of production. For Hochschild, emotion is a personal resource that women must self-exploit more than men. It nonetheless remains a psychophysical fact, socially manipulated, rather than a discursive practice that constructs women as more emotional than men.

In sum, social science disciplines women and their psyches. It constructs emotion as an individual and intrapsychic phenomenon and evidences the same concern as lay discourse with the emotionality of women – its frequency, its intensity, its virtues as an emblem of female gender identity, but most of all, its danger and implicitly the need for its control.

Personalization

I now return to the question of how these cultural notions about the emotionality of women, articulated in scientific discourse, are related to everyday discourse. The rhetoric of control that we first looked at was shown to reflect, in multiple and complex ways, relations of power between men and women, and to reflect them in ways that can be said, in large measure, to reproduce the "emotional female." By looking closely at some more microscopic aspects of the interview talk, however, we can see that gender differences are minimal, a fact that may speak to the gaps and fissures in the construction of a hegemonic discourse.

In two of the series of interviews, people were asked, first, to describe recent experiences with each of several common emotions and, second, to talk about how they feel about their work and family lives. In an analysis of a sample of 286 randomly selected interview statements that include direct reference to emotions, I have focused on the degree to which the statement "personalizes" the emotion experience – that is, on a variety of ways emotions, even as they are discussed, can be distanced from the self. It might be expected that women would use more personalizing and immediate syntactic forms if they operate following the cultural model in which women are more emotionally expressive and have a more emotional self-identity.

Personalization, or a nondistancing discursive strategy, was indexed by four speech patterns (see Table 4.1), which will now be discussed.

Table 4.1. *Personalization in syntax*

1. *Present Tense*
   "I *get* [or *am*] angry whenever someone talks to me that way."
   Others
   "I *was* very angry."

2. *Experiencer of the emotion discussed*
   Self, as subject of emotion experience
   "*I'm* very anxious about it."
   Self, as object of emotion experience
   "It's making *me* angry just talking about this."
   Other person (male, female, or gender unspecified)
   "*My father* was very annoyed with me for going into that field."
   Unspecified
   "*It* was a very strong feeling of hate."
   "And *that* developed a certain amount of hate toward that individual
      because of the fact that he . . ."
   None – emotion as an abstract entity
   "Well, hate and frustration usually go hand in hand, I would say."
   " 'Love' would be, I think, a good catchall phrase because . . ."

3. *Cause or elicitor of emotion*
   Self
   "They were angry at *me*."
   "*I* just kind of giggled and made her even angrier."
   Other person
   "I hate *her* because she was mean enough to tell me that."
   "I'm deathly afraid of *dentists*."
   Event
   "The most anxious moment I had . . . was *my first performance with the . . .
      Choral Society*."
   "I hate *going out* unless I really have to."
   Object
   "He loves *books*.
   Unspecified
   "*Lots of little things* are frustrating."
   "I can't talk anymore, I start screaming to begin with, when I'm really
      angry."

4. *Negation*
   "I [or she] was*n't* angry."

1. The present tense rather than the past or conditional tense (e.g., "I *get* [or am] angry whenever someone talks to me that way" compared with "I *was* very angry"), is used. Tense obviously does several things to the meaning that audiences can make of a statement about emotion. First, it can move the emotion experience farther away from or closer to the self or another in time. Second, it can either generalize or particularize the experience; the use of the present tense, for example, can often include the implication that the emotion is habitually experienced by the subject. On both of these counts, the stereotype would lead us to expect more use of the present tense by women speakers. In fact, there is no difference between male and female speakers in the interview sample in the use of the present tense. If anything, men as a group make slightly (insignificantly) more use of it.

2. Another element of a personalizing strategy might include the use of syntactic patterns that more directly portray the speaker as the experiencer of the emotion. Statements were coded as portraying the experiencer as the self, as another person (male, female, or gender unspecified), or as leaving the experiencer unspecified (e.g., "*It* was a very strong feeling of hate" or "And *that* developed a certain amount of hate toward that individual because of the fact that he . . .") or the emotion as an abstract entity with no particular experiencer (e.g., "Well, hate and frustration usually go hand in hand, I would say" or " 'Love' would be, I think, a good catchall phrase because . . ."). The category of self was further broken down by whether the self was portrayed as subject or object of the emotion experience (e.g., "*I'm* very anxious about it" compared with "It's making *me* angry just talking about this"). The belief in women's emotionality might lead to the expectation that women would more often portray the self (particularly the self as subject rather than object) as the experiencer of emotion, whereas men would portray the other as the experiencer or leave the latter ambiguous.

In the interview sample, it is *not* significantly more common for women, in their discussions of emotion, to focus on the experiencing self as the subject versus the object of the emotion, nor is it more common for men to leave the experiencer unspecified or abstract. In addition, neither women nor men are more likely to portray others as opposed to the self as the experiencer of the discussed emotion. Women and men speak more alike than differently in this sample when discussing the experiencer of emotions.

3. Statements about emotion usually contain an implicit or explicit etiology, that is, they specify the cause (usually by specifying the object)

of the feeling. Personalizing strategies might include identification of either the self or, secondarily, another person as the ultimate cause of the emotion (rather than the use of syntactic patterns that obscure or fail to identify the cause). Statements were coded as portraying the cause as either the self (e.g., "They were angry at *me*" or "*I* just kind of giggled and made her even angrier"), another person (e.g., I hate *her* because she was mean enough to tell me that" or "I'm deathly afraid of *dentists*"), an event (e.g., "The most anxious moment I had . . . was *my first performance with the . . . Choral Society*" or "I hate *going out* unless I really have to"), an object (e.g., "He loves *books*"), or as leaving the cause unspecified (e.g., "*Lots of little things* are frustrating" or "I can't talk anymore, I start screaming to begin with, when I'm really angry") (cf. Shimanoff 1983). Given the associations between gender and affect I noted earlier, we might expect that women more than men would see other people as intimately involved in their own emotion experience and themselves as evoking emotion in others, rather than seeing events as triggering emotion in themselves or failing to specify a cause. The latter strategy can be associated with the view of emotion as nonsensical, irrational, or without ascertainable cause. In fact, there are no significant gender differences in the use of personal versus impersonal causal attribution, nor do women use self versus other attributions more than men.

4. Finally, a number of statements about emotion in the interviews are essentially denials of emotion in the self or the other (e.g., "I [or she] was*n't* angry"). The stereotype might lead us to expect more negation in general from men and more negation of particular kinds of female-linked emotions (which include most emotions except anger) by men and of male-linked emotions (notably anger) by women. Here again, women's and men's speech are indistinguishable in terms of the proportion of emotion states that are negated as they are discussed.

The absence of extensive differences might be attributed to the special nature of the people interviewed, all of whom agreed beforehand to talk with a stranger about emotion. The results are consistent, however, with a study of gender differences in emotion language use by Shimanoff (1983), who did a similar analysis of the tape-recorded natural conversations of a number of American college students and married couples, and found few differences in male and female conversations that included reference to emotions.[9] The results are also consistent with the trend in studies of psychological and linguistic sex differences in general, which have tended to show far fewer differences than researchers both expected – on the basis of cultural stereotypes about distinctive male and female styles of thinking, behavior, and speech – and then often found in self-fulfilling fashion. The absence of differences is more significant given the syntactic nature of the evidence examined; Shibamoto (1987) has concluded that gender differences that are not a response to audience expectations about particular gender identities are more likely to be found in syntactic patterns of use because they are typically outside of our awareness and hence of our easy manipulation, unlike semantic patterns such as those having to do with the notion of "control" we examined earlier.

Conclusion

In all societies, body disorders – which emotion is considered to be in this society – become crucial indicators of problems with social control and, as such, are more likely to occur or emerge in a discourse concerning social subordinates. Foucault has made the claim that power creates sexuality and its disciplining; similarly, it can be said to create emotionality. The cultural construction of women's emotion can thus be viewed not as the repression or suppression of emotion in men (as many laypeople, therapists, and other commentators argue) but as the creation of emotion in women. Because emotion is constructed as relatively chaotic, irrational, and antisocial, its existence vindicates authority and legitimates the need for control. By association with the female, it vindicates the distinction between and hierarchy of men and women. And the cultural logic connecting women and emotion corresponds to and shores up the walls between the spheres of private, intimate (and emotional) relations in the (ideologically) female domain of the family and public, formal (and rational) relations in the primarily male domain of the marketplace.

Rubin has remarked of sexuality that "There are historical periods in which [it] is more sharply contested and more overtly politicized" (1984:267). Emotionality has the same historical dynamism, with shifting gender relations often appearing to be at the root of both academic and lay struggles over how emotion is to be defined and evaluated.[10] In other words, the contemporary dominant discourse on emotions – and particularly the view that they are irrational and to be controlled – helps construct but does not wholly determine women's discourse; there is an attempt to recast the association of women with emotion in an alternative feminist voice.

Feminist treatments of the question of emotion (e.g., Hochschild 1983;

Jagger 1987) have tended to portray emotions not as chaos but as a discourse on problems. Some have contested both the irrationality and the passivity of feelings by arguing that emotions may involve the identification of problems in women's lives and are therefore political. Talk about anger, for example, can be interpreted as an attempt to identify the existence of inappropriate restraint or injustice. Sadness is a discourse on the problem of loss, fear on that of danger. By extension, talk about the control of emotions would be, in this feminist discourse, talk about the suppression of public acknowledgment of problems. The emotional female might then be seen not simply as a mythic construction on the axis of some arbitrary cultural dualism but as an outcome of the fact that women occupy an objectively more problematic position than does the white, upper-class, Northern European, older man who is the cultural exemplar par excellence of cool, emotionless rationality. According to a feminist analysis, whether or not women express their problems (i.e., are emotional) more than men, those women's audiences may hear a message that is an amalgam of the orthodox view and its feminist contestation: "We (those) women are dangerously close to erupting into emotionality/pointing to a problem/moving toward a social critique."

Notes

An earlier version of this chapter was presented on the panel "Emotion and Discourse" at the annual meetings of the American Anthropological Association, Chicago, November 18–22, 1987. The draft has benefited greatly from the comments of Lila Abu-Lughod and Steven Feld. The research on which this chapter is based has been conducted with grants from the State University of New York Foundation and the National Institute of Mental Health and with the help of many people. Kathryn Beach, Robin Brown, Paula Bienenfeld, and Walter Komorowski assisted in interviewing and transcription, and the expert analytic work of Angela Carroll and Marion Pratt helped give the chapter its form.
1. The actual process by which these models of gender and emotion are acquired is a fascinating but unexplored question. We might expect that it includes, in part, the child's reasoning from the culturally assigned authority and control of the male teacher to a lack of emotion, the latter perhaps already having been learned to require "strength" and "control" to master – in other words, to generalize from the dominant position of males to a presumed lack of emotion (a process that might also have occurred in her teachers' views of themselves).
2. The method used in looking at the transcripts draws on recent developments in the "cognitive" study of cultural meaning. These focus on the analysis of extended and relatively natural conversations for the cultural knowledge or cultural models (Holland and Quinn 1987) evident, if not always explicitly stated, in them. By looking at such things as syntax, metaphor, or the

propositional networks underlying the sensibility of sentence order, it is possible to draw inferences about the kinds of models individuals are using or, perhaps more aptly, to draw inferences about the kinds of inferences listeners can make about what the speaker has left unsaid but likely wants understood.

3. There are 180 instances in those parts of the women's transcripts analyzed so far, and 85 instances in the men's, with each set of transcripts being of approximately equal length.

4. I have found Woolard's (1985) analysis of the nature of hegemonic and oppositional forms of language use very productive in formulating what I have to say here.

5. Martin (1987) has examined the American discourses on reproduction and women's bodies and has rigorously uncovered the contradiction between a view of uterine contractions during childbirth as involuntary and a view of the woman as in fact in control of the labor process. The women she interviewed about their birth experiences spoke very similarly to the women described in this chapter about their sense of control over the physical process and over their cries of pain and pleasure during labor and birth. She notes a class difference, however, with middle-class women speaking with more approval of control than working-class women. We might then expect men also to express more concern with and approval of control of emotion, which is not the case here. This is certainly a problem worthy of more study, particularly a delineation of what kinds of control of which domains appear to emerge from what kinds of experience within hierarchical systems.

6. Acknowledgment of one's emotionality may mean very different things to female and male audiences. Women may announce to each other shared identity and solidarity, while asserting difference, submission, or defiance when making similar statements to men.

7. Abu-Lughod's (1986) study of the Awlad 'Ali represents the most detailed and eloquent example of how, in another cultural system, the particular *kinds* of emotions allocated to and voiced by women articulate with other aspects of their ideological and social structural positions.

8. This group of studies obviously follows in the tradition of centuries of expert explanations of hysteria. Although there have been many versions of the explanation (such as one nineteenth-century account that diagnosed its origins as an empty womb and a childhood where the restraint of emotion was not taught [Smith-Rosenberg 1972]), they have been organized around the connection between female physiology and mood.

9. Shimanoff (1983) found that male and female speakers did not differ in the number of affect words they used, in the tense, valence, or source (similar to the notion of "elicitor" used here) of statements about emotion. She did find, however, that males made more reference to their own emotions than to those of other people when compared with females.

10. The resurgence of interest in emotion in the late 1970s and 1980s across the social sciences may in part be the result of the feminist movement's revalorization of all things traditionally associated with women (Margaret Trawick, personal communication). Changing gender relations may also be at the root of the reinvigoration of a long-standing Western discourse on the value of emotional expression; the current debate pits expressionists, for whom healthy emotions are vented ones, against those who would dismiss the latter as "self-indulgent" or "immature." This debate no doubt draws

90   Catherine A. Lutz

in a complex way, in each concrete context in which it occurs, on the gender ideologies and conflicts of the individual participants.

References

Abu-Lughod, Lila. 1986. *Veiled Sentiments: Honor and Poetry in a Bedouin Society.* Berkeley: University of California Press.
Archer, John, and Barbara Lloyd. 1985. *Sex and Gender.* Cambridge: Cambridge University Press.
Asad, Talal, ed. 1973. *Anthropology and the Colonial Encounter.* New York: Humanities Press.
Babchuk, Wayne, Raymond Hames, and Ross Thompson. 1985. Sex Differences in the Recognition of Infant Facial Expressions of Emotion: The Primary Caretaker Hypothesis. *Ethology and Sociobiology* 6:89–101.
Birnbaum, D. A., T. A. Nosanchuck, and W. L. Croll. 1980. Children's Stereotypes About Sex Differences in Emotionality. *Sex Roles* 6:435–43.
Bowlby, John. 1969. *Attachment and Loss,* Vol. 1. London: Hogarth Press.
Cancian, Francesca. 1987. *Love in America: Gender and Self-Development.* Cambridge: Cambridge University Press.
Chodorow, Nancy. 1978. *The Reproduction of Mothering.* Berkeley: University of California Press.
Deaux, K. 1984. From Individual Differences to Social Categories: Analysis of a Decade's Research on Gender. *American Psychologist* 39:105–16.
Fausto-Sterling, Anne. 1985. *Myths of Gender: Biological Theories of Women and Men.* New York: Basic Books.
Foucault, Michel. 1980. *The History of Sexuality,* Vol. 1. New York: Vintage.
Gottlieb, Alma. 1987. American PMS: A Mute Voice. Paper presented at the annual meetings of the American Anthropological Association, Chicago.
Haan, Norma, Robert Bellah, Paul Rabinow, and William Sullivan. 1983. *Social Science as Moral Inquiry.* New York: Columbia University Press.
Hall, J. 1978. Gender Effects in Decoding Nonverbal Cues. *Psychological Bulletin* 85:845–75.
Haraway, Donna. 1986. Primatology Is Politics by Other Means. In Ruth Bleier, ed., *Feminist Approaches to Science.* New York: Pergamon Press, pp. 77–118.
Hochschild, Arlie. 1983. *The Managed Heart: Commercialization of Human Feeling.* Berkeley: University of California Press.
Holland, Dorothy, and Naomi Quinn, eds. 1987. *Cultural Models in Language and Thought.* Cambridge: Cambridge University Press.
Jagger, Alison. 1987. Love and Knowledge: Emotion as an Epistemic Resource for Feminists. Ms. in possession of author. Department of Philosophy, University of Cincinnati.
Jordanova, L. J. 1980. Natural Facts: A Historical Perspective on Science and Sexuality. In Carol MacCormack and Marilyn Strathern, eds., *Nature, Culture, and Gender.* Cambridge: Cambridge University Press, pp. 42–69.
Kirkpatrick, John. 1987. Representing the Self as 'You' in American Discourse. Paper presented at the annual meetings of the American Anthropological Association, Chicago.
Lutz, Catherine. 1988. *Unnatural Emotions: Everyday Sentiments on a Micronesian Atoll and Their Challenge to Western Theory.* Chicago: University of Chicago Press.
Maher, Vanessa. 1984. Possession and Dispossession: Maternity and Mortality

in Morocco. In H. Medick and D. Sabean, eds., *Interest and Emotion*. Cambridge: Cambridge University Press, pp. 103–28.

Martin, Emily. 1987. *The Ideology of Reproduction: The Reproduction of Ideology*. Paper presented to the Upstate New York Feminist Scholars' Network, September.

Montagu, Ashley, ed. 1978. *The Learning of Non-Aggression*. Oxford: Oxford University Press.

Parsons, Talcott, and Robert Bales. 1955. *Family, Socialization, and Interaction Process*. Glencoe, IL: Free Press.

Rosaldo, Michelle Z. 1984. Toward an Anthropology of Self and Feeling. In R. Shweder and R. LeVine, eds., *Culture Theory: Essays on Mind, Self, and Emotion*. Cambridge: Cambridge University Press, pp. 137–57.

Rosaldo, Renato. 1977. The Rhetoric of Control: Ilongots Viewed as Natural Bandits and Wild Indians. In B. Babcock, ed., *The Reversible World: Symbolic Inversion in Art and Society*. Ithaca, NY: Cornell University Press, pp. 240–57.

Rubin, Gayle. 1984. Thinking Sex: Notes for a Radical Theory of the Politics of Sexuality. In Carol S. Vance, ed., *Pleasure and Danger: Exploring Female Sexuality*. Boston: Routledge & Kegan Paul.

Ruddick, Sara. 1980. Maternal Thinking. *Feminist Studies* 6:70–96.

Sampson, E. E. 1981. Cognitive Psychology as Ideology. *American Psychologist* 36:730–43.

Scheper-Hughes, Nancy. 1985. Culture, Scarcity, and Maternal Thinking. *Ethos* 13:291–317.

Scheper-Hughes, Nancy, and Margaret Lock. 1987. The Mindful Body: A Prolegomenon to Future Work in Medical Anthropology. *Medical Anthropology Quarterly* 1:6–41.

Shibamoto, Janet. 1987. The Womanly Woman: Manipulation of Stereotypical and Nonstereotypical Features of Japanese Female Speech. In S. Philips, S. Steele, and C. Tanz, eds., *Language, Gender, and Sex in Comparative Perspective*. Cambridge: Cambridge University Press, pp. 26–49.

Shields, Stephanie A. 1987. Women, Men and the Dilemma of Emotion. In P. Shaver and C. Hendrick, eds., *Sex and Gender*. Newbury Park, CA: Sage Publications, pp. 229–50.

Shimanoff, Susan. 1983. The Role of Gender in Linguistic References to Emotive States. *Communication Quarterly* 30:174–9.

Smith-Rosenberg, Carroll. 1972. The Hysterical Woman: Roles and Role Conflict in 19th-Century America. *Social Research* 39:652–78.

Stoler, Anne. 1985. Perceptions of Protest: Defining the Dangerous in Colonial Sumatra. *American Ethnologist* 12:642–58.

Strathern, Marilyn. 1980. No Nature, No Culture: The Hagen Case. In Carol MacCormack and Marilyn Strathern, eds., *Nature, Culture, and Gender*. Cambridge: Cambridge University Press, pp. 174–222.

Taussig, Michael. 1984. Culture of Terror – Space of Death. Roger Casement's Putumayo Report and the Explanation of Torture. *Comparative Studies in Society and History* 26:467–97.

Whatley, Marianne. 1986. Taking Feminist Science to the Classroom: Where Do We Go from Here? In Ruth Bleier, ed., *Feminist Approaches to Science*. New York: Pergamon Press, pp. 181–90.

Williams, Raymond. 1977. *Marxism and Literature*. Oxford: Oxford University Press.

Woolard, Kathryn. 1985. Language Variation and Cultural Hegemony: Toward an Integration of Sociolinguistic and Social Theory. *American Ethnologist* 12:738–48.

5. Topographies of the self: praise and emotion in Hindu India

ARJUN APPADURAI

Topographies of the self

This chapter explores a specific modality of verbal interaction in Hindu India – praise – in order to construct an argument about the variability of the relationship between language, feelings, and the topography of the self in human societies. In contemplating emotional life in any culturally specific setting, it seems important to note that emotions have a linguistic life and a public and political status that frequently engender formulaic modes of expression. Yet, it also seems that emotions, unlike other phenomena, appear to have a basis in embodied experience, thus inclining us to see them as rooted in some elementary biophysical repertoire that is both limited and universal. To ignore completely this second aspect of emotion is to run the risk of deconstructing emotion altogether as a distinctive phenomenon to be investigated. In the argument that follows, I will try to show that praise in Hindu India is a form governed by the regularities in performance of a culture-specific and conventional activity, like many other linguistic activities. But I will also try to show that praise in Hindu India is, in Bourdieu's sense, a regulated, improvisatory practice (Bourdieu 1977), which depends on a particular *topography of the self* that underlies its public expressions.

This topography, properly understood, leads us to a second issue. Much recent discussion, several chapters in this volume, and my own previous work (Appadurai 1985) take the view that our current common sense about intention and expression, about "real feelings" as opposed to "voiced sentiments," about superficial statements that conceal "real" and "inner" emotional states is, as is so often the case, merely *our* embodied *doxa* misrepresented as general theories about the relationship between affect and expression (Abu-Lughod 1986; Lutz 1988). Such ideas are not only part of emotion talk in the contemporary Anglophone world but are also anchored in the New Testament, where, for the first time in Western history, a major normative claim was made about the separability of act and actor, intention and action, "inner states" and "outer forms." Although these Christian ideas have undergone many changes and spawned many conflicting intellectual offspring, Western discourse has continued to build on this normative break. What has gradually evolved is a complicated repertoire of discourses about the "individual," the "self," and "personality," with the last term serving as the most recent, and most technical, bridge between the first two.

An exploration of this Judeo-Christian story and its many twists and turns over the last two millennia is beyond the scope of this chapter. It does, however, seem possible to identify an elementary Western topography of the "person" (a relatively neutral term for the anthropologist) in which the biologically anterior "self" (where the intertwined processes of ontogeny and phylogeny play themselves out), through the vicissitudes of the trajectory of "personality development," becomes a recognizable though idiosyncratic moral unit, the "individual." This view is a kind of master trope within which more specialized discourses (religious, therapeutic, and legal) contest each other on matters of detail.

This topography is anchored in a spatial image of layers, of which the affective bedrock is seen as simultaneously the simplest, the most general, and the most directly tied to the somatic side of personality. Thus, most Western metatheories of personality are doomed to remain parochial, since they ask cross-cultural questions without any consciousness that their constraining master image itself needs to be interrogated before serious comparative questions can be asked (Lutz, this volume).

I would suggest that such topographies of the self, whether or not they are articulated in elaborate cultural discourses (and metadiscourses), are variable cultural phenomena. We need to deepen our understanding of *this* variation if we are to retain the force of the insight (exemplified throughout this volume) that emotions are discursive public forms whose special power does indeed draw on embodied experience, without implying any parsimoniously describable universal biological substrate. But this demonstration cannot, at least for the anthropologist, be primarily experimental or deductive. It has to be ethnographic, and anchor itself in interpretations of existing forms of performance in particular cultural settings, as a way of exemplifying alternative topographies of the self. In analyzing the pragmatics of praise in Hindu India, I seek to sketch the outlines of one such culturally specific topography. In particular, I shall argue that praise is *not* a matter of *direct* communication between the "inner" states of the relevant persons, but involves the public negotiation of certain gestures and responses. When such negotiation is successful, it creates a *"community of sentiment"* involving the emotional participation of the praiser, the one who is praised, and the audience of the act of praise. Praise is therefore that set of regulated, improvisatory practices that is one route to the creation of communities of sentiment in Hindu India.

The genealogy of praise in the Indic context

As is the case in Christianity and Islam, so in the Hindu world the paradigmatic or prototypic act of praise is the praise of the divine. In the Hindu case, as opposed to that of Islam and Christianity, there is a combination of subordination and intimacy, which Babb (1986) has recently called "hierarchical intimacy." The praise of the many incarnated forms of divinity in Hinduism is a central, highly developed part of the ritual process. *Stōtra* (a term whose linguistic features I shall discuss shortly) refers to a ritualized and usually textualized recitation of praise. It is a major part of the relationship of devotee to divinity in all the major traditions of Hinduism. In some contemporary contexts where Sanskrit has left a strong imprint on the regional languages, the technical, ritual concept of *stōtra* imbues more everyday usages. Thus an everyday Tamil word for praise is *stōttiram*.

Although this is not the place for an extended history of the concept and practice of *stōtra* in Hinduism, four things are worth noting about its cultural construction. First, it makes praise a ritual offering. Second, it puts praise into a formulaic and an aesthetic framework. Third, its main device is description (often through hyperbole) of the positive qualities of the god or goddess in question. Fourth, praise in the *stōtra* is associated with the public expression of the emotional bonds of devotee and deity. *Stōtra* thus is a mode of praise that is ritual, aesthetic, hyperbolic, and emotional. This ritual mode underlies a very large part of the corpus of devotional (*bhakti*) poetry in both North and South India. What is important about this cultural paradigm is that it involves both *interaction* and *assessment:* Thus praise involves intimacy between the subject and the object of praise, while also implying a certain distance. I now turn to some further implications of the involvement of praise with the attitude of a devotee to divinity.

As with other ritual and rhetorical forms in Hindu India, there is in praise a logical concatenation of attitudes to divinity and to royalty, the latter being seen as mortal vessels of universal sovereignty. The praise of kings thus is a perfectly acceptable and highly developed cultural mode and is to be seen in various types of panegyric and eulogy, starting with the earliest literatures. Such praise, which also tends to the formulaic and the hyperbolic, can sometimes take the form of an extended opening portion of inscriptions recording a royal act of generosity.

These written prefaces (Sanskrit: *praśāsti*) have not been extensively studied, since historians have generally been more interested in the acts or events recorded in the main body of the inscriptions.[1] The rhetoric of these praise texts is complex and is historically and regionally variable, but some general points can be made. In most of these "praise prefaces" the central objective is to identify and glorify the reigning sovereign and, when not the same as the sovereign, the donor whose act is being recorded. The identification is usually done through genealogical and chronological statements, often involving chains of names, that stretch back to divine ancestors. The genealogical claims are themselves a form of glorification. A typical strategy is to present an extended series of names, some of which are titles (*viruṭu*). The Dravidian word *viruṭu*, which in historical contexts generally means 'title' or 'emblem', has the more general etymological connotations of honor, pedigree, panegyric, and praise. All these names, many of which have identifiable meanings, are themselves expressions of positive qualities, potencies, or achievements.

Of course, there are many cultures in which praise is an onomastic principle. In South India, royal names or titles, often self-conferred, are complex words or sets of words that refer to specific recent acts of valor, generosity, or piety. These complex, self-conferred titles are both records and advertisements of royal achievements. When the donor whose action is being recorded in an inscription is the same as the king who is being praised, these *praśāsti* constitute a culturally appropriate formula for self-praise for those who rule. Even here it is possible that there are sacred models, such as the self-celebrating epiphany at the end of the *Bhagavad Gita*, in which Krishna stages an enormous spectacle of his powers and forms to Arjuna.

These *praśāsti* forms tell us that the pragmatics of praise in the Indic context has something to do with boasting, boosting, competing, elevating, and inflating. In the Indo-Aryan languages, there is a semantic distinction between those forms deriving from the Sanskrit root *stu* (whose Vedic context places it explicitly in a ritual and hymnal context) and those forms (such as the Hindi and Gujarati *praśansa*) deriving from the

Sanskrit *śansa*, which has the far more secular connotations of commendation, applause, fame, and glory. In the standard dictionary of the Dravidian languages, of the twenty-one relevant entries, five are semantically neutral, but of the remainder, twelve have very secular overtones (again having to do with flattery, boasting, elevating, and publicizing), and only four are clearly linked to adoration, worship, prayer, and so forth (Burrow and Emeneau 1961).

It is, of course, dangerous to infer contemporary semantic realities from such etymological patterns, especially given the complicated lexical histories compressed into various dictionary entries. Nevertheless, it seems reasonable to argue that, at least in the Indo-Aryan languages, there are *two* clusters of meaning surrounding acts of praise: a primary cluster derived from Vedic ritual and hymnal practice and a secondary cluster pertaining to praise in everyday life. In the Dravidian case, the relative priority of these two clusters is less clear, and it is conceivable that the ritual or worship-oriented sense of praise is a product of interaction with North Indian traditions and practices, and that the earlier, classical Tamil universe is oriented to praise as panegyric rather than to praise as worship.

But it is also clear, in both the Indo-Aryan and the Dravidian cases, that there is no sharp break between the two semantic clusters and that each derives some of its pragmatic force from the other. The two subfields converge in the praise (or self-praise) of kings, where the pragmatic lines between praise as adoration, praise as honor, praise as worship, praise as flattery, and praise as naming are difficult to draw (Bharati 1970).[2] This pragmatic sense of praise could be extended from kings to all *patrons*, as in the following typical benediction appearing at the conclusion of each section of an eleventh-century Jaina text from Delhi, in which the poet praises his patron, a Jaina merchant (Cohen 1979:1.21.18): "May Sri Nattala, whose fame, appearing like the moon, shines on the earth; because of whom bards have become seekers of the wish-fulfilling tree; by whom speech is uttered free from error; who is beloved of the people, illustrious, pious, and incomparable, be victorious!"

The patron (*yajamāna*) of any ritualized or aesthetic activity is the situational incarnation of the god-king. Thus, the ideological and rhetorical forms associated with the praise of patrons (which we have from a huge variety of paintings, texts, sculptures, and inscriptions associated with Hindu "art") can be seen as paradigmatic of the attitudes expected from inferiors toward their superiors in all domains of life. But in making the move from highly stylized, fixed forms of expression to everyday ones, we enter a cultural field of greater ambiguity.

Praise and dependence

One consequence of the resilience of the value placed on the formulaic praise of superiors is that flattery is a prominent part of everyday public behavior in India. In this respect, praise (or, more exactly, flattery) is one of the standard means not simply to mark hierarchy but to mark dependence. Flattery is typically part of the rhetoric surrounding a "big man," whether the big man is a politician, a film star, a business magnate, a village headman, or a charismatic religious leader. Of course, such a rhetorical stance occurs in many societies, but it has a particular flavor and structure in Hindu India.

Earlier, I observed that the *stōtra* combines the texture of ritual, aesthetic, hyperbolic, and emotional modes of expression. Public flattery is perhaps most easily seen in the politics of contemporary India. The praise heaped upon Indira Gandhi by her followers, themselves often leaders of substance in their own regions and contexts, frequently shocked outside observers. Such flattery was an important part of public demonstrations of dependence and adoration (touching her feet, asking her blessings on various enterprises, anticipating her moods, and so forth) that could easily be construed as simple, self-interested groveling. But in India, these demonstrations are an important part of a tradition of adoration of and interaction with the glory of the superior.

What we see in political behavior can also be seen in less formal contexts involving superiors and their clienteles, where flattery takes on immense proportions. Today, given how far removed many of these contexts are from the authority of ritual and the splendor of the court, Indians themselves have developed a certain ambivalence about public flattery and the forms of dependence that it implies. One sign of this ambivalence is the colloquial Hindustani term *chamcha* (literally, 'spoon'),[3] which is applied in a derogatory way to those dependents of any celebrity who specialize in echoing, praising, and transmitting his or her views without any whiff of critical independence. Yet, such hangers-on, whose sole function is to provide a continuous flow of praise, are an integral part of most groups surrounding celebrities in India. It may appear at first sight that this "groupie" phenomenon is an accompaniment of stardom and power in many cultural settings. But I would argue that its special diacritic in Hindu India is its unconscious anchoring in the living logic of worship.

For those who lack the privilege of constant contact with a superior, there is another, less direct mode of praise. This mode involves praising the good deeds, capabilities, powers, and reputation of the superior to somebody else, outside the physical presence of the superior. Although not, therefore, a direct act of adoration, it is not flattery either. Again, it applies to major rulers, deities, saints, patrons, and "stars" of every sort. It involves singing their praises, not so much in the form of names and qualities as in narrative forms, focusing on specific achievements of the superior to which the speaker is able to testify. It is a form of reputation building (for both the speaker and the big person spoken of) whose cultural logic has hardly been explored.

In this indirect form of praise, too, there is a special bond between the speaker and the object of praise, for its narratives frequently put the speaker in a privileged relationship to the superior. This privilege takes two forms. The first involves the action worthy of praise, which marks the speaker as a worthy recipient of the superior's favor. Stories about the miracles worked by a saint, the gifts given by a philanthropist, the boon granted by a specific deity, the financial help given at a time of crisis by a politician, the secret lifesaving act by a filmstar – all these usually involve the speaker as a direct beneficiary. The second form of privilege is epistemological: It marks the speaker as someone who knows something special and who has the privilege of passing it on. Witness and transmission, insofar as they underlie such indirect forms of praise of a superior, are fundamental parts of the cultural construction of reputation in contemporary India. In this process, praise, witness, rumor, and narrative come together. This configuration, which today applies to all sorts of celebrities, stars, and big men and women in the making, relies on spontaneous narratives of praise that continue (as in the past) to generate texts: stories, poems, songs, and prayers of praise. The mode of praise here is not direct flattery but publicizing, which is directed not to the emotional satisfaction of the superior but to the increment of his or her following.

Sometimes, in the making of such reputations, the teller of the story (if you will, the publicist) tells it in the full knowledge that word of his or her acts will eventually return to the superior who is the object of such praise. Such strategies of circumlocution are typical of small communities (families, neighborhoods, devotional groups, offices, work groups and so forth) where circles of communication are finite, and acts of reputation building have an excellent chance of benefiting the transmitter as much as the subject of the act. Also true of such small communities of interaction is the distortion of messages that occurs, and credit for a reputation-building act for the publicist may not be registered appropriately. But the hope that your superior will hear of your praise, and thus think better of you, is not crudely manipulative (as with alternative topographies of the self, which permit both acts and judgments of hypocrisy),[4] but a mixture of adoration and expectation of reward that characterizes Hindu ritual generally. Praise of the superior is, therefore, part of a complex series of acts of mutual benefit that characterize the ethos of Hindu worship itself.

But how do superiors construe their own capability to praise their inferiors and dependents? In general, direct praise of inferiors and dependents is as uncommon as the praise of superiors is common. There are stories in the Hindu tradition in which deities express their admiration for particularly remarkable devotees and acts of devotion. But in everyday life, it is not in good taste for the superior to sing the praises of dependents directly. But here we need to discriminate among several situations.

In the domestic situation of most Hindu households, parents do not praise their children directly, for this would be seen as inviting the free-floating malevolence of the "evil eye," a topic on which I shall shortly have more to say. But although it is considered important for parents to deprecate the virtues and abilities of their children to outsiders, such outsiders are certainly not prevented from seeing or hearing the children demonstrate their skills or accomplishments in drawing, singing, schoolwork, or domestic arts. Such demonstrations raise difficult dilemmas for guests or observers, who have to calculate their responses carefully. To withhold all praise is tantamount to an insult. To praise too directly and in too fulsome a manner raises the specter of the evil eye. The solution generally is to separate the act from the actor and to praise the accomplishment as if it were distinct from the actor. Thus, praising the product or performance (the painting, the cooked dish, the song, the dance) rather than the performer is perfectly appropriate. This stricture applies only in the physical presence of the object of praise, where the dangers of the evil eye are greatest. When the child is physically not present, there is greater latitude, although even here the problem of the evil eye is not entirely absent.

From the point of view of the guest or visitor in a domestic setting, relatively loose constraints on the praise of children are much more stringent in regard to wives, and women more generally. Especially for adult males who are not regularly involved with the household, praise of women, whether direct or indirect, whether of person or of performance, must be extremely muted. Even thanks for hospitality, which is in any case complicated (Appadurai 1985), are rendered to the male host rather than to the female hostess and cook. If praise is ever directed to the women of the household, it has to be brief, casual, and product oriented, rather than oriented to the female or females of the house. In the latter case, not only is there the danger of the evil eye, but also there are the sexual implications of praise, which endanger conventions of modesty in the South and of honor, reinforced by the impact of Islam, in the North. Women are generally expected to be invisible providers of good things and good works, for which they cannot easily be praised.

The evil eye, which I have now mentioned several times, generally applies to vulnerable creatures, who are dependent on the nurturance and protection of superiors. The best examples of this category are children and domestic animals such as cattle. When such vulnerable creatures are especially beautiful, innocent, weak, or fortunate, they are seen as natural magnets of envy, desire, and ill will, with fuzzy boundaries between these sentiments. Beautiful children, healthy cattle, attractive daughters, and devoted sons are typical targets of these emotions. But the evil eye is invoked largely in those situations where the phenomenology of emotions is ambiguous, where acclaim might mask envy, gratitude might disguise desire, and congratulation might conceal ill will. There is no explicit indigenous theory about the relationship between emotional ambiguity and the evil eye, but it seems to be a plausible interpretive link.

David Pocock has noted, in a West Indian rural setting, that the evil eye is a culturally organized interpretation of envy and that, sociologically, it is most likely to be imputed in those situations where "those who should be equal are not so in fact" (1973:39). Pocock also suggests that *najar* (the evil gaze) is not to be feared, in a hierarchical society, between those whose status is different and clearly defined. But there is reason to suppose that this view cannot be generalized, and that the link between emotional ambiguity and the evil eye is a more subtle one. To make this case, it is worthwhile to examine begging as a social phenomenon in India.

Begging, like many other activities in India, is an organized occupational activity. Although it is increasingly a phenomenon of pauperization and proletarianization in urban India, there is a recognized cultural place for it and a recognized cultural idiom for its practice. Begging is a legitimate (even if devalued) activity for two reasons. First, it partakes of the emotional and ritual ethos of worship, with the beggar playing the role of the worshipper. Second, in its open admission of the radical dependence of the beggar on the goodwill of others for his subsistence, it carries some of the moral authority of asceticism, and in many cases "beggars" and "ascetics" are not clearly distinct categories. The widespread fear of both beggars and ascetics is tied up with the magical power of words, in which blessing and cursing are two sides of the same coin (Peter van der Veer, personal communication).

Although there is a great deal of regional and situational variation in how begging is practiced and perceived, the central verbal tactic of beggars is to *bless* and *praise* their human targets while asking for food or for money. This practice could be labeled "coercive subordination," for in blessing and praising their (potential) benefactors, beggars seek to trap them in the cultural implications of their roles as superiors, that is, in the obligation to be generous. The coercive element is also expressed in the *open* way in which beggars reveal their desire to benefit from the greater good fortune of their fellows. In India, when desire is so open, can malice be far behind? Indeed, in crowded public situations, beggars can often be seen (and heard) to express their resentment of rebuffs by mumbling abuses and curses (the inverse of praise and blessings), particularly when they have been rebuffed in a cruel or insulting manner.

Begging is an exaggerated and intensified enactment of forms of dependence and types of interaction that are widely institutionalized in Indian society. The parallels between benefactors and gods, the coercive and reciprocal implications of praise, the link between praise and the desire for the good things in life, the fine line between desire and envy, the hidden threat of abuse beneath the external profession of praise, are all factors on which beggars depend to exploit the emotional ambiguity that links praise – through envy – to the evil eye. The ambiguity lies in the fact that praise can be a celebration of dependence *or* a subtle (and coercive) complaint about it. Beggars, who rightly see themselves as having little (transactionally) to lose, given the speed, number, and impersonality of their encounters, frequently rely on this ambiguity in their practices. Thus, some beggars look threatening while they utter paeans of praise; or they exaggerate the mechanical and impersonal formalities of their verbal routines; or they violate canons of physical contact by touching their targets on their arms or thighs rather than on their feet or not at all. In playing with this gestural and verbal repertoire while uttering formulas of praise, beggars *deliberately* enact the ambiguity of their emotional relations to their potential benefactors. Thus their performance underlines the fact that praise is not a matter of *direct* communication between the inner emotional states of the parties involved but of a publicly understood *code* for the negotiation of expectations and obligations. This public play of affect involves a distinct topography of the self, and a related aesthetics of transaction, that can best be appreciated by considering two further arenas in India: the world of appraisal and the world of appreciation.

But before going on to discuss these two arenas, it is worth remarking that there are many contexts in which praise is not seen as a vehicle for the sentiments of the evil eye: The praise of superiors, the praise of inanimate objects, and the praise of nonintimate inferiors are examples of such contexts. Thus, if you praise as a good worker a farm laborer who works for another man, you might do so in a patronizing way, and this is not regarded as endangering the worker. We might conclude that when objects or persons are seen as relatively invulnerable to envy, desire, or ill will, or when the emotions appropriate to them are seen as relatively unambiguous, the evil eye is not thought of as a likely accompaniment of acts of praise. But the praise of objects brings us to the distinction between praise as *adoration* and praise as *appraisal*.

Appraisal and the world of things

I have so far discussed *praise as interaction* in two modalities: one that is ritual in orientation and whose paradigm is the worship of the divinity; and one that has to do with applause, publicity, and reputation, and seems typical of the followers of leaders, big men, and big women. But there is another axis of discrimination in regard to praise, and here we must distinguish praise as a mode of interaction from praise as a mode of assessment. By looking at praise between putative equals (especially in the context of marriage) and between unequals, I shall show that praise reveals some of the ambiguities inherent in all public codifications of affect.[5]

In India, praise as assessment is most often seen in the relationship between equals. It arises in contexts where praise as adoration and praise as applause are equally out of place. It is also prone to be expressed especially in regard to things. Praise as assessment is likely to occur in contexts with a commercial component, either generically, as in the contexts of shops, bazaars, and markets, where buyers and sellers are equals (even if their larger social identities are disparate); or when contractual arrangements are being negotiated; or, most revealingly, in the transactions and negotiations that accompany marriage. I shall use this last context to explore the link between praise, assessment, and the world of things.

Marriage negotiations in Hindu India, especially among upper-caste groups that have elaborate dowry practices and other related gift transactions tied up with affinity, belong to a class of events that I have elsewhere called "tournaments of value" (Appadurai 1986). They are agonistic encounters, outside the sphere of normal economic practice, where negotiations take place over objects of prime value, with subtle and long-term implications for day-to-day economic well-being. In the particular tournament of value constituted by Brahman Hindu marriage in Tamil South India, praise is an important rhetorical component of the status contests that characterize both the negotiations that precede marriage (May 1986) and the marriage itself (Appadurai 1981). Praise has special political overtones in the context of marriage because marriage always involves the effort of bride givers (in India, by definition, of lower status) to dignify their temporary deference to the bride-receiving family. Both the gifts that accompany marriage and the individuals involved in the marriage are subject to very complicated mutual assessment.

In the first place, a subtle battle of assessment is involved on the very first occasion when members of the prospective groom's family visit the home of the potential bride. On these delicate occasions, the entire rhetorical posture of the bridegroom's party can be summed up as appraisal (or evaluation, or assessment). The home of the bride's family is assessed, as are the things on display within it, including furniture, wall decorations, and utensils. More personal possessions, especially jewelry and clothing worn by the female members of the household, are also on display for assessment. Last but not least, the prospective bride and her accomplishments are displayed for assessment. The exchange of words on such occasions is a very subtle commentary on this traffic in things, images, and sense impressions.

For the potential bride's family, there is usually a maximum effort to let their house, their possessions, and their carefully decorated daughter speak for themselves. When they themselves speak, they tread a thin line between humility (which is expected of them as prospective bride givers) and self-advertisement. The latter is accomplished subtly by referring to well-placed relatives, influential friends, and their own economic stability. More important, they make comments from time to time that allude to the culinary (or musical or housekeeping) skills of their daughter or of the women of the family in general. On the bridegroom's side, there is a greater sense of command and assurance and a more brazen tendency to assess their environment, including the human beings in it. Questions about material possessions set the stage for later, hard-nosed negotiations about what the bride's parents will do for their daughter. Even those positive comments made by the bridegroom's party in praise of the material lives of their hosts are meant to be acts of appraisal, signs of evaluation.

At the marriage itself, a good deal turns on the material display of the dower: the utensils, the jewelry, and the clothing provided by the bride's family for the couple and especially for their own daughter. Here assessment becomes an instrument of status politics in the most direct manner. Members of the bridegroom's family often do not hesitate to assess openly the possible weight of the metal in utensils, the heaviness of silk saris, and the possible cost of specific pieces of jewelry. These actions, and the often deprecatory verbal accompaniments to them, are the negative side of praise as assessment and are frequently the starting point of bitterness between the two families, which can result in long-term discord and sometimes in the abuse or death of the bride.[6] Such public, detailed, and intensive assessment of material objects, as part of the social reproduction of groups, has other general implications (see Breckenridge 1986) that lie outside the scope of this chapter.

It is sufficient to note that praise as assessment of material possessions is most intense in the context of dowry-centered marriages, but it can also be seen in a wide range of social interactions between persons who are, roughly speaking, in the same social class. Thus, whenever families and social groups reach the economic level where part of their household inventory of possessions is clearly for display and not simply for subsistence, their social interaction acquires the dimension of appraisal. More than elsewhere in the world, in Hindu South Asia it is culturally acceptable to scrutinize, and preferably to handle physically, the special possessions of the person you are visiting; to inquire after the "cultural biographies" (Kopytoff 1986) of their possessions; and, if possible, to ascertain their original cost. There is also an equally acceptable set of devices to fend off such questions, to give vague replies, and to avoid offering information to the questioner. But the form of the negotiation is culturally sanctioned, and neither side can easily take offense. Here too praise plays an active role, for statements of admiration and encomium can, and often do, precede more pointed evaluative inquiries. Here praise is a gentle, polite way of introducing potentially impolite queries.

It is worth noting that the more "personal" the things in question, the more careful the acts of praise and assessment must be. What can easily be said or asked about a radio, a car, a bicycle, or a cigarette lighter can less easily be said or asked about a piece of jewelry, a piece of clothing, or a utensil in active use. In these latter cases, acts of praise begin to approach praise of the owner and to raise the possibility of envy or desire directed at this person. This marks the boundary at which acts of praise cannot lightly be made or construed. Yet, praise of any thing or possession (whether made as a grudging act of appraisal or as a display of genuine enthusiasm) is preferable to direct praise of a person, unless the person is an obvious superior. With superiors, praising their possessions would most likely be taken amiss, since it implies an inappropriate evaluative stance on the part of the inferior. By extension, the positive assessment of the material possessions of an inferior would be regarded either as patronizing or as sarcastic, but in either case as not in very good taste.

In general, the praise of things exemplifies one mode of praise, which is evaluative, whereas the praise of persons exemplifies another mode, which is interactive. But since persons and things have qualities that link them, every act of evaluation has something interactive about it, just as every interactive act of praise is the product of some sort of appraisal. This situation both resembles and contrasts with that of more egalitarian societies, where there may be explicit sanctions against creating emotions of awe or envy in others by showing them one's possessions (Catherine Lutz, personal communication). In both cases, what is important to note is that praise is governed by regularities of discourse and embodied strategies of interaction that do not assume anything critical about the "inner" states of the actors. What the relationship then *is* between expressions and emotions can best be seen by turning to the domain of aesthetics and performance.

Appreciation and performance

Throughout this chapter, I have noted that praise, in both formalized and everyday settings in India, has something of the formulaic and the hyperbolic about it. To the observer–analyst, it often appears exaggerated, formal, and unrelated to the emotional interior of the person who praises. This problem of the emotional authenticity of praise (see also Irvine, this volume) is best tackled by looking at the major area where Indians have reflected on emotion and appreciation: the emotional and aesthetic theory of *rasa*, the master theory of aesthetics in Hindu thought.

As every student of Indian poetics and aesthetics is aware, *rasa* is a peculiarly elusive concept, partly because its assumptions are very different from those of Western common sense regarding the relationship between feeling, gesture, and performance. Yet the theory of *rasa* contains clues not just to Indian ethnopoetics but also to praise in everyday life and the topography of self that underlies it. Before I use the concept of *rasa* to illuminate the pragmatics of praise, I will outline its elements in the Indian learned tradition.

Indian aestheticians have singled out eight feelings (*bhāva*) that all persons experience in their lives: love, mirth, grief, energy, terror, disgust, anger, and wonder (see Brenneis, this volume). In the poetic context, each of these is transformed into a corresponding mood (*rasa*), a generalized, impersonal feeling capable of being understood by other persons in similar states. In drama, these moods are expressed in a publicly understood set of gestures, and both the dramatic performance and its critical analysis involve the appraisal of these gestures. The consequences of this appraisal for dramatic performance are neatly captured by A. K. Ramanujan (1974:117–18):

> The actor, as in a Stanislavsky school, must study the physical stances and expressions that are functions and reflections of the mood, even glandular secretions of tears and contractions of the solar plexus: one feels grief because he weeps, joy because his face glows and his eyes dilate. It is a form of physical imagining, as in the story of the village idiot who found the missing donkey by imagining where he would go if he were a donkey. The emotion produces tears and gestures; cannot the gestures reproduce the emotion? And the reader and the spectator in his turn goes through the incipient gestures and tensions in himself: the mood creates a condition in which the reader or spectator reconstitutes his own analogous private, incommunicable, and forgotten feelings into this impersonal expression. They are transmuted into the mood. This he enjoys, and thus he can enjoy, for example, grief.

Let me gloss this discussion of the portrayal of emotion in Indian poetics by noting that it has a special set of pragmatic assumptions. The key assumption is that the actor evokes certain feelings in the viewer by exteriorizing his or her own emotions in a particular formulaic, publicly understood, and impersonal way. The object is to create a chain of communications in feeling, not by unmediated empathy between the emotional "interiors" of specific individuals but by recourse to a shared, and relatively fixed set, of public gestures. The creation of shared emotions is thus unyoked from the emotional authenticity of any particular person's feelings. Praise in Hindu India partakes of this set of assumptions concerning performance and feeling. Praise is measured by the "community of sentiment" it evokes and creates, and not by the authenticity of the link between the private (or idiosyncratic) emotions of the praiser and the object of his or her praise.

In the classical theory of *rasa*, particularly as formulated by the eleventh-century Kashmiri Saiva theorist Abhinavagupta, the relation between emotion and aesthetics takes an elaborate form and is expressed in interesting ethnopsychological terms (Gerow 1974:220–1). The theory is based on intuition, on the generalization of character, of event, and of response, and has been described by Edwin Gerow as a statement of radical antirealism. In Abhinavagupta's formulation, *rasa* is a transcendent mode of apprehending the work of art, to which normal modes of awareness are obstacles. Gerow (1974:224) has this to say about the "inversion of emotion" in Abhinavagupta's view of the aesthetic response:

> The entire drama has now been translated from the theater to the audience; the theater is no longer "object," but pretext for the interior play whose success is nothing but a state of mind, cleverly evoked through suggestion, realized as those latent aspects of the audience's emotional being that are the common and recurrent heritage of mankind. These aspects are implied by and present in every emotional circumstance, every concrete emotional situation, but are never, in ordinary life, grasped in themselves, apart from their specific determinants. It is the function of the play, of linguistic art, so to free the very conditions of emotional life; and it is precisely in this sense that the *rasa* is not a concrete emotion (*bhāva*), but rather the inversion of an emotion; the specific determinants of the emotion (place, time, circumstance, etc.) are so cast as to appear themselves as function of the latent emotional state, and are generalized.

Gerow also points out that the theory of *rasa*, which posits a state of consciousness more real than the work of art itself, has clear philosophical links to the theory of levels of reality contained in the philosophy of

Advaita Vedanta. *Rasa* may be said to anticipate and prefigure *mōkśa* (spiritual liberation). But later in the history of Hindu devotionalism, particularly in the writings of the Bengali Vaisnavas of the sixteenth century, a curious reversal occurs whereby *mōkśa* "has not only become an ideal open to all men, recast as the perfection of the most human of relations, love, but this new 'emotional' transcendence, *bhakti*, has become the essence of *rasa*" (Gerow 1974:226).

Gerow's statement of both the classical theory of *rasa* and the inversion of emotion on which it is founded – and the reversal of the theory in Bengali Vaisnavism, where *mōkśa* itself is seen as an emotional state, an eternal version of the experience of *rasa* in art – provides the basis for making a plausible interpretive link between the vagaries of *rasa* theory in Indian history and the significance of praise in Hindu life. To substantiate this intuition, I will return to the topic of begging, which was discussed earlier in relation to the evil eye. This large interpretive leap from *rasa* theory to the cultural logic of begging in India is justified because begging is a highly organized performance and, in its most common forms, has a large audience. Beggars are often consummate actors who have developed their own style – composed of verbal, gestural, and kinesthetic elements – for approaching their potential benefactors. Although the benefactors are not always willing participants in these small performances, both positive and negative responses to beggars have acceptable cultural forms. Since the "interaction rituals" (Goffman 1967) involved in begging are public and highly orchestrated, they are not completely removed from the arena of aesthetic performance. The second justification for using begging as an everyday extension of the underlying logic of *rasa* theory is that begging, too, involves the public negotiation of emotional expressions.

The beggar's praise is no more intended to represent his "inner" feelings to his audience than are the gestures of the actor on the classical stage. As in *rasa* theory, what beggars do, by drawing on a publicly negotiable set of expressions, is to draw the audience (and their potential benefactor, who is sometimes the *sole* member of the audience) into a "community of sentiment" whose pragmatic consequence (if the performance is skillful) is that the benefactor bestows some favor on the beggar. Why can we not simply say that the beggar is a flatterer who plays upon the ego of his target? Because begging in India usually involves not only a tale of woe (this is hardly a unique feature of begging in India) but also a fairly elaborate performance of "coercive subordination." Such coercive subordination, when it does work, does so partly because it is rooted in the general understanding of praise as a key to reciprocity between superiors and inferiors; partly because of the hidden threat of the evil eye; and partly because "communities of sentiment" can be created in India by the skillful orchestration of specific gestural elements without reference to the "inner feelings" of the actors. The fact that both the beggar's performance and his audience's response appear mechanical and unsentimental does not disprove my interpretation, any more than the ritualized collective wailing accompanying death in many societies suggests that the participants are in no way sentimentally involved. In fact, the more deeply shared the ethos and the code, the more matter-of-fact, or "mechanical," the performance can afford to be.

In the creation of "communities of sentiment," standardized verbal and gestural forms are used, and there is no assumption of any correspondence between the words and gestures and the internal emotional world of the "actor." What matters are the emotional *effects* of praise, which, when it is properly "performed," creates a generalized mood of adoration or admiration or wonder that unites the one who praises, the object of this praise, and the audience, if there is one. At the same time (and here the *bhakti* connection is relevant), a special emotional bond is created with the object of praise itself. But the emotional landscape implied by such acts of praise is not built on the idiosyncratic, biographical, experiential, "inner" feelings of Western common sense. It is constituted of the emotional effects created by the public negotiation of the words and gestures of praise.

Of course, the verbal and gestural forms of praise in everyday life do not have the aesthetic rigor or the ritual predictability of art or worship. Thus, the emotional impact of specific acts of praise in ordinary life can often be weak, ambiguous, or, for lack of a clear frame, unfocused. Still, when praise is directed at a benevolent superior, something of the aesthetic and emotional communion implied by the concept of *rasa* is, I suspect, present. To the extent that formulaic public praise of superiors is considered credible and pleasurable, it is probably due to this cultural conception of the construction of emotional and aesthetic satisfaction.

Praise in Hindu India is one aspect of the critical evaluation of texts, persons, and deeds, and it is an important part. Such criticism is intended to deepen, rather than to abort, the social bonds between the subject and the object of criticism. It suggests an idea of emotional and aesthetic communion between audience, artifact, and ultimate reality, which differs from those assumed and created by most varieties of post-Renaissance Western critical theory. A great deal more accounts for the

Indian attitude toward traditional objects, whether human or textual, than can be discussed here. Ideas about originality and authorship, commentary versus criticism, and the inherent prestige of the past all would need to be carefully worked out to account for the Indian "critical" temper. The idea that praise is a complex devotional, evaluative, and interactive act should be an important aspect of such an account.

Still, it is important to recall that praise in ordinary life is not always a matter of communion, devotion, appreciation, and adoration. We have seen already that praise can, in relations with equals and inferiors, be a more ambiguous rhetorical device, reflecting envy, inappropriate desire, or anger. But even in these cases, it is still a form that is regarded as having effects on the extralinguistic world. Directed at the wrong object, or as a direct expression of inappropriate "personal" emotions, praise is dangerous, duplicitous, even damaging. But whether it makes or breaks the bonds between the speaker, the audience, and its referent, praise is never a neutral, descriptive act. It always has the ability to affect and create things in the world. The everyday challenge for Hindus is to assess correctly the meanings of the forms of praise they witness and to predict prudently the results of the forms of praise they produce.

Praise is thus not a matter of linking the emotional "interiors" of actors by breaking through the public veil of language, of gesture, and of communication. It is rather one of the varieties of improvisatory practice that, in Hindu India, can create sentimental bonds quite independent of the "real" feelings of the persons involved. Such bonds are part of the politics of everyday life, and such politics is cultural and not biological, since its messages and its media are publicly expressed, construed, and appraised.

Notes

This chapter is dedicated to Thomas Zwicker, who died in Ahmedabad on October 29, 1985. It was first delivered at a conference on the emotions in India, organized by Pauline Kolenda and Owen Lynch in December 1985. I am grateful to all the participants at that conference for their suggestions, and especially to Frederique Marglin, who served as commentator on this chapter. I am also grateful to Owen Lynch for his detailed critique of an earlier draft. Finally, I thank Lila Abu-Lughod, Richard Cohen, Dilip Gaonkar, Catherine Lutz, and Peter van der Veer for helping me to sharpen what was previously a rather diffuse argument.
1.   The word *praśasti* is derived from the Sanskrit *śansa*, which in turn accounts for the term *praśansa*, a standard lexeme for 'praise' in several modern Indo-Aryan languages, including Hindi, Gujarati, and Marathi. The praise (*praśasti*) portion of inscriptions is particularly elaborated in the royal inscrip-

tions of eighth- to sixteenth-century South India, parts of which were successively under Pallava, Chola, and Vijayanagara rule.

2. I am grateful to Kirin Narayan for drawing this source to my attention.

3. I have neither heard nor read anything about the etymology of this term. I suspect that it implies the idea of "feeding" praise to one's superior, as well as the derogatory, even polluting, identification of one human being with an instrument put into another human being's mouth.

4. The subject of hypocrisy, on which I am currently working, brings together a number of complicated cross-cultural issues involving the topography of the self, the problems of staging and representation, and the authenticity of public expressions, which cannot fully be engaged here.

5. The etymological roots of the English word "praise" are clearly economic and imply assessment in a framework that involves commerce, calculation, and exchange. This original sense of the English word "praise" has been lost in most contemporary uses, but there is a dimension of praise that is not unrelated to it, even in contemporary Western practice.

6. I refer here to the phenomenon of "bride burning," which, especially in North India, has drawn a great deal of attention both in the press and among feminist groups. It is widely agreed that these deaths are often the end point of a trajectory of abuse of women by their husband's families, fueled by the massive inflation of dowry demands in contemporary urban India.

References

Abu-Lughod, Lila. 1986. *Veiled Sentiments: Honor and Poetry in a Bedouin Society.* Berkeley: University of California Press.

Appadurai, Arjun. 1981. Gastro-Politics in Hindu South Asia. *American Ethnologist* 8, 494–511.

   1985. Gratitude as a Social Mode in South India. *Ethos* 13:236–45.

   1986. Commodities and the Politics of Value. In A. Appadurai, ed., *The Social Life of Things.* New York: Cambridge University Press, pp. 3–63.

Babb, L. A. 1986. *Redemptive Encounters: Three Modern Styles in the Hindu Tradition.* Berkeley: University of California Press.

Bharati, A. 1970. Pilgrimage Sites in Indian Civilization. In J. W. Elder, ed., *Chapters in Indian Civilization.* Dubuque: Kendal/Hunt, pp. 83–126.

Bourdieu, Pierre. 1977. *Outline of a Theory of Practice.* Cambridge: Cambridge University Press.

Breckenridge, Carol. 1985. The Social Use of Everyday Objects in Hindu South India. In L. Chandra, ed., *Essays in Honor of Pupul Jayakar.* Delhi: Agam Kala Prakashan, pp. 57–66.

Burrow, T., and Emeneau, M. B. 1961. *A Dravidian Etymological Dictionary.* Oxford: Clarendon.

Cohen, R. 1979. The Pasanahacariu of Sridhara: An Introduction, Edition and Translation of the Apabrahmsa Text. Ph.D. dissertation, University of Pennsylvania.

Gerow, Edwin. 1974. The Rasa Theory of Abhinavagupta and Its Applications. In E. Dimock, ed., *The Literatures of India: An Introduction.* Chicago: University of Chicago Press, pp. 216–27.

Goffman, Erving. 1967. *Interaction Rituals.* New York: Anchor Books.

Kopytoff, Igor. 1986. The Cultural Biography of Things. In A. Appadurai, ed., *The Social Life of Things*. New York: Cambridge University Press, pp. 64–91.

Lutz, Catherine. 1988. *Unnatural Emotions: Everyday Sentiments on a Micronesian Atoll and Their Challenge to Western Theory*. Chicago: University of Chicago Press.

May, L. 1986. Arranging Marriages: Negotiation and Decision-Making in South India. Ph.D. dissertation, University of Pennsylvania.

Pocock, D. 1973. *Mind, Body and Wealth*. Oxford: Basil Blackwell.

Ramanujan, A. K. 1974. Indian Poetics: An Overview. In E. Dimock, ed., *The Literatures of India: An Introduction*. Chicago: University of Chicago Press, pp. 115–18.

6. Shared and solitary sentiments: the discourse of friendship, play, and anger in Bhatgaon

DONALD BRENNEIS

This chapter is intended to complement – in a highly tentative way – current research on relationships between discourse and emotions. I have been guided to the perspective I will propose by the people with whom I have worked: rural, Hindi-speaking Fiji Indians. I will provide a brief ethnographic account of some of the notions through which they inform their own understandings of talk and sentiment. The methodological core of my approach is a consideration of a local rhetoric and aesthetics: In what terms do Bhatgaon villagers interpret, evaluate, and shape their experience, and how are such practices enacted through discourse? My discussion will draw primarily on village men's accounts and behavior. This is not, however, due solely to my being a male ethnographer in a somewhat sex-segregated community. Rather, as I will later argue, these local theories of emotion and experience – and the ways in which they take shape in ongoing discourse – are critical elements in the definition and politics of gender in Bhatgaon.

Before moving to a discussion of the Fiji Indian case and its possible implications, I want to highlight two areas in which recent ethnopsychological research and work in the study of language and emotion or affect have led to important reformulations that are particularly relevant to my argument. First, it has become increasingly evident that understandings of the locus and genesis of emotional experience vary considerably across cultures. In contrast to the usual Western notions of the locus of emotion being within the individual, for example, in much of the Pacific, "emotion words . . . [are] statements about the relationship between a person and an event" (Lutz 1982:113). As Myers (1979) and others have demonstrated, there is often a critical relational dimension in local theories of the emotions. Indeed, "feelings" often provide a social rather than an individual idiom, a way of commenting not so much on oneself as on oneself in relation to others.

Second, we have a much subtler understanding of some of the critical ways in which language and emotion are entwined. A number of studies have focused on semantic dimensions of emotion vocabularies in different cultures (e.g., Lutz 1982; Myers 1979). Starting with local terms, such studies illumine considerably the varied ways in which discourse apparently concerned with emotion operates. Other studies have focused more on those pragmatic, prosodic, and other communicative devices conventionally associated with the expression of emotion in particular communities. How do speakers evince their feelings? Through what "plops, squeaks, croaks, sighs and moans" (Mithun 1982, cited in Irvine 1982), to mention only a few possibilities, are feelings conveyed? The question of expressive devices is not limited to speakers; scholars as diverse as Osgood (1960) and Besnier (1989, n.d.) have considered stylistic features of the written encoding of emotion.

Irvine (1982) provides a particularly helpful consideration of oral expressive devices, as well as a discussion of the descriptive and analytical questions they suggest. One issue raised by Irvine (1982:34) is that of what she calls "sincerity." How do we, whether as outside observers or community members, know that we are hearing a true account of a speaker's feelings? The issue becomes especially complicated in societies like the Wolof, where intermediaries such as griots are often used to express their clients' outrage while those for whom they speak sit nearby, expressionless (Irvine 1982:40).

Both the emotion vocabulary literature and that concerned with expressive devices raise questions about the representation of emotion in discourse. In the lexical approach, the focus is on discourse *about* emotion. The expressive literature focuses more on discourse *as* emotion, that is, as the enactment or representation of particular feelings. In this consideration of the multiple roles of discourse, a more general premise of the ethnography of speaking is evident: Language is about something, does something, and is something in itself; the content and conduct of emotional communication are integrally related.

Emotion discourse as relational practice

A central feature of the preceding studies is that their explicit focus is almost exclusively on questions of emotional expression, on the senders of affect-laden messages. There often seems to be an implicit assumption that the problematic issues lie in the relationship between the internal state of the original "feeler" and the form and content of his or her message. In other cases (see, e.g., Abu-Lughod 1986; Lutz 1987), speakers' intentions and the discursive strategies they employ in pursuing those ends have been highlighted; the rhetorical motivation of emotional performances is a central concern. In both kinds of study, however, the individual speaker – whether expressive or calculating – occupies center stage. Little overt or detailed attention has been paid to the questions of how those messages are received and how they might affect their auditors.

Let me take several somewhat extreme examples from the ethnomusicological literature to suggest some possible problems with a solely sender-focused model. *Qawwali* is a genre of Sufi Muslim devotional music common in Pakistan and India (Qureshi 1983). Professional *qawwali* musicians use a range of performance devices not to express their own sense of religious ecstasy but to draw it forth from members of the congregation. They themselves can succeed at this only when they remain unmoved movers, their music evoking powerful and culturally valued experiences in their listeners. Similarly, performers at the Kaluli *gisalo* are primarily concerned with their effect on their audience's emotional responses; "when textual, musical, and performative features properly coalesce, someone will be moved to tears" (Feld 1982:216).

The evocative possibilities of performance are clearly not limited to music. Shifting back to language, it is not always speakers who are moved; rather, they often attempt to engender in others particular kinds of experience. Self-expression is not at issue, but the discourse is no less "emotional." A concern with speakers, their rhetorical intentions, and the communicative devices through which they deploy emotional idioms to pursue their goals, however, must be complemented by attention to their audiences and to those local theories and understandings that inform their responses. If emotional rhetoric works, how does this happen? Audiences are not solely targets; they are, rather, active interpreters, critics, and respondents.

Such instances – in which performers are themselves dispassionate but their listeners moved – are extreme cases. I use them to suggest that, in most emotion discourse, language is expressive, affecting, and constitutive, displaying a speaker's state and influencing to some degree that of his or her audience. Just as there is often a relational dimension to local conceptions of the emotions, so also, I suggest, might emotion discourse helpfully be conceptualized as an interactional process.

Even if an audience remains silent, members construct their own experience of what occurs, attributing particular states, degrees of sincerity, and so on, to speakers or other senders. Radway's (1984) thoughtful examination of women's practices in reading, evaluating, and responding to romance novels is a particularly striking example of the constitutive work that audiences do. Similarly, several more ethnographic studies (Duranti and Brenneis 1986) demonstrate the very active roles that audiences play in events as diverse as Zinacanteco gossip sessions and California church services. A concern for audience response is implicit in many treatments of emotion discourse, as in Irvine's discussion of the "sincerity" question mentioned earlier, where the use of griots "may perhaps weaken the affective load" (1982:40). How the "load" is evaluated can only be understood by taking an audience's or receiver's perspective into account. In many cases, audiences become more active, speaking as interlocutors, expressing their own feelings, subtly transforming preceding speakers' constructions, or evincing their disbelief, sympathy, or appreciation.

In a recent article (Brenneis 1987), I have suggested the notion of "social aesthetics" as a rubric for those shared theories through which members of the village audience evaluate the style, coherence, and effectiveness of particular events. Such a social aesthetics delineates, albeit at times inchoately, the standards to which a verbal performer is held accountable (see Bauman 1977; Hymes 1975) and in terms of which a particular rhetorical strategy either succeeds or fails. Such aesthetic theories of coherence and beauty are linked to ethnopsychological notions of personhood, emotion, expression, and experience, as well as to local ways of making sense. They also, to quote Herzfeld, "correspond intelligibly with local social theory, with indigenous ideas about meaning, and with criteria of style, relevance and importance" (1985:xv).

Such a social aesthetics informs the ways in which audience members make sense of and experience others' performances. The efficacy of discourse – ritual, political, emotional – lies largely in how compelling its audience finds it to be; central to a local social aesthetic are the criteria that underlie such determinations. This focus on "experienced" dimensions of discourse further addresses a recurrent problem in anthropological considerations of emotion that Abu-Lughod points out in her chapter in this volume: an implicit cognitivist inclination that results in our "assimilating emotion to thought." "Feeling" is represented primarily as a way of interpreting and understanding the world, even if an initially surprising one. Although there is an important cognitive dimension in the notion of social aesthetics – and in the Bhatgaon villagers' model that informs it – it occupies neither a clearly demarcated nor a privileged position. Emotions are not solely "about" the world; they also help constitute it. Similarly, emotion discourse is not solely referential. It is more than a vehicle for the representation of feeling and for the comprehension of the world through emotionally framed schemata. A consideration of audience theories can help illumine the ways in which emotion discourse not only argues but also is felt and catalyzes response.

I would suggest that, just as ethnopsychological research has illumined the cultural construction of emotion and experience, a consideration of emotion discourse needs to take into account the social aesthetics of particular communities as they bear upon questions of experience and personhood, expressiveness, and evocation. In some communities, a sender-focused model may at times be appropriate; in others – or at least in some domains within those groups – evocation rather than expression may be at the core of local theory. One would expect, in fact, that in most societies a complex of notions would obtain. Rarely, I expect, would some relational dimension be absent.

One potentially valuable focus for such analysis is the communicative event, especially those events that local people consider to be salient, consequential, or beautiful. As White suggests in his chapter in this volume, we need to learn considerably more about the "articulation of ethnopsychologies of emotion with social institutions." Communicative events are indeed critical points for such articulation, as already elegantly shown by, among others, Rosaldo (1984) and Abu-Lughod (1986).

In the remainder of this chapter, I outline briefly some aspects of social aesthetics and emotion theory in Bhatgaon. I am particularly concerned, as Bhatgaon villagers themselves are, with the aesthetic, experiential, and emotional dimensions of communicative events.

A Fiji Indian aesthetics

The system of social aesthetics in Bhatgaon has a number of distinctive elements. First, the underlying system focuses primarily on the organization of performance as social practice. As such, performance almost inevitably involves more than one actor; one can rarely conduct emotional discourse by oneself. This premise underlies a common aesthetics for verbal and musical events alike. A second distinctive element of Bhatgaon social aesthetics is that it makes an explicit link between theories of performance and the language of emotion and experience. It is indeed difficult to separate ethnopsychological from aesthetic notions;

in articulating the bases of their enjoyment or appreciation of particular events, villagers also articulate their sense of self and experience.

Third, aesthetic theory in Bhatgaon is internally complex and multivalent. Although the means through which different experiences are effected are relatively invariant, the characteristics of those contrasting experiences differ in systematic ways. Rather than embodying a particular focal principle, as, for example, honor in thirteenth-century Iceland (Bauman 1986) or manhood in rural Crete (Herzfeld 1985), a Bhatgaon social aesthetics holds that different orienting values come into play in different kinds of events. The Bhatgaon situation also differs from that of Egyptian Bedouins described by Abu-Lughod (1985), where two "discrepant discourses on emotion" expressing quite different sentiments coexist. The contrasting experiences encompassed by Bhatgaon local theory, rather, are all included within the same broader discourse.

In Bhatgaon villagers' discussions of emotions, two features are salient. First, the word in local Hindi for emotion (*bhaw*) is the same as that for gesture or display. Bhatgaon social aesthetics explicitly links feeling and display. Second, none of these "feelings" seem to be individually experienced, at least as people spoke of them. *Bhaw* ('feelings') are not viewed as internal states. Rather, moods seem to be located in events themselves.

Bhaw is most frequently used in compound constructions in religious discourse, as in *prembhaw* (*prem* 'amity'), which carries the multidimensional meaning of (1) a situation of interpersonal amity, (2) the display of the mutually respectful and amiable demeanor that embodies this amity, and (3) the experience of that state. *Prembhaw* is definitively associated with the weekly meetings of religious groups and linked through those events with such performance genres as *parbacan* ('religious speeches') and *bhajan kavvali* ('*kavvali*-style hymns'). It is also said to characterize the relatively rare *pancayat*s, public occasions for the mediation of potentially consequential conflicts, organized by the religious associations. Moral didacticism – the willingness to teach and be taught – is a critical component of *prembhaw*. Clearly defined solo turns, a focus on moral and spiritual improvement – on the message – and the willingness of others to attend to what an individual is saying or singing are among the features encoding *prembhaw* and enabling its experience. It is critical to note that these are features that cannot be enacted by an individual alone; the discourse of amity is necessarily interactional.

Another frequently discussed *bhaw* is *tamashabhaw*, best translated as a situation of playfulness or fun, the associated experience, and those elements that instantiate it. An evening's session of conversation, especially when the talk turns to *talanoa* ('gossip'), is a prime occasion for such playfulness. Similarly, the raucous but ritually critical singing of *cautal* hymns during the *Holi* festival is a ritual event definitively linked with *tamashabhaw*. The conventional features of *tamashabhaw* – those that engender its experience – include a fast interactional tempo, a participatory structure in which a number of people take part, and a system of turn allocation among performers allowing for considerable overlap. When such elements are present in an event, it can be "read" as playful; the stage is set for the experience of social pleasure. That it is *social* pleasure, that is, an experience that can be had only in the company of and with the cooperation of others, is again critical.

The Bhatgaon aesthetics and the system of ethnopsychological theories intertwined with it are social theories in two senses. First, they are shared understandings, the emerging product of ongoing social learning, negotiation, and modification. Second, they include necessarily interactive behavior for their enactment and experience. Important emotional experiences in Bhatgaon are located in events themselves, especially in the constellations of persons and performance styles conventionally associated with their different varieties.

Anger: the solitary sentiment

To suggest that only shared, socially constructed emotions are given full value as *bhaw* is not to claim that Bhatgaon villagers do not recognize individual feeling. Personal emotional states – individualized, transient, situationally specific – are devalued, but they are acknowledged obliquely. Typical of such passing sentiments is anger, the Hindi word for which, *qussa*, also means 'fist'. The link between feeling and gesture is evident here in a particularly concrete iconic way.

True *bhaw* are 'built' or 'made' (*banana, karna*). In the religious talks definitively linked with *prembhaw* ('amity'), for example, speakers frequently use the phrase *prembhaw banana cahiye* ('we must build amity') in describing the goals of the worship sessions. Similarly, an oral invitation to drop by a friend's house is often defined as a chance to 'make' *tamashabhaw* ('fun'). On the other hand, *qussa* ('anger') – never recognized as *qussabhaw* – 'happens' to one (*qussa laqye*). It is an individual phenomenon, the experience of which is implicitly considered to be beyond one's own control, although its expression may be restrained. The source of *qussa* is considered to lie in specific situations. For example, the discovery of a neighbor's bullock browsing in one's rice field often leads to anger, as does a direct accusation of some wrongdoing on one's part. Some persons are considered more likely to express *qussa* than others. One who is constitutionally prone to manifest anger is considered a *kara admi* ('hard man') or *kara aurat* ('hard woman'). Such persons are also characterized as *sidha* ('straight'); they are considered to be dangerously direct. Although *qussa* may 'happen' to anyone, not all individuals will reveal it.

Levy (1984) has suggested that certain emotions may be "hypercognized" in a culture; that is, to quote Ochs, they are "the objects of considerable attention and knowledge . . . [and are] richly expressed within the culture" (1986:254). Other emotions are, in contrast, "hypocognized," receiving little attention. Although Levy's original focus was on the relative salience and degree of elaboration of emotions within particular cultures, his initial distinction has been refined in a variety of ways. Besnier (1989, n.d.), for example, has shown how an emotion that may be hypocognized in some media or performance genres may be quite marked in others; letters home in Nukulaelae encode considerable affect that is noticeably lacking in face-to-face conversation and other oral practices.

Clearly, such emotions as amity and playfulness, those recognized and constructed as *bhaw* in Bhatgaon, are hypercognized, the core of a rich complex of theories and practices. Anger, individually enacted and expressed, is asocial and in some senses accidental. It is taken as happening to people, some of whom may be constitutionally more susceptible to it than others. Anger is hypocognized, recognized only in passing comments, and not lexicalized as a salient and valued emotion, that is, not treated as a *bhaw*.

There are two levels at which this particular distribution can be interpreted. One is in terms of the kinds of emotions themselves. It is critical to note that the hypercognized emotions require joint performance and construction, whereas such trivialized sentiments as anger are defined as individual. Beyond this, however, there is no "social" and socially valued variety of anger. Anger poses real dangers for villagers. That it is hypocognized and is not a subject for shared enactment fits well in a community where a tender and easily endangered egalitarian ideology informs the daily life of adult males.

A second interpretive tack is to consider the discourse involved. *Bhaw* demand shared performance; in their formal and stylistic characteristics, they instance and index the various kinds of sociability that define them.

Such solitary sentiments as anger, however, are seen in Bhatgaon as individually enacted. Such individual enactments are also relatively un-ambiguous; a fist, whether literal or figurative, requires little interpreta-tion in Bhatgaon. Further, such interpretation is neither called for nor allowed. Responding to anger is difficult and potentially dangerous. The social–individual dimension is critical in sorting out richly elaborated and downplayed emotions in Bhatgaon. Beyond this, however, the shared or individual nature of the discourse embodying these emotions is criti-cal to their recognition and experience.

Event, emotion, and gender in Bhatgaon

Focusing on those communicative events in which *bhaw* figure critically is effective not only as a heuristic device or starting point for under-standing emotion discourse in Bhatgaon. Such events are indeed the only contexts in which these elaborated, coperformed emotions are pos-sible. Here the intimate link between local theories of emotion and the forms of discourse associated with them is central. *Prembhaw* – the shared amity that both promotes solidarity and redresses the damage caused by individual anger – can be 'built' only through joint effort and, usu-ally, only in particular kinds of events, especially those sponsored by religious associations. Although *tamashabhaw* can be enacted in a wider range of contexts, from public festivals such as *Holi* to evenings at home, it also requires coperformance.

Central to such events is their "participation structure" (Philips 1982), the range of likely or appropriate performers and the roles they are ex-pected to take; gender is a critical determinant of such structure in Bhat-gaon. Active participation and, in most instances, even audience mem-bership in the occasions with which *prembhaw* is definitively associated are, by and large, restricted to males. Only among the reform Hindu group – and then only at special meetings – are women expected to be present or encouraged to speak. Gender is the basis of exclusion (see Foucault 1972:216; Lederman 1984:103), not only from these events but from the highly valued emotions that can only occur in them as well. The participation structure of the events linked to *tamashabhaw* is some-what less restrictively ordered. During the *Holi* celebration, for example, both men and women are expected to participate, although only men perform the raucous songs central to the festivities. Even domestic en-actments of *tamashabhaw* are limited by avoidance rules precluding the participation of younger women; in those "fun" evenings in which I was involved, female participation was generally limited to women considered my elders.

Several points are critical here. First, the egalitarian ethos informing adult male relationships in Bhatgaon is rarely considered to extend to women. Some male villagers, particularly members of the reform Hindu congregation, claim that women are men's spiritual equals and should be afforded the chance to develop their capacities through joining in worship. In practice, however, a concern for sustaining equality is – from the male villagers' point of view, at least – solely a male matter. In the management of disputes, for example, insults against women are redefined as attacks on their male kin; it is male standing that is endangered (Brenneis 1980).

As in those North Indian communities from which their forebears emigrated, Bhatgaon villagers reckon kinship patrilineally. There is little genealogical depth, however, and the large corporate kin groups common in North India do not exist. Marriage is village exogamous and residence virilocal. Young women marry into Bhatgaon and find themselves, initially at least, strangers in their husband's households and in the social world of village women. The first few years of marriage are generally spent in a joint household in which the new wife is subject to her mother-in-law and her older sisters-in-law. However, although initially isolated, young wives get to know women beyond the household fairly rapidly. They may, for example, accompany their husbands or female affines on visits to other households or take part with other women in preparing special feasts or attending weddings.

Oldest sons and their wives and children are most likely to remain permanently with the son's parents; most younger brothers establish new households within three or four years. Men generally attribute such household division to enmity between the coresident sisters-in-law. A frequent comment is *bese qussa, bese jagara* ('too much anger, too many fights'). Even if two coresident brothers are known to have been disagreeing about a shared household budget, for example, their wives' apparent antipathy is publicly defined as the real cause of the split. Women's anger – not men's arguments – leads to disruption in such situations.

It is not that women are thought to have a monopoly on anger; it is, rather, that they are considered to have fewer emotional or practical alternatives to its expression than do men. Although social disruption within the family is often attributed to women's anger, another common source of trouble – particularly between unrelated individuals – is the socially pleasurable but injudicious gossip of men (Brenneis 1984). Women are not considered prime offenders here, perhaps because men are more likely to disregard what women have to say than the commentary of other males.

Finally, the social lives of women in Bhatgaon are in many ways opaque to males, whether villagers or ethnographers. It was inherently impossible for me to participate in all-female events or to interview a wide range of women in any depth. Such extended discussions as I was able to have with appropriate female friends – as defined through fictive kinship – suggest several tentative conclusions. First, the women with whom I spoke appeared to share without evident irony in the discourse concerning *bhaw*. They saw those hypercognized emotions as indeed valuable. Second, I received no inkling of a complementary set of emotion theories held by and concerning women. This could reflect my inability to work extensively with women. Emotional notions linked to such themes as nurturance and compassion might well figure strongly in female theory and practice, but I have no evidence.

In sum, then, women are, by and large, excluded from the particular events linked with the highly valued and inherently social *bhaw*. In addition, the discourse of these elaborated emotions in Bhatgaon can be jointly created only in such contexts. The *bhaw* depend on shared discourse for their expression and experience; women are much less likely to take part in such discourse and, consequently, in those emotions culturally defined as worthy and beneficial. From the standpoint of local theory, women rarely have the opportunity to build or create such experiences. This suggests two major implications. First, if one is concerned with emotion discourse as constituting commentary on social relationships, women's exclusion from 'amity', for example, serves as an idiom for their exclusion from the socially valued world of religious community. In an odd way, that this religious community is primarily male is almost incidental. The gender-based distinction is hidden in a putatively gender-indifferent view of the emotions, a practice that leads to this distinction's being taken for granted rather than overtly articulated. Second, if one takes emotion discourse *as* emotion, as helping to shape and constitute individuals' lives, women may well be excluded from these socially valued experiences.

Although both men and women have such hypocognized feelings as anger 'happen' to them in situations where they are not emotional actors but passive recipients, it is primarily men who can jointly engender friendship and play. In contrast to the striking split in Western ideology between reason and emotion and the corresponding association of emotion with the female (Lutz, this volume), in Bhatgaon neither the distinction nor the distribution occurs. Instead, men generally control the discourses through which socially significant emotion is realized.

Note

I would like to thank Geoffrey White and Catherine Lutz for including me in the original symposium, and Catherine Lutz and Lila Abu-Lughod for their perceptive and very helpful comments on earlier drafts. Susan Seymour and Sheryl Miller provided the forum in which my initial understandings of the gender dimension first emerged, and various other Pitzer colleagues, especially Ronald Macaulay and Dan Segal, provided useful criticism.

References

Abu-Lughod, Lila. 1985. Honor and the Sentiments of Loss in a Bedouin Society. *American Ethnologist* 12:245–61.
  1986. *Veiled Sentiments: Honor and Poetry in a Bedouin Society.* Berkeley: University of California Press.
Bauman, Richard. 1977. Verbal Art as Performance. In R. Bauman, ed., *Verbal Art as Performance.* Prospect Heights, IL: Waveland Press, pp. 3–58.
  1986. Performance and Honor in 13th-Century Iceland. *Journal of American Folklore* 99:131–50.
Besnier, Niko. 1989. Literacy and Feelings: The Encoding of Affect in Nukulaelae Letters. *Text* 9:69–91.
  n.d. Reported Speech and Affect on Nukulaelae. Ms, Department of Anthropology, Yale University.
Brenneis, Donald. 1980. Strategies of Offense Choice: Malice and Mischief in Bhatgaon. *Canberra Anthropology* 3:28–42.
  1984. Grog and Gossip in Bhatgaon: Style and Substance in Fiji Indian Conversation. *American Ethnologist* 11:487–506.
  1987. Performing Passions: Aesthetics and Politics in an Occasionally Egalitarian Community. *American Ethnologist* 14:236–50.
Duranti, Allessandro, and Donald Brenneis, eds. 1986. *The Audience as Co-Author. Text* (Special Issue) 6:239–347.
Feld, Steven. 1982. *Sound and Sentiment: Birds, Weeping, Poetics and Song in Kaluli Expression.* Philadelphia: University of Pennsylvania Press.
Foucault, Michel. 1972. *The Archaeology of Knowledge and the Discourse on Language.* New York: Pantheon.
Herzfeld, Michael. 1985. *The Poetics of Manhood: Contest and Identity in a Cretan Village.* Princeton: Princeton University Press.
Hymes, Dell. 1975. Breakthrough into Performance. In D. Ben-Amos and K. Goldstein, eds., *Folklore: Performance and Communication.* The Hague: Mouton, pp. 11–74.
Irvine, Judith. 1982. Language and Affect: Some Cross-Cultural Issues. In H. Byrnes, ed., *Contemporary Perceptions of Language: Interdisciplinary Dimensions.* Washington, DC: Georgetown University Press, pp. 31–47.

Lederman, Rena. 1984. Who Speaks Here? Formality and the Politics of Gender in Mendi, Highland Papua New Guinea. In D. Brenneis and F. Myers, eds., *Dangerous Words: Language and Politics in the Pacific.* New York: New York University Press, pp. 85–107.

Levy, Robert. 1984. Emotion, Knowing and Culture. In R. Shweder and R. LeVine, eds., *Culture Theory: Essays on Mind, Self and Emotion.* New York: Cambridge University Press, pp. 214–37.

Lutz, Catherine. 1982. The Domain of Emotion Words on Ifaluk. *American Ethnologist* 9:113–28.

  1987. Goals, Events and Understanding in Ifaluk Emotion Theory. In D. Holland and N. Quinn, eds., *Cultural Models in Language and Thought.* Cambridge: Cambridge University Press, pp. 290–312.

Mithun, M. 1982. The Synchronic and Diachronic Behavior of Plops, Squeaks, Croaks, Sighs and Moans. *International Journal of American Linguistics* 48:49–58.

Myers, Fred R. 1979. Emotions and the Self: A Theory of Personhood and Political Order Among Pintupi Aborigines. *Ethos* 7:343–70.

Ochs, Elinor. 1986. From Feeling to Grammar: A Samoan Case Study. In B. Schieffelin and E. Ochs, eds., *Language Socialization Across Cultures.* Cambridge: Cambridge University Press, pp. 251–72.

Osgood, Charles. 1960. Some Effects of Motivation on Style of Encoding. In T. A. Sebeok, ed., *Style in Language.* Cambridge, MA: MIT Press, pp. 293–306.

Philips, Susan U. 1982. *The Invisible Culture: Communication in Classroom and Community on the Warm Springs Indian Reservation.* Chicago: Longmans.

Qureshi, Regula. 1983. *Qawwali:* Making the Music Happen in the Sufi Assembly. In B. Wade, ed., *Performing Arts in India.* Lanham, MD: University Press of America, pp. 118–57.

Radway, Jane A. 1984. *Reading the Romance: Women, Patriarchy and Popular Literature.* Chapel Hill: University of North Carolina Press.

Rosaldo, Michelle Z. 1984. Toward an Anthropology of Self and Feeling. In R. Shweder and R. LeVine, eds., *Culture Theory: Essays on Mind, Self, and Emotion.* Cambridge: Cambridge University Press, pp. 137–57.

7. Registering affect: heteroglossia in the linguistic expression of emotion

JUDITH T. IRVINE

Introduction

"Linguists of all breeds seem to develop cold feet when it comes to discussion of the expression of emotion in language," remarks W. O. Beeman in a recent paper (Beeman 1988:9). The problem, he suggests, is that affectivity is seen as "soft" and "idiosyncratic," contrasting with reference and cognition, and therefore with the rule-governed structures on which linguistics as a discipline has principally focused. Beeman attributes these assumptions to the emergence of transformational-generative theory in 1957, with its explicit definition of linguistics as a cognitive discipline; but similar ideas can be found in the traditions of Saussure and Bloomfield, and in many other disciplines as well. It is not only Chomskyan linguists who have supposed that affectivity belongs to an "expressive" (nonreferential) dimension of language, that it pertains to individuals rather than speech communities, and that it is largely a property of *parole* rather than of *langue*. Shweder (1984) and others have argued that an emphasis on cognition and rationality – and a marginalization of affectivity – have increased in the social sciences generally since World War II.[1]

Although acknowledging that some languages do provide phonological and morphological devices marking emotional states in speaking (Henry 1936; Stankiewicz 1964), for the most part linguists have seen "expressive phenomena" as marginal to the main body of the grammar. Yet, two of linguistics' most stellar figures, Jakobson (1960) and Sapir (1921, 1927), thought otherwise: Affect, or emotion, according to them, was a fundamental dimension of human life and a factor cross-cutting all levels of linguistic organization. More recently, a growing literature on such diverse aspects of linguistic structure as word order, verb voice, quantifiers and deictics, right and left dislocation, and so on indicates a

126

connection with affect, even though the authors of that literature have not always foregrounded this point. Whether recognized as such or not, the evidence has begun to accumulate that would support the incorporation of affect more centrally in models of communication (see Ochs 1988 for a review and discussion of this literature).

Equally important to Sapir was the question of how much the communication of emotion is culturally constructed and culturally variable. Although lively debates on this subject have existed for decades, for much of that time empirical studies tended to focus on nonverbal, expressive gestures and "paralanguage" (voice quality and dynamics). Anthropological studies arguing for cultural variability in the construction of emotion turned, instead, to the emotion lexicon (see Rosenberg, this volume); but these labels for describing and reporting feelings have usually been studied at some remove from the emotional performance itself. Studies on the use of a wider set of linguistic resources, during affective performance and in connection with cultural differences, are only now beginning to appear (see e.g., Abu-Lughod 1986; Beeman 1988; Brenneis 1988; Irvine 1982; Ochs 1988).

It is only recently, then, that scholars have begun to take an interest in extensively pursuing and substantiating a view once articulated by Sapir (1927, 1930): that emotional expression is pervasive in linguistic structure, and that the communication of personality and emotional states is culturally organized in a speech community.[2] In this chapter, I take up Sapir's theme of the conventionality of affective performance and follow it in relation to the linguistic concept of "register" – a coherent complex of linguistic features linked to a situation of use. What I suggest is that many of these "varieties according to use" (Halliday 1964) have an affective dimension that organizes some of their linguistic characteristics. The study of registers is a convenient way to look at the verbal aspects of affective display, because it suggests a set of complementary representations of feelings that are conventionalized among a community of speakers. Where my discussion differs from Sapir's is in its greater emphasis on an interactional approach and, more importantly, in foregrounding the organization of diversity in a community's conventions of affective performance.

The ethnographic case to be drawn on for this discussion concerns styles of speaking in a rural Wolof community in Senegal – styles that relate to the representation of affectivity, on the one hand, and of social rank, on the other. To emphasize the role of affect and personality in these linguistic registers is not only consonant with a Wolof cultural scheme, but is also useful as a way to understand the registers' system-aticity and their relation to cultural images of persons. Those images, as we shall see, form an organized set, as do the linguistic forms that display them.

Indeed, the importance of complementarities – in affectivity, in social differentiation, and in linguistic form – in this case is one of the reasons for focusing on registers. The concept of register is inherently hetero-glossic (i.e., suggesting a plurality of "voices" in the Bakhtinian sense): By definition, there is always a *set* of registers, not just one. As opposed to the notion of a "language" with an assemblage of expressive devices all equally available to each speaker as he or she goes through the full gamut of feelings, "affective registers" suggest a set of different repre-sentations of emotion – a set that may be culturally defined and linked to cultural conceptions of the diversity of persons, personalities, and situations.

In short, the communication of feeling is not merely a property of the individual, or a function of transient irrational impulses, or an unruly force operating outside the realm of linguistic form.[3] Instead, it is so-cially, culturally, and linguistically structured, and we cannot ade-quately interpret individuals' behavior as emotional expression until we understand some of that framework.

Register, dialect, and the contextualization of emotion

Entering the vocabulary of American linguists only relatively recently, the term "register" is most closely associated with a British school of linguistics, particularly the work of M. A. K. Halliday and his followers. It derives (Halliday 1978) from that school's interest in the ways speech is affected by the "context of situation," a notion prominent in the writ-ings of J. R. Firth and, earlier, in Malinowski's writings on language. As defined by Halliday (1964), a register is a linguistic "variety according to use," in contrast to a "dialect," which is a "variety according to users." Although American linguists (and sociolinguists) for a long time tended to prefer the more general terms "linguistic variety" and "code," "reg-ister" is now becoming widespread.[4]

In the usage of most linguists, registers are styles of speaking whose grammatical configurations overlap; that is, they are styles that are lin-guistically distinguishable, but only as varieties of one encompassing "language." Of course, the same could be said for dialects. The defini-tional difference between dialect and register is functional, rather than formal: Which dialect you use is determined by your geographical and social affiliation (especially your locus of origin); which register you use is determined by the social activity you are engaged in (i.e., the properties of your situation, whether it is something already given or something you are trying to create).

In Halliday's view, this functional distinction has consequences for registers' (and dialects') formal properties: According to him, the registers of a language tend to differ from one another primarily in semantics, whereas the dialects tend to differ from one another in phonetics, phonology, and "lexicogrammar" (Halliday 1978:35). Yet, even if such tendencies can be identified in some cases – and they do not apply conveniently to the Wolof registers to be described – the fact remains that the differences among registers are not actually limited to semantics, however broadly semantics is defined.[5] There are also grammatical, phonological, and phonetic differences.[6]

The questions, then, are what all the various linguistic devices making up a register have to do with one another; what governs their distribution; and how tightly they cohere. Some sociolinguists have described the linkage of devices in a register in terms of "co-occurrence rules" (Ervin-Tripp 1972). But however useful such rules might be for descriptive purposes, what is still needed is some sense of what motivates them – in what sense a register may be systematic, its devices having some coherence, and how much coherence they must have.

My suggestion here is that one of the principles underlying a register's co-occurrence rules can be coherence of affective performance – a principle governing prosody as well as vocabulary choice and sentence composition. The connection with affect is often explicit. In Javanese, for example, speakers apparently conceive of the available language levels as registers whose use depends on one's assessment of a situation, particularly the relationships among its personnel and the appropriateness of displaying affect. The higher, more "polite" levels are considered depersonalized, regulated by an ethic of proper order, peace, and calm; in them one "does not express one's own feelings" (Wolff and Poedjosoedarmo 1982:41). The lower, "coarser" levels, on the other hand, are the "language . . . one loses one's temper in" (Errington 1984:9).

There is also a sense in which the Javanese language levels distinguish categories of speakers. People do not control all levels equally well. Geertz (1960) describes Javanese social ranks as differing significantly in the range they control within the total repertoire, the more "polite" levels being more associated with persons of traditional high rank. As images of "refinement" and affective display, then, the language levels evoke both the situations characteristically evoking such responses and the persons characteristically manifesting them.

As the Javanese example illustrates, the distinction between dialect and register, although a useful analytical starting point, becomes more complicated as soon as one looks more closely at a particular speech community. Although there are several reasons for this, some of the most important ones have to do with the cultural structuring of "voices" associated with social groups. Images of persons considered typical of those groups – and the personalities, moods, behavior, and settings characteristically associated with them – are rationalized and organized in a cultural system, and become available as a frame of reference for one's own performance and for interpreting the performances of others. This system informs the style switching that all speakers engage in.

Thus our verbal performances do not simply represent our own social identity, our own feelings, and the social occasion here and now. They are full of allusions to the behavior of others and to other times and places. To put this another way: One of the many methods people have for differentiating situations and marking their moods is to draw on (or carefully avoid) the "voices" of others, or what they assume those "voices" to be. The concept of register, then, although initially defined in terms of situation rather than person or group, in fact draws on cultural images of persons as well as situations and activities.[7] There is no contradiction between the situational, or contextual, focus and a connection with the cultural construction of emotion and personality.

Actually, the situational focus in the concept of register is part of what makes it compatible with recent anthropological approaches to the study of emotion, which have often emphasized a contextual approach. Although our own society tends to locate emotion firmly within the individual (as a matter of internal psychobiology and biography), other cultural systems may locate it in social relations or in the relationship between a person and an event (Brenneis, this volume; Lutz 1982; Myers 1979). In such cases – or for the scholars similarly disposed to construe emotion as socially shaped – the social situations in which emotions variously arise or are displayed, and the social relations experienced by and partly defining the self, become critical for emotional understanding. As Lutz and White (1986:419) note, in such views "actors understand emotions as mediating social action: they arise in social situations and carry implications for future thought and action. Emotional understandings, then, are not seen as abstract, symbolic formulations – not 'thinking about feeling' so much as thoughts which are necessarily linked with social situations and valued goals that give them moral force and direction."

But perhaps the most important reason the concept of register may be useful in the ethnographic study of the cultural construction of emotion is the emphasis on the role of conventionality, linguistic and otherwise, in affective display. Such conventions, linguistically expressed, represent a cultural construction of available emotions, personalities, and so on that are linked to other dimensions of culture and society. Independent, in a way, of what a person may "actually" feel at a particular moment, they nevertheless represent the resources the person has to draw on for affective display, the terms in which his or her behavior will be interpreted by others, and the framework of interpretation for the experiencer as well. Moreover, as Abu-Lughod (1986:241) has noted, the expression of feelings has relevance not only for the person expressing them but also for the audience and the furtherance of social relationships: "sentiments can be used to symbolize something about the person expressing them." Communicative forms are not merely the "expressive" result of psychological processes internal to the communicator; they are also forms of social action.[8]

Wolof registers and affectivity

Let us turn now to a consideration of styles of speaking in a rural Wolof community.[9] The Wolof language has relatively little geographical dialect differentiation, although urban usage has come to differ somewhat from rural 'true Wolof' (*wolof piir*). Differing forms of talk do exist on the rural scene, however. Informants in a Wolof village identified two styles of speaking, *waxu gewel* and *waxu géér*, which they linked with differences in affectivity and in social rank. One of these (*waxu géér*), a laconic way of speaking, is conventionally associated with high-ranking nobles, because these persons are assumed to be its typical users; the other style (*waxu gewel*), hyperbolic and high in affectivity, is conventionally associated with the lower ranks, particularly the "griots" (praise singers, speech makers, and bards).

Why call these forms of speaking "registers"? Although *waxu gewel* and *waxu géér* may look at first like social dialects – distinct linguistic varieties associated with distinct social groups, the nobles and griots[10] – it turns out that speakers from all social categories use both ways of speaking, depending on the situation. In practice, therefore, these ways of speaking operate as registers, resources on which any speaker may draw to define the situation and the relationships at hand. Moreover, the Wolof labels do not mark two absolutely distinct varieties so much as they point to the poles of a behavioral continuum or range of possibilities.

In what follows, I shall describe the linguistic phenomena involved, their relation to affectivity, and their role in social interaction. Before doing so, however, it is useful to set the cultural scene. A Wolof ideology of language and social rank rationalizes the differentiation of ways of speaking and their connection with rank and situation. Images of affectivity and impulsivity, manifested in verbal behavior as well as in other forms of activity, are central to this cultural scheme.

Ethnographic background: a Wolof ideology of rank

Like many other peoples in the western sahel and savanna region of Africa, the Wolof traditionally were organized in a complex system of social stratification, usually termed a "caste" system in the African ethnographic literature. It is a system of ranked groups and subgroups, occupationally specialized and strictly endogamous. Although undermined by government policies and other factors, the caste system retains considerable importance in rural communities, and even on the urban scene, according to some observers.[11] The material presented here is drawn mainly from fieldwork in a Senegalese village of some 1,200 people (in the 1970s, when most of the relevant fieldwork was done).

In Wolof village society, differences in rank are an acknowledged value that organizes all sorts of social activities and interactions, ranging from economic specializations and exchange to the regulation of marriage, and including social contact and conversation. Of the low-ranking castes, the most numerous and conspicuous is the bardic caste, or griots, whose specializations are public speech making, praise singing, music, and the rhetorical and communicative arts in general. To some extent, however, the rhetorical specialty is a prerogative of all nonnoble castes, because all of them can substitute for griots or participate along with griots on occasion. Moreover, in a way, the image of the griot publicly eulogizing, persuading, and entertaining the noble is only the crystallization, on the level of caste differences, of a cultural convention associating certain kinds of verbal performances and conspicuous verbal activity with rank differences small or great.[12] The difference in verbal behavior associated with griots and nobles serves as a cultural prototype, I believe, for the organization of talk among any interactants should their differences in rank become relevant.

A connection between differences in rank, behavior, and affectivity is fundamental in this ideological formation. Central to it is the idea that people are inherently unequal, having different constitutions that govern their feelings and motivations and make them behave in different ways. These different behavioral dispositions incline their bearers to differing but complementary forms of action, whence arise the occupational specializations of the caste system. Since disposition and personality are thought to be inheritable, personality of differences follow genealogical lines, especially the lines of caste endogamy. One's constitution – the biological, emotional, and moral qualities one derives from ancestral inheritance and from childhood experience – is the source of one's *naw* 'temperament' or 'capacity for emotionality'. Persons of the same rank are *nawlé* 'castemates', who resemble one another in temperament and moral status.[13]

These temperaments contrast, according to informants, between degrees of affectivity and impulsivity, on the one hand, and restraint and torpidity, on the other. Restraint, self-control, and *sangfroid* are normative characteristics of the nobility, who are supposed to be more solid, stable, and "heavy" than the typical lower-caste person, who is "lightweight," volatile, even frenetic. On a symbolic level, the contrast is sometimes described in terms of weight, sometimes in terms of differences in the viscosity of body fluids, and sometimes in terms of the elements – earth, air, fire, and water – as if the various castes consisted of these, or resembled these, in different degrees, balances, or emphases. Thus the nobles' self-control is like the stability of earth, as compared with the other elements, supposedly more prominent in lower castes: air, which (in this cosmological scheme) suggests a capacity for frenetic movement; fire, which symbolizes anger, the warmth of passion, and a consuming greed; and water, which symbolizes fear (but also, in a more positive sense, the cooling of anger).[14]

Of the lower castes, the griots, in particular, have the image of high affectivity and excitability; as volatile and theatrical personalities; and especially as people who excite others. High-ranking nobles are conventionally associated with self-control, but also with lethargy and blandness. Their restraint (*kersa*) may "make them reluctant to say bad things," as some villagers said, but (they continued) it also makes them reluctant to say or do much of anything. It takes a griot to make life interesting and attractive and to keep the high nobles awake. Just as a rush of air stirs a fire, so the breath of the griots' utterance rouses passion and energy in the noble, to the point where creative action becomes possible. The "hot" elements in the noble's temperament, ordinarily dormant, are thus activated.

This complementarity is illustrated in a frequent image in Wolof oral poetry and epic narrative, where a slumbering king must be wakened by an orchestra of griots playing drums and iron clappers lest his royal duties go unfulfilled. (The same image is cited for village-level political assemblies today, where a group of griots punctuate the political speeches with drum rolls and cheers "because otherwise the chiefs would fall asleep.") Once roused, the king may be moved to great deeds – the greater because of the seriousness and weightiness of his personality – but griots are needed to stir him to that point.

If griots are thought of as people who easily express their own feelings and who stir the feelings of others, the affectivity of their behavior is shaped by their rhetorical and aesthetic skills. Related, on the conceptual level, to the "lighter" elements' capacity for motion, fluency of expression is at least as important in the image of the griot as is lack of inhibition, from which it is in fact inseparable. Not only verbal expression is involved: Griot women are supposed, for example, to be the best dancers, since high-caste women are "too stiff" and "too ashamed" to perform in the sexually suggestive manner deemed the most skillful.

As for that 'shame' (jom) and its experiential concomitant ruus ('to feel ashamed') – these can perhaps best be understood as deriving from the interactional model of emotional experience that seems to be important in the Wolof cultural scheme. As informants explain them, the actions that give rise to a feeling of shame are not necessarily inherently bad (although they may be); rather, they are witnessed actions inappropriate to one's rank. Thus the acts one would be ashamed to do include behavior that might be quite proper in private or if directed toward superiors, but shameful if witnessed by a public that includes lower-ranking persons.[15] Fluent, voluble public speaking is an example: When addressed by griot to noble, the interaction of their naw operates to constructive effect, overcoming the noble's torpor; if addressed in the other direction, the interactive effect would be destructive to both. The noble would fail to maintain restraint, and the griot's own self-control supposedly would be too fragile to withstand the force of the noble's breath. As a result, the griot would be imperiled – made vulnerable to self-destructive impulses and to attack by witches and nefarious spirits – whereas the noble would be ashamed and might even suffer some loss of rank.[16]

The difference in "weight" between high and low ranks thus affects the consequences of emotionally expressive behavior, as well as its likelihood of occurrence. Although griots may easily express emotionality, their feelings do not bear the heavy social import that high nobles' feelings do. The high nobility are administratively and economically responsible for large numbers of dependents; their actions, and the sentiments leading to their actions, are seen culturally as more consequential. One of the griot's main roles, therefore, is to express the ideas and feelings of nobles – to communicate for them energetically and persuasively, especially in the public arena. Griots are expressive vehicles, and much of what they express is not ultimately their own. It is, instead, supportive repetition, persuasively elaborated and charged with excitement. As a historian and repository of folklore, the griot is the repeater of the voices of tradition and the ancestors; as a public spokesperson for a noble, he or she repeats and elaborates an idea the noble may have whispered in the griot's ear only a moment ago.

Wolof villagers summarize these aspects of the griot's role with the term *jottali* 'transmission', which must be understood as supportive, charged, and elaborated repetition. It is essential to what the griot does, and therefore to the nature of the "griotlike" style of speaking. The cultural framework suggests that sentiments are most constructively, persuasively, and even effectively expressed when routed through a speaker of lower rank than their originator. The forms of talk considered to have the greatest emotional charge thus include those performance genres in which griots specialize and that exemplify "griot talk." Moreover, the process of repetition, whether it concerns repetitive constructions within an individual speaker's turn at talk or repetition by other speakers, is considered to heighten the emotional effect.

Linguistic varieties

The two labeled styles of speaking mentioned earlier, *waxu gewel* and *waxu géér* – 'griot talk' and 'noble talk,' respectively – can now be considered against this cultural background. The linguistic phenomena that constitute these registers are found in all aspects of verbal performance, from prosody, phonetics, morphology, and sentence structure to turn taking and the management of conversational discourse. We shall see that the contrasting images of nobles and griots – in terms of affectivity, rhetorical fluency and aesthetics, and elaborated repetition – shape many characteristics of the registers.[17]

Table 7.1. *Prosodic contrasts*

	"Noblelike" speech	"Griotlike" speech
Pitch	Low	High
Voice	Breathy	Clear
Volume	Soft	Loud
Contour	Pitch nucleus last; little dynamic range	Dynamic and pitch nucleus first; wide dynamic and pitch range
Speed	Slow	Fast

Despite their connection with caste images, in practice these varieties are not associated exclusively with a speaker's absolute rank (griot or noble). Instead, they are used as a range of registers signaling *relative* rank (of the speaker as compared to the addressee or relevant other) and signaling types of situations – those in which differences of rank are to be attended to. Except for the extreme ends of the register continuum, all speakers use all the rest of the range, depending on their relation to a particular addressee and situation. A person of noble rank uses a "griotlike" style of speaking when addressing a noble kinsman from whom he or she wants to ask a favor, for example. Thus the registers invoke a kind of metaphor of high and low ranks – and a model of affective relations – in order to define (in this case) an act of petitioning and to make the petition persuasive.

Let us now examine the linguistic characteristics of these registers in more detail. Following this description of the registers, some text and transcript examples will show them in actual use.

Prosody. In some respects, prosodic features provide the most striking differences between "griotlike" and "noblelike" registers. The differences are not only obvious to an observer but salient to Wolof villagers themselves, who explicitly call attention to the pitch, speed, volume, and quantity of talk as defining characteristics of the registers. Voice quality (breathiness) and intonational contour observably differ, along with the other characteristics just cited. Table 7.1 summarizes these features.

As Table 7.1 shows, what informants are identifying as two forms of talk are actually two poles of a continuum; no specific demarcation point distinguishes one form from the other.[18] For example, there is no absolute decibel level above which all utterances are "griot talk" and below which they are all "noble talk"; there are only differences relative to one another and established locally, in a particular situation. In all these prosodic phenomena, the registers are mirror images of one another, emerging (and diverging) when, and to the extent that, differences in rank emerge as important.

The most extreme versions of the "griotlike" prosody are found in those public situations where the greatest differences in social rank are most pertinent. Political meetings, villagewide celebrations, and the feasts given by prominent families to mark major life events are good examples. The griot stands and shots as loudly as possible to the assembled crowd; he sways and jabs at the air with dramatic and forceful gestures, pointing at his addressees and holding up the money he has received in largesse. The veins in his forehead and neck stand out from the effort of the performance. His voice rises into falsetto pitch, and the rate of his utterance increases to more than 300 syllables a minute.[19] Meanwhile, the higher-rank persons present, especially the highest nobles, remain seated, silent, and motionless, until moved to some action such as handing the griot a gift or (at a political meeting) making a terse comment.

Even in conversation, prosody observably shifts along with changes in topic, affective tone, and attention to rank. For instance, one evening a certain noble was sitting in my house, along with a few other nobles, chatting about politics. It was early in my fieldwork, and I was trying to elicit talk for the tape recorder, without yet having developed much sense of the appropriateness of different kinds of talk for different speakers. Unaware that village nobles do not normally engage in public oratory of any sort, especially on their own account, I asked him to give me an example of a political speech. After some mild teasing by the others and general amusement at the idea that he might do such a thing, he identified one of the few appropriate contexts for such talk, offering comments about what he would do if he were made an official representative of his village charged with welcoming important visitors at the next political assembly. His voice dropped to a basso profundo, and the rate of his utterance slowed to fewer than 60 syllables a minute. Attention having been called to his rank, he spoke in the most "noblelike" prosody possible, short of refusing to speak at all.

Phonology. Informants do not seem to be as explicitly aware of phonological contrasts in registers as they are of the prosodic ones; at least, they are not as likely to describe them. Still, some phonological differences are observable, and I have heard them parodied by teenagers imitating the voices of older people or taking parts in dramatic skits. Moreover, villagers suggested that a certain type of stammer (dër), in which "the tongue sticks in the mouth," often afflicts persons of extremely high rank, whose tongues are not agile and whose utterance is not rhetorically fluent.[20]

Many of the phonological differences between the two registers seem to be related to differences in the tempo of speaking. The articulation of sound may be affected either by the haste of extremely rapid speech or by the drawl of very slow speech. Compared with the less extreme portions of the register continuum, the most rapid "griot speech" performances tend to elide segments in unstressed syllables. In a few words, an unstressed syllable may be elided or omitted altogether. "Noble speech," in contrast, drags out its vowels and tends to affricate its consonants, even though the overall number of words is far fewer. When the highest-ranking nobles in town speak in this style, the general effect is of drawling and low-pitched mumbling, an effect further exaggerated by practices such as holding the hand over the mouth while talking or turning and lowering the head so that the voice will be muffled by a bulky neck scarf.

To the Western observer accustomed to the notion that voice belongs to the powerful, there is something surprising about the Wolof high noble's mumbled, muffled speech and, as one might call it, "conspicuous disfluency." Yet, there is a sense in which power is indeed displayed in this form of talk – the power to command the audience's attention. The people who speak in the most extreme versions of this style are those whose high status and authority are unambiguous. Although they speak little, their right to the floor is unquestionable; other people seem always to reserve part of their attention for watching whether the highest-ranking one present is about to speak. When the high noble does begin to say something, an immediate hush falls, no matter what the level of chatter was before. Everyone leans forward, straining to make out what is being said. This is quite different from audience behavior at griot performances, where people of medium and low rank often continue to converse among themselves, and the griot's shouting is in some respects an effort to gain attention.

The disfluency of high nobles, and the effort necessary to understand it, derives not only from slow speed or physical barriers like hands or scarves, but also from the phonological rules this register involves. Although both "noble speech" and "griot speech" could be said to make

Table 7.2. *Phonological contrasts*

"Noblelike" speech	"Griotlike" speech
Feature contrasts	
Contrasts in vowel length and consonant length not clearly maintained	Contrasts in vowel length and consonant length clearly maintained
Nonnasal stops affricated and/or prenasalized, e.g.: [p] → [φ] [b] → [β], [mb], [mβ]	Stops in stressed syllables, and all "fortis" stops, energetically articulated
"Breathy" or "creaky" (laryngealized) articulation of voiced stops	Voicing contrasts in syllable-initial consonants, and all "fortis" stops, clearly maintained
Elisions in unstressed syllables	
Stresses not clearly marked (little difference between stressed and unstressed syllables)	Stressed syllables clearly articulated; elisions in unstressed syllables: "Lenis" final stop (in unstressed syllable) → Ø (especially if voiceless)
	Unstressed CV# → C#
	Initial [k] in unstressed syllable → [ʔ]
Vowel height	
Some lowering of vowels?	Some fronting and raising of vowels, especially before palatal glides

phonetic alterations, if the speech of citation forms or even of calm conversation among castemates were taken as a standard, "griot speech" apparently remains more faithful to the underlying system of significant contrasts. For example, griots uttering the extreme forms of "griot speech" always maintained contrasts in vowel length (which are very important in Wolof), even if some of the short vowels had to disappear altogether. In the most extreme "noble speech," however, distinctions of vowel length tended to disappear in the mumbling drawl.

A summary of the phonological differences I have observed in these registers is outlined in Table 7.2.

The variations described in Table 7.2 seem to apply only to the most extreme ends of the register continuum, although there are some other forms of phonological variation (e.g., further differences involving vowel height) that seem to be connected with age and gender more directly than with rank or with these registers, and thus apply throughout the

continuum. Clearly, therefore, much more detailed examination of phonological variation in Wolof in general, as well as in these registers, could
and should be done.

Morphology and syntax. The differences in fluency and level of excitation
that we have noted so far in prosody and phonology also show up in
the registers' morphology and syntax. "Griot speech," the hyperbolic,
elaborated, verbose variety, is replete with emphatic devices, parallelisms, and ideophones. Its grammatical constructions are thus consistent
with the emphatic intonational pattern and dramatic gestures, and with
the image of the griot as poetically skillful, affectively charged, and conspicuously talkative. "Noble speech," on the other hand, is terse and
bland. It is also less fluent in that sentences may be left incomplete and
agreement rules are not consistently followed.

Differences in fluency and grammatical "correctness" – as well as in
aesthetics and vividness of speech – are manifested in several ways. For
example, these differences are relevant to a morphological variation that
seems to differentiate the two registers.[21] The forms concerned are variations in noun class assignment – where one tends to assign a noun,
among the classes *bi, gi, si, ji, wi, mi, li,* or *ki,* so labeled according to the
form of the proximal determinant used with them. In principle, classes
are assigned on the basis sometimes of semantic subtleties such as connotations of an object's size, sometimes of consonant harmony (thus
soràngs si 'the orange [near me]'), and sometimes simply of historical
convention. "Noble speech" and "griot speech" differ not only in which
class markers tend to be assigned, but also in the consistency of class-
marking agreement rules, and in whether the determinants and relativizing constructions that would require overt class marking are present
at all.

My attention was first called to this matter by informants' reports that
the Wolof kings and high nobility of former times used to use the "wrong"
class markers. They had to make mistakes in minor points of grammar,
because correctness would be an unnecessary frill, an emphasis on fluency
of performance or performance for its own sake, which would not be
appropriate – or perhaps even possible – for these highest of nobles.
(The same was true for religious ascetics, who were too concerned with
otherworldly matters, and communion with God and the prophets, to
have room in their minds for forms of talk associated with the rhetoric
of this world.) In practice, "noble speech" uses few class markers. When
markers do appear, they are quite often those that informants of all so-

cial categories label "wrong" in elicitation sessions; there is a relatively heavy use of the *bi* class, which is semantically more neutral than others; and agreement rules are not consistently followed.

In contrast, griots' class markers, especially as used in public performance, are generally assumed by others to be grammatically "correct" even when they actually deviate from historically attested forms (Irvine 1978). It is also assumed that they involve some aesthetic principle or semantic subtlety, even when the audience cannot identify what that semantic effect is.

Another aspect of rhetorical fluency concerns the completeness of sentence structures. Whereas the sentences of "griot speech" are well formed, complete, and often elaborate, with relative and conjoined clauses, "noble speech" shows false starts, unfinished sentences, and a tendency to use simple, unmarked constructions with few modifiers. Again, the Wolof kings of former times provide some illustrations of "noble speech" patterns. Consider, for instance, the speech of the king of Saloum, recorded about 1865 when he paid a formal visit to the Catholic mission at Saint-Joseph de Ngasobil, which was then headed by the missionary linguist Mgr. Alois Kobès. The missionary archives (Abiven n.d.) describe the visit as follows (my translation from the French; Kobès's Wolof transcription is unaltered):

> The king has a birth defect: he stammers a great deal ordinarily, but it is to be noted that he stammered rather more in speaking to Monsignor. . . . [When he saw a statue of Jesus open and shut its eyes and move its arms,] the king said (stammering): "Lì, lì, lì, lì, ma gìs . . . yépă, du du dara, lef là, lef l'angi" ("Everything I have seen until now is nothing, this is the thing" – of all the other things in the mission.)

Rendered in modern orthography,[22] the king's utterance looks like this:

Li, li, li, li   ma gis – yëpp,   du du
This this this this I   see   everything neg neg
This – this – this – this I see – everything, it's not –

dara,   lëf   la,   lëf   laanggi.
nothing thing obj. foc. or NCM? thing pron + presentative it's
nothing, that thing, that is the thing.

Although Kobès's translation may well represent the import of what the king meant to say, his actual sentence is less well formed. The stammer we see here looks much like the false starts and incomplete structures observable in the speech of a modern village chief (see the transcript in the later "Examples" section) and other high nobles. Of all these high-ranking people it is said that their tongues lack agility, their bodies lack liveliness (unless aroused by a griot), and their minds are preoccupied with weighty matters.

Although stammering and other disfluencies may lead to some repetition of initial elements, this should not be confused with the parallelistic constructions found in "griot talk." The constructions of "griot talk" are never syntactically disfluent. Quite distinguishable from false starts and incomplete constituents, they represent instead complex (multiple-clause) sentence structures and regular processes of morphological reduplication. Reduplication is a word-formation process in Wolof that, for verbs, suggests continuous or repetitive, intensified action. For example, *crab-crabé*, a verb formed from a reduplication of the French loan word *crabe* 'crab', means 'continuously, repetitively, or strikingly move sideways, crab fashion'. It is a word I have encountered only in bardic performances, although Wolof audiences did not find it obscure. It is interesting to contrast these reduplicative and repetitive forms with constructions involving the suffix *-aat* (as in *dellusiwaat* 'return here again', *waxaat* 'speak again', etc.), which refer to a repeated action but apparently bear no connotations of register difference.

That these reduplicative verb forms involve connotations of intensity, vividness, and continuous action makes their frequency in "griot speech" consistent with other features of the register: its frequent use of emphatic devices (including those that result in cleft sentences and other complex structures), of the "explicative" and continuative auxiliaries, of ideophones (intensifiers), and of a verb–complement construction that most often conveys vivid details of sound and motion. All these features relate to a conception of the griot as much involved with excitement, noise, and frenetic activity.

Table 7.3 summarizes the morphological and syntactic constructions characteristic of the two poles of the register continuum.

Lexicon. The preceding discussion of morphology and syntax has necessarily touched on several aspects of lexical choice that differentiate these Wolof registers. Thus we have already seen that the affectively charged register, "griot speech," is characterized by frequent use of spatial deictics, especially in their "emphatic" forms; by verbs formed from morphological reduplication (such as *topp-topp* 'continually and intensely

Table 7.3. *Contrasts in morphology and syntax*

"Noblelike speech"	"Griotlike speech"
Emphatic devices	
Unmarked (subject-verb-object) order of basic constituents; sparse use of focus markers	Left dislocations, cleft sentences; heavy use of focus markers (subject focus, object focus, and "explicative" verbal auxiliary)
Sparse use of spatial deictics and determinants	Frequent use of spatial deictics, especially their "emphatic" forms[23]
Sparse use of modifiers	Ideophones (intensifiers); more use of verb–complement construction *né* _____, which often conveys details of sound and motion
Parallelisms	
Little use of parallelism	Repetitive and parallel constructions (e.g., parallel clauses)
Few reduplicated forms, especially in verbs; no novel use of morphological reduplication.	Frequent use of morphological reduplication, especially in verbs, including novel word formations
Disfluencies	
Noun classification system: choice of class marker "wrong" or semantically neutral; avoidance of markers when possible; incomplete or inconsistent concord	"Correct" class markers; principles of consonant harmony and semantic subtlety; more use of markers; consistent and complete concord
Incomplete sentence structures; false starts	Well-formed sentence structures

pushing'); and by continuative and explicative verbal auxiliaries (*di* / *i*, *dëfë* / *dëf* / *daa*). Similarly, emphatic particles such as *de* 'indeed' and *dàll* 'really' are also frequent in this register and more rare in "noble speech."

Other relevant lexical choices include the use of vivid vocabulary, especially in the representation of motion (e.g., *jéllanyo* 'toss about'; *mbentalé* 'shaking out, as when shaking skirts to get the dust off'; *nappaaje* 'squash with the foot'; *sa jód-a-jód, ak sa jëd* 'your stiff strutting and stamping'); the representation of noise (*mu dox di xabat-xabatja* 'she walks around making a slishy-sloshy sound'; *né ngërëp!* 'went crashing down WOMP!'); or the description of strong affect (*saalit* 'tremble in a frenzy of fear'; *sënggëm jooy* 'hunch over weeping'). Ideophones (*sedd guii* 'extremely cold'; *nyuul kuuk* 'extremely black'; *wex tàll* 'extremely bitter'; etc.) and hyperbolic expressions such as *ba dee* 'to death' (*ma ree ba dee* 'I died laughing') or *ba reey* 'till killing' are also characteristic.

Honorific and eulogistic expressions, especially in forms of address (praise naming) and expressions of thanks, are part of the "griot speech" register too. Indeed, because of the ideological connection between affectivity and rank, it is somewhat arbitrary whether we call this a hyperbolic, affectively charged register or an honorific register, whose use implies taking on a low-ranking role for oneself and enthusiastically imputing a high-ranking role to someone else. However, the "griot speech" register may be employed to express anger as well as enthusiasm. In the case of anger, of course, honorific expressions will not occur, except sarcastically ("F- N- [praise name], you're just like an outhouse: you never lie, you never tell tales"). Sometimes derogatory nicknames and insulting labels will be used where, in a praise performance, praise names and eulogizing expressions would have been employed.

In contrast, the laconic register, "noble speech," tends toward a bland and affectively neutral vocabulary. This does not necessarily mean a general semantic neutralization, however. Nouns labeling detailed classifications of the natural world, such as the botanical or zoological lexicon, and those classifying the social world in a formal sense (without any particular attitudinal load), may be found just as frequently in this register as in the other. What differentiates the registers has to do with affect and public performance, not with one's knowledge about the world.

Discourse management and interactional devices. The register differences so far described are systematic in their connection with affectivity and rank, and with the Wolof cultural ideas that interpret these in the form of the images, or behavioral stereotypes, of griot and noble. The same ideas apply, too, to the management of discourse: the conversational roles available to participants and the distribution of rights to the floor. I have described some of these patterns of interaction in other papers.[24] For the present, I would like to emphasize a few aspects of the interactional system. One (already mentioned) is the use of repetition to express supportive agreement with one's interlocutor; the other is the frequent use of conversational intermediaries and spokespersons to relay a message through third parties, even when the message source and its target are physically copresent. Both of these patterns are connected with the image of the griot as repeater, supporter, and transmitter of messages from higher-ranking persons whose dignity precludes publicly expressing their own sentiments or arguing on their own behalf.

The village chief, for example, almost never speaks aloud in a public gathering, such as a public political meeting or a religious event held in the central plaza of town. As his brother commented to me, "He [the chief] ought not to speak in the public plaza; he ought not to speak in front of many persons. He is a chief and a great *marabout* [religious leader], and he would be ashamed." If a high-ranking person needs to communicate something to a large group, or to some other person of similarly high rank, he or she must resort to an intermediary, someone of lower rank (often a griot), to perform the communicative task. The noble says something quietly to the intermediary, perhaps whispering in his or her ear; the intermediary then repeats the message loudly and more elaborately, relaying it to its intended receiver.

This pattern is widespread in the western Sahel. It is attested as early as 1506, when the Portuguese geographer Fernandes described the use of speech intermediaries among the Wolof and Manding, in groups as small as three and even when all parties were present together (Fernandes 1940:77–8). Similar reports have been made by many observers through the years; for example, David Gamble (1967:75) notes that when a daughter or wife of a chief comes on a visit, she is accompanied by a retinue including griot women; the high-ranking visitor makes only a few formal remarks, the lighter parts of the conversation being conducted by her companions "on her behalf."[25] Since a high-ranking host or hostess has griot spokespersons too, a formal visit may involve double intermediaries. On one such occasion I was present when a particularly important chief received another chief in his house. Each had his griot mediator, and after the initial greetings the conversation was entirely taken over by the griots, who conversed with each other on their nobles' behalf. The chiefs themselves simply sat in silence.

Not only chiefs, but high-ranking Wolof villagers in general, rely heavily on intermediaries, occasionally even double intermediaries, in situations they consider formal or important, and when they must address a message to the public, to a stranger, or to someone of equally high rank. For instance, any public announcement (of a birth, a death, a religious celebration, an upcoming meeting, etc.) must be relayed through a griot. Similarly, when important visitors come to his household, a high-ranking noble does not greet them directly but calls on an intermediary – a griot, a slave, a son, or a wife – to do so and to mediate the conversation; only after some time (if at all) will the noble directly address the visitors himself. Large-scale or ceremonial occasions are not the only relevant ones for verbal intermediaries. For example, an elderly woman with an eye problem – someone I knew quite well – came to me for medication, bringing along her young nephew so that she would not have to petition me directly. "She needs . . . this thing," announced the nephew loudly, pointing to a tube of eye medicine, while his aunt stood by in silence.

More striking examples for a Western reader, perhaps, than intermediaries who relay requests, announce decisions, or conduct political negotiations are cases where the intermediary's role is to express strong emotion. One afternoon, a group of women (some five nobles and two griots) were gathered near a well on the edge of town when another woman strode over to the well and threw herself down it. All the women were shocked at the apparent suicide attempt, but the noble women were shocked in silence. Only the griot women screamed, on behalf of all.[26]

Examples: the registers in use

Now that the linguistic features of the registers have been described, it remains to consider some recorded instances of their use. I have chosen three examples: two that represent public, mixed-caste situations and one that comes from a more intimate gathering of castemates. The public cases illustrate broad contrasts between the behavior of high and low castes: All the talk occupying the public "stage" is spoken by low-caste persons, and all is "griot speech"; high-caste sponsors and addressees are completely silent. The types of affect – anger and enthusiasm – are quite different in the two cases, however. In the more private context represented by the third example, the behavioral contrasts are less extreme, but we can see both registers emerge even though everyone present is of the same caste.[27]

Example 1. The text materials that follow are excerpts from an insult session at a high-caste wedding (all come from the same wedding). At these sessions, low-caste women, especially griots, insult the bride and her kin, expressing jealousy and anger on behalf of the bride's high-ranking cowives. Lines of text initially shouted out by a low-caste solo speaker are repeated many times by a chorus of low-caste women, who are eventually joined by most of the audience (the assembled public). The meter of the text lines is picked up and repeated by griot drummers, whose rhythmic energy is supposed to stir the crowd to ever-higher levels of angry shouting, creative verbal fluency, and aggressive, sexually suggestive dancing. Meanwhile the bride, to whom this tirade is addressed, sits with downcast eyes, silent and motionless, demonstrating her strength and self-control to the extent that she remains unmoved by the barrage of angry noise and activity directed at her. And the high-ranking cowives, whose anger is being expressed, usually also remain quietly in the background.[28]

These texts are examples, then, of "griot speech." Uttered at high pitch and high volume, their rhythm and articulation are nevertheless very precise, and their sentences are well formed. Notable as well is the use of emphatic forms, insulting labels ('crazy person', 'leper', 'witch', 'thief'), vivid description (including "quoted" wailing), and the reduplicated *jeex-a-jeex* 'all thoroughly worn out'. In the free translation, I have tried to replicate the emphases as much as possible by *underlining* emphasized forms. I have not included the many repetitions of text lines.

A

Man   du ma wujjee   ak   ab doff! Lee   mu
I (emph) neg I   be cowife with det. crazy now (elided form) she
I won't be cowife with a crazy person! Now she's whipping me
ma ritax aw yett!   Sa-i   baay woo na la,
me whip det. stick, cane your pl. father call   you
with a cane! Your fathers summoned you,
kii   défë xonqx,   kii   défë nyuul
this person (emph) expl. red   this person (emph) expl. black
this [child] is *red*, *this* [child] is *black* –
– toskàn   ginaar laa   ci   xamoon! Lingéér
have hatchlings chicken obj. focus + I about knew   queen
I've only heard of that when *chickens* hatch! [Even] the queen
di   xaxaar doomam – di   ci   wax,
cont. insult child her   cont. about say
would insult her own child [if she behaved like that] – saying,
waa waa waa! lu ma xam, laa   ci   wax! Kii
waa waa waa what I   know obj. focus + I about say this person (emph)
Waa waa waa! What I know, I'm going to tell! *This* person
motu   ma wujj! Ab sacc la!   Bàjjoam
not worthy I   cowife det. thief focus womb her
isn't worth being my cowife! She's a thief! Her womb
neexul! Boo   dëbb,   doxatt! Xari,
displease when you pound (grain) fart   [bride's name]
is disgusting! When you pound [grain], you fart! Xari [bride],
ngga ber   ngatan,   ba sa-b sàr
you put aside [child's] cot till your mattress
you have put aside your childhood cot, now your [big] mattress

jeex-a-jeex!
be totally finished
is all worn out!

B

Jabari   faj-mer   la   – nun,   ka   nu bëggoon
wife of assuaging anger   obj. focus we (emph) that person we wanted
She's the consolation-prize wife – the person *we* wanted

dikkul!   Xari C-,   jabari faj-mer   ngga –
arrive not [bride's name] wife of assuaging anger you (obj. foc.)
didn't show up! Xari C- [bride], you're the consolation-prize wife

nun,   la   nu bëggoon dikkul!
we (emph) obj. foc. we wanted   arrive not
– the one *we* wanted didn't show up!

C

Xari   yow,   doomi   gaana, setub   dëmë yi!
[bride's name] you (emph) child of (pl.) leper grandchild of witches
Xari [bride], *you* are the child of lepers, the grandchild of witches!

Example 2. This example is an excerpt from a griot's public performance of praise oratory on the occasion of a feast sponsored by a wealthy noble. The noble sponsor remains secluded (thus, silent and invisible) inside his house, while griots and guests assemble in the compound yard. A griot orator declaims the genealogy, family history, and great deeds of the sponsor and his family with high pitch, loud volume, and great rapidity; from time to time, he pauses while a chorus of other griots sings a verse of more conventional praise for the sponsor's patrilineage. The more enthusiasm the griot can express, and the more he can stir the crowd to admiration of the sponsor, the more moved the sponsor will be and the more enhanced will be his rank (because of the recognition by others, and because of the immanent presence of ancestors addressed and invoked by the griot). What the noble is moved to is more effective social action, including the greater display of material generosity.

The following text represents a few moments of solo oratory. It illustrates "griot speech" as the expression of intense enthusiasm. Note that to use extended forms of personal names and to invoke ancestral names – both of which are done here – is to express special enthusiasm and praise. Other characteristics of the discourse include emphatic forms, reduplicated forms (*baaxabaax, metti ba metti, baribari*) and parallelisms, and much description of motion, often with the continuative auxiliary *di / i.* The griot's quotation of a proverbial expression, *jàmbaar xam na la xeex di faj,* shows him speaking on behalf of noble forebears – the source of proverbial sayings – at the same time as he addresses the particular noble sponsor and his ancestors.

Maissa Moxurija Ali, Moxurija Ndumbe Jeey, Mori Taaw Njaay Fall
[name, extended]   [name, extended]   [name, extended]
    "   "   "

– waaw, nyoom,   warees na léén-a   tudd
 yes them (emph) ought hort. you pl. + obj. focus name
– Yes, *them,* you really ought to name them

bu baaxabaax!   Ndax nyoom   séén maam
exceedingly well, thoroughly because they (emph) their ancestor
in most glorious detail! Because it is *their* ancestor

la   nyu dakkilin   tabala!   Sànniko soxo
obj. foc. we rapidly beat drum for praise hymn fire off bullets
to whom we drum paeans of praise! Fire off the sacred bullets!

bi yaram! Nyu né ko borom gànnaay! Nyu né jàmbaar xam na
 sacred they say him owner battlefield they say hero knows
For he is called "Owner of the Field of Battle"! He is called

la xeex di faj!   Alpaaq la
what fight cont. cure   [name] you
"Hero Who Brings the Battle to a Glorious Close"! Alpaaq [name]

nyibbisi, Alpaaq séén   maam! Ba mu demee ca xaré ba
return here [name] your (pl.) ancestor when he went to war that
is incarnate in you, Alpaaq your forefather! When he went to war

– bi mu metti ba metti – mui dóór rek
which it hurt till hurt he cont. strike only
– where pain piled on pain – he had only to strike and [his

nyui   dee! Nyui   daanu! Nyu baribari   di
they cont. die they cont. fall they multitudinous cont.
enemies,] they would die! They would fall! In multitudes they would

saalit!   Jàmbaar, mooi   xam
tremble in frenzied fear Hero he (subj. foc.) cont. know
tremble in a frenzy of fear! The *hero, he* knows

la xeex di faj!
what fight cont. cure
what brings the battle to a glorious close!

Example 3. The following conversation is drawn from a much more private, casual situation. The assembled company – a small group – are all castemates (nobles),[29] and nothing earthshaking transpires. Still, the conversation illustrates, in a small way, some of the differences between registers and how the registers can be drawn on according to topic, affectivity, participants, and other emergent properties of a situation.

The setting is the village chief's courtyard one summer evening. Several villagers of noble rank, the chief himself, and I are sitting around chatting; there is no special reason for the gathering other than sociability. After some trucks are heard in the distance, the conversation turns to the varying skills of drivers. MF, a young man whose family belongs to a royal patriclan, claims that drivers who work for the nearby phosphate mine are better trained than others. In support of this allegation, MT, a man whose family, although of noble caste, is a client of the chief's, entertains the group with a short narrative. Thus MT, perhaps the lowest-ranking man present, takes on a griotlike speaking role with his narrative as he attempts to lend persuasive support to MF: [A note on transcript conventions: / / = overlapped transition; large brackets = simultaneous utterance.]

MT: Xamxam   ci   li   nyu xam né, *nyoonyu!*
      knowledge of what they know   those people (emphatic)
      The *knowledge* they have, *those* people!

MF: E – Tingééj [? indistinct]
           [name of town, also known as Rufisque]
      Eh – [the ones in] Rufisque. [?]

MT: Xamxam,   xamxam   dàll la nyu ko   am, ba m' ko doylé
      knowledge knowledge really they it   have till it suffices
      They *really* have enough *knowledge*

      ci diggïnte,   diggïnte,   aa//
      between   between
      [to drive] between – ah –

Chief: // [indistinguishable] Mariama,   yów fi
                                            [JTI]   you here
                                    Mariama [JTI], you

      de   woon sax. [pause]   ⎡ Fekk fu   kenn du nyu-i xam fu –
      emph were even   find where noone   they know where
      were   here then. [pause]   Turns out nobody knows where –
MT: diggïnte   Tingééj ak Ndar.
                                   between   [place] and [place]
                               – ⎣ between   Rufisque and Saint-Louis.

Chief: li   ca –   li nyu-i ci – jogé ba xam – [pause]
      what at   what they about set out till know
      what – about what –   get to know – [pause]

> li   ci   de   wonee –
> what about emph was shown
> what was indeed shown –

MT: A!   A – a –

       Ah!   w-   w-

am   nggoonent, da nyu fi   musa am
an   afternoon   expl they here once have
One afternoon, they once had here

benn, benn, benn kii   bu fu –   bu ko musa riix ci
one   one   one machine rel. where rel it once stick in
a, a *machine* where – that got stuck in a

genn   kekk. [pause] kaay topp ko, topp-topp-topp-topp-
one(aug) mudhole   come push it   push continually
a big *mudhole*. [They] come and push it, pushing pushing

topp-topp – mu nyàngg   – mu nyimé
pushing   it suddenly active it manage
pushing – it suddenly moves – it manages to

tabasiku!
suddenly disengage
burst out!

KN: A bon nak –
     well thus
     Well then –

MT: Bon nak, bu nyu jubuló,   demal ci biir   nger,
     well thus when they straighten go caus. in middle highway
     Well then, when they straighten up, they make it go in the
     middle of the highway,
     kii   bu nyu-i   law!
     machine rel they cont. touch
     the machine they were handling!

MT's narrative uses a number of emphatic devices: the particle *dàll* 'really', the numerals *benn* and *genn* 'one' (outside any context of actual counting), an augmentative noun class marker (*gi*, incorporated in the numeral *genn*) for *kekk* 'mudhole', syntactic focusing devices, repetitions and the reduplicative form *topp-topp* 'continually and energetically pushing', and vivid vocabulary. He repeats MF's *tingééj* and KN's *bon nak*; and he uses a dramatic prosody, with wide-ranging pitch and stress contours. In contrast, the utterances of the chief – apparently the main target of MT's rhetorical effort, the person who is to be persuaded – display a flat intonational contour and what might be considered conspicuous disfluency, with his mumbling and incomplete constructions.[30]

Even on a quite ordinary social occasion, then, and when the speaker is not himself a griot, the attempt to persuade and entertain one's interlocutors carries implications of rank and bears overtones of the griot's affectively charged, theatrical manner. To put this another way, the attempt at persuasion is an effort to bring about affective involvement in one's listeners. Since this is a griot specialty, even the noble speaker echoes a griot voice.

Summary

In sum, I have suggested that the linguistic phenomena comprising two labeled Wolof registers cohere in terms of affectivity and ideas about the nature of high and low ranks. These phenomena concern all aspects of the linguistic system, although some aspects are more salient to Wolof villagers than others; and the principles governing the differences between these registers also reach beyond them to organize patterns of social contact and conversation. There are no absolute boundaries between these registers and no linguistic feature that, in isolation, categorically identifies a stretch of talk as belonging to one variety or the other. Yet, the varieties are systematic: They reflect consistent patterns of contrast that emerge in the course of interaction.

Thus the characteristics that distinguish "griot speech" from "noble speech" all involve contrasts in affectivity (hyperbolic versus restrained) and rhetorical elaboration. They are rooted in images of persons, whose voices a speaker echoes when he or she echoes their social roles. These images are coherent, even if they are sometimes attenuated, echoes of another's voice. The co-occurrence of linguistic characteristics in a register, and the association of register with social role, are not arbitrary. Instead, they are products of a Wolof cultural association between social ranks and affectivity.

Whether this kind of connection would apply to the sociolinguistic organization of registers in other cultural systems is not clear, and space does not permit the examination of this issue. Some interesting cases for comparison might include Javanese language levels (mentioned earlier); Samoan registers (Ochs 1988); registers in Fijian Hindi (Brenneis 1988); and perhaps, from European material, the linguistic expression of the "royal rage," or heroic anger, if information is available. These cases make convenient comparisons with Wolof because all involve relations between affect, speaking, and social rank – although the particulars of the connection can be expected to differ.

Conclusion: complementarities and dialogic relations

The system of sociolinguistic registers I have outlined in the preceding pages is based on cultural assumptions that link affectivity inextricably with social structure – and therefore with the discourses in which society enacts, constructs, and reproduces its relationships. For Wolof villagers, social differentiation, conceived as a differentiation of ranks, is fundamentally based on the differentiation of affective modes and the control, expression, and channeling of affectivity. Although rank has many dimensions for the Wolof, including differences in wealth, political authority, genealogy, and moral stature, all of these are connected, in the ideology of the system, with affect, impulsivity, and self-control. Like their neighbors the Fulani, described by Paul Riesman (1983), Wolof nobles rationalize their claim to superiority over lower ranks in terms of sangfroid and restraint.[31]

Despite the moral weight nobles attach to differences in emotionality and its expression – and their view on these moral implications is not wholly shared by the lower ranks – no Wolof villager suggested that the high ranks could be self-sufficient or that society could function if everyone behaved like the highest nobles. As members of this Wolof community see it, society *is* differentiation, and high rank cannot be expressed if there is no one to take on "lowering" tasks. As one high-ranking elder argued, only a balance and an interaction between the high and the low, the calm and the impulsive, can make social action possible. Comparing the impulsive energy (*fit*, residing in the liver) that different personalities and ranks possess and control in different degrees to the engine of a car, he asked me: "Which would you rather have – a car that does not move, or a car that can only go a thousand kilometers an hour?" (I didn't know.) "Neither one. One would crash, and the other would never start. Either way, you would never get to Dakar." What you need, he concluded, is both a strong engine and a good set of brakes. The two are complementary in that both are necessary for the well-being of the whole and its potential for constructive action.

In Wolof discourse, this complementarity has several facets. The first of these is the complementarity of "personalities" or affective images associated with different social ranks, the high and the low. I have argued that the registers described here represent the voices attached to those images, voices that a speaker takes on in different social situations and for different purposes, whatever his or her own rank. The second facet is that these voices necessarily interact: They are mirror images of one another, and like mirror images they cannot exist in isolation. Although there can be conversations in which register differences are minimized, there is no Wolof discourse in which everyone present uses, say, extremely "griot-like" speech; even if all the audible talk that occurred were in the *waxu gewel* register, the silence of the audience would represent the *waxu géér* side of the coin. It is the contrast between them that organizes Wolof discourse, and organizes it to some effect (as, for instance, when the griot animates a noble and moves him or her to action, or simply when a speaker takes on griotlike rhetoric in an effort at persuasion).

As the prototype of the verbal intermediary – the message bearer – the griot faces in two directions: toward the message's source and toward its destination. It is the same for the griot's emotional expressiveness and for hyperbolic speaking that takes on the griot's "voice." The griot is both excited by others and exciting to them: There is a double complementarity. On the one hand, we have the relation to the addressee, in utterances that attribute some emotion or personality to him or her and stimulate the addressee and/or the audience to some feeling and action. The griots' praise oratory is a good example of discourse oriented in this direction. Extravagantly praising an addressee, it arouses feelings of family pride. To experience those feelings intensely supposedly "strengthens" the addressee and moves him or her to praiseworthy acts (such as distributing largesse). The audience, too, is moved and persuaded oƒ the respectability of the person being praised. Although the discourse is replete with signals of high affect, it is not really the griot's own feelings that are particularly at issue (see also Appadurai, this volume).

On the other hand, we have the relation between a speaker and the source of the message: the person whose ideas and sentiments the intermediary expresses. In the Wolof communicative system, the displayer of affect (or the person who expresses an idea) need not be the same person who supposedly possesses it. A griot may display emotion on behalf of a noble, to whom the emotion is attributed but who sits by impassively. If a high-ranking woman remains silent while griots express her anger at her husband's having taken a new wife, the sentiment is nevertheless attributed to her, not to the griots themselves. The songs and wailing of the griots who serve as public mourners when an important person dies also express the family's feelings in this way; so too does the intermediary who loudly expresses cordiality to a visitor on a host's behalf. Again, although the discourse is charged with high affect, the speaker's own feelings are not the ones principally being expressed.

I have called all these relations – between contrasting registers, between the contrasting social personae they represent, between the contrasting roles organizing a social situation, and between the expressor and the owner of a sentiment – "complementarities." This term expresses a Wolof sense of mutual necessity about these contrasts, but it is not otherwise ideal, for it may suggest that there is no difference in power or value between the contrasting forms. Moreover, it may suggest a certain social completeness and harmony, a sense that all of society has been comfortably accounted for, that may suit the views of Wolof nobles but cannot suit everyone else. In particular, the *jaam* – the former slaves – are poorly accommodated in the set of registers described here. Aligned with griots in many respects because of their low rank, aligned with nobles in other respects,[32] but unlike either in having been unfree, the *jaam* in some sense perhaps have no "voice" in the Wolof system at all.

"Heteroglossia" and "forms of dialogicality" might be better terms to describe the discourse relations in this system. Although they do no better than "complementarities" in attending to differences in power or value, at least they do not seem to imply that such differences do not exist or that structured coexistence is necessarily harmonious. What is useful about them, too, is that they call attention to the fact that discourse *is* a matter of relations – a matter of social relations and social situations. In doing so, they invoke an anthropological literature that calls into question monologic models of language and their analogues in models of society (Hill 1985). It is clear that monologic models of language, for all their usefulness in other arenas, cannot comfortably accommodate an organization of registers and their uses such as we have seen in Wolof.

The affective registers I have described in this chapter concern the organization of verbal means through which Wolof speakers display emotion and in terms of which Wolof audiences interpret emotional display. I have not much treated questions about what emotions Wolof speakers "really feel" or to what extent such questions, which assume some level of affectivity independent of its expression and of its cultural construction, make sense. I would like to conclude by pointing out, however, that seeing the discourse of emotion as essentially dialogical may have some implications about emotion itself – particularly an implication that a view of emotion may need to be relational as well. An approach that locates emotion only within the individual, rather than in the relationships between persons or between persons and events, suggests a monologic discourse and will not apply well to the case at hand.

As proponents of a contextual approach to emotion have suggested, the feelings one experiences in a given situation are not just primally "there," but are experienced in relation to something – indeed, to many things, including the possibilities of expression, the feelings one attributes to others with whom one interacts, and the feelings one attributes to others with whom one may be associated. Moreover, the possibilities of expression include not only one's own performance, but the performances of others who serve as one's expressive vehicle. Actually, we know little about the subjective dimension of these relayed performances. If these possibilities of expression have different social consequences, can the feelings they express be the same?

To speak like a griot, if (for example) you are not one, is to forego the option of having your feelings expressed by a specialist whose performance skills, you may believe, exceed your own. Instead, you take on the mantle of the griot's supposed emotionality, and you contrast yourself with some more restrained interlocutor. Whether or not you "really feel" the particular emotion you display, your subjective experience presumably includes knowing that you sound like a griot (about whose emotionality you have certain beliefs). Your attitude toward griots, and toward being for the moment associated with them, must color your feelings toward other aspects of the situation. If you *are* a griot, an equally complex contextualization applies, including your attitudes toward the person whose feelings you perform and toward the person you arouse, as well as your attitude toward the griot status you are for the moment typifying.

With Wolof villagers, it would be difficult even to approach a discussion about the subjective experience of emotion without bearing some of these relations in mind. It seems to me, however, that the point is not limited to this ethnographic case. One cannot experience a situation only in itself, without also being influenced by feelings about the social voices talking in it and about it, and by feelings about the roads not taken.

Notes

1. See also Ochs 1988.
2. Although Sapir did not exclude the possibility of some biologically based

level of emotional universals and temperamental tendencies, he argued nevertheless that both the expression of feelings and the notion of what feelings and personalities there are to be expressed are subject to the conventions of a cultural system and the organization of linguistic form. It is only in terms of these conventions that the behavior of individuals can fully make sense.

3. Lutz (1986) argues that these assumptions, and the contrast between emotion and thought, are deeply embedded in the Western world view of the person, of social life, and of morality. Although she writes from the perspective of cultural anthropology, psychology, and philosophy, the relevance to linguistics is obvious.

4. The terms "style" and "language level" are also relevant, although not identical to "register." "Language level" is used principally for cases like Javanese, which has a labeled set of linguistic varieties ranked according to refinement and respect conveyed for the addressee and/or the referent. "Style" is a term that has many usages, including situational variety, but also including the notion of an individual's style (his or her personal speech characteristics) and even (in the work of Labov) degrees of self-conscious attention to talk.

5. When Halliday (1978:35) says that registers tend to differ in semantics, he adds "and hence in lexicogrammar, and sometimes phonology, as realization of this." But he does not tell us how this works or why phonological differences should be seen as the "realization" of semantic differences.

6. Consider, for example, the "language levels" of some Indonesian languages, such as Javanese. Named linguistic varieties conveying degrees of politeness, refinement, and respect for the addressee and/or referent, the Javanese language levels are perhaps an especially formalized instance of register differences. Linguistically, the language levels have been described as differing mainly in lexicon (including sets of lexical substitutions) and in some special affixes. But recent work has pointed out that they also differ in prosody and morphophonemics, although these aspects have been little studied (Errington 1984:9).

7. Although register is defined in terms of situational context, the connection with affect and the cultural construction of the person has not been utterly absent from linguistic discussion of what registers are. Halliday writes, for example, about the "degree of emotional charge" in participants' relationship as a situational factor contributing to register choice (1978:33); and Firth speaks of "treating personality and language in society as a sort of basis for linguistics with a sociological component" (1957 [1950]:189).

8. See also the discussions of "sincerity" and affect in Irvine (1982) and Abu-Lughod's discussion (op. cit.) of "hypocrisy."

9. The largest ethnic group in Senegal, the Wolof population now stands at over 2 million – urban as well as rural and elite as well as peasant. Before the French colonial conquest in the late nineteenth century, they were politically organized in a set of kingdoms whose history dates back to the thirteenth century, when a Wolof state first emerged within the Empire of Mali.

Most of the fieldwork on which this chapter is based was carried out in 1970–1, 1975, and 1977 in a village in the Préfecture de Tivaouane, Senegal. I also returned there briefly in 1984. Thanks are due to the National Institute of Mental Health, the National Science Foundation, and Brandeis University for financial support of that research; to the Institut Fondamental d'Afrique Noire and the Centre de Linguistique Appliquée de Dakar for institutional sponsorship; and to my village hosts for their hospitality and intellectual assistance.

10. The Wolof labels even derive from these groups: Literally, *waxu gewel* means 'griot talk' and *waxu géér* means 'noble talk'.

11. See, e.g., Silla 1966.

12. Note that people can also be ranked within a caste according to genealogical purity and seniority, age, gender, wealth, and other factors, although the outcome of all these criteria need not be obvious.

13. Although *nawlé* usually refers to similarity of caste rank, because of the moral ingredient it is sometimes translated as 'co-religionary'. For a discussion of *naw* and *nawlé*, and of a Wolof metaphysics that links personality and status to the composition of the liquid elements of the body, see Marone (1969).

14. These symbolic connections also underlie caste-linked occupations, so that the nobles' affinity for earth supposedly makes them especially suitable for farming and land administration, whereas the griots' affinity for air is connected with their verbal activities. Similarly, blacksmiths supposedly have an affinity for fire, as do tanners (who work with fiery acids) and potters, whereas fishermen have an affinity for water. Within the high (noble) ranks, distinctions are sometimes drawn between clerics (*sériñ*), on the one hand, and princes and commoners, on the other. In addition to their role as land administrators, the princes (*garmi*) and, in somewhat different ways, the commoners and military slaves (*ceddo*) whom they command also engage in warfare; their temperament is ''hot'' compared with that of the ''cool'' clerics.

15. Also acts that cannot appropriately be witnessed by one's castemates or superiors.

16. Note the expression *nit kii dokna sama naw* 'this person has curdled my *naw*', relating to interaction considered emotionally destructive.

17. Not all possible feelings or expressive devices are caught in this particular net, only the ones constituting images of nobles and griots and thus relevant to the two registers named after them. In an earlier paper (Irvine 1982), I outlined some aspects of the linguistic expression of affect in Wolof. Only in the discussion of prosody and discourse management, however, did I allude to the registers of ''griot speech'' and ''noble speech'' being described here. Although some of the other devices mentioned in that paper are included here, not all of them clearly sort out into these two registers.

18. Pitch is a partial exception. In male speech one can distinguish falsetto from normal voice, and falsetto is linked exclusively with extreme renderings of ''griot talk.'' Pitch distinctions also apply within normal voice, however, and are involved in the less extreme versions of the ''griotlike'' register. They also apply within normal voice for female speakers, although one form of female utterance representing extreme emotionality is ululation.

19. The highest rate I have recorded and done a syllable count for came out to 386 syllables per minute. These rates are maintained over several minutes; they include pauses for breath intake. Were such pauses not included in the count, the rates would be higher.

20. See later comments on the stammer of the king of Saloum.

21. I say ''seems to'' because it is somewhat difficult, for statistical reasons, to tell whether the particular type of variation primarily characterizes situations or social groups. Variation in Wolof noun class morphology is dis-

cussed in detail in Irvine (1978) and is related to historical changes in the linguistic system. Although the discussion in that paper is framed largely in terms of social categories (age, caste, and gender), part of the argument rests on the idea that each speaker controls more than one variant of many of the nouns concerned. The variation can therefore be thought of in relation to registers that carry different connotations of social identity and intention – that represent different "voices" in the community – and are differentially drawn on by speakers according to their own social situation.

22. The orthography used in this chapter is based on the official system developed by the Centre de Linguistique Appliquée de Dakar and adopted by the Republic of Senegal in 1971. It is a phonemic system whose phonetic values are fairly transparent. A few symbols may require some explanation: *c* and *j* are palatal affricates; among the vowels, *é* = [e], *e* = [ɛ], *ë* = [i], *a* = [ʌ], *à* = [a], *o* = [ɔ], *ó* = [o].

23. This and some other features of "griot speech" seem to occur less often in griots' formal performance of historical narrative. There is some intersection of genre features with register, therefore, that needs to be more carefully examined.

24. See, e.g., Irvine (1974) on Wolof greetings, Irvine (1980) on directives, and Irvine (1979) on the organization of talk in political meetings.

25. According to Gamble, women of slave status may serve as intermediaries too. For some other comments on griots as intermediaries, see Diop (1981) and Camara (1976).

26. See Camara (1976) for a useful discussion of intermediaries among the Malinke and the vicarious expression of emotion, particularly anger.

27. Because of problems of presentation, the transcriptions I provide here do not show prosodic features or phonetic detail. Their illustration of register differences is thus limited to morphology, syntax, lexicon, and (to a small extent) discourse management.

28. There is a distinction here between the bride's actual cowives (women already married to the bride's husband) and her classificatory cowives (other women married into the husband's household – e.g., his brother's wives). The classificatory cowives may take part in the performance, usually as part of the crowd who eventually repeat lines of text.

29. Because I myself was classified as high caste, the only situations I observed that I can characterize as completely caste internal are those where everyone else was high caste too. No situations in which I was present to record and take notes can be considered wholly low caste.

30. It is perhaps a little unusual that the chief speaks as much as he does, disfluent or not. Notice, however, that he addresses me, not the other villagers, whom he more clearly outranks.

31. Among the Fulani studied by Riesman, the lower ranks consist of former slaves; among rural Wolof, there is a broader range of lower ranks, including slaves as well as other groups. Wolof discussions of emotionality usually focus on griots rather than on slaves.

32. A *jaam* is a person whose ancestors were once higher-ranking but were demoted, either because they were captured in battle or because they sold themselves for material goods. Should any *jaam* manage to buy back their freedom – theoretically, although seldom practically, a possibility – they would ascend to their ancestors' free rank. Since slavery has been illegal in Senegal for a considerable time, these principles represent the conventional calculation of social rank, not a legal status.

160   Judith T. Irvine

References

Abiven, Père O., compiler. n.d. *Annales religieuses de Saint-Joseph de Ngasobil, 1849–1929.* Dakar: Archives, Archevêché de Dakar.

Abu-Lughod, Lila. 1986. *Veiled Sentiments.* Berkeley: University of California Press.

Beeman, William O. 1988. Affectivity in Persian Language Use. *Culture, Medicine and Psychiatry* 12:9–30.

Brenneis, Donald. 1988. Shared and Solitary Sentiments. *Working Papers and Proceedings of the Center for Psychosocial Studies* 23. Chicago: Center for Psychosocial Studies.

Camara, Sory. 1976. *Les Gens de la Parole.* The Hague: Mouton.

Diop, Abdoulaye-Bara. 1981. *La Société Wolof: Tradition et Changement.* Paris: Karthala.

Errington, Joseph. 1984. *Language and Social Change in Java.* Athens: Ohio University Center for International Studies.

Ervin-Tripp, Susan. 1972. On Sociolinguistic Rules: Alternation and Co-Occurrence. In J. Gumperz and D. Hymes, eds., *Directions in Sociolinguistics: The Ethnography of Communication.* New York: Holt, Rinehart, & Winston, pp. 213–50.

Fernandes, Valentim. 1940. *O Manuscrito "Valentim Fernandes."* Lisboa: Academia Portugesa da Historia. (From a work dated 1506–10.)

Firth, J. R. 1957. (1950). Personality and Language in Society. *The Sociological Review* 42(2):8–14.

1957. *Papers in Linguistics 1934–1951.* London: Oxford University Press.

Gamble, David. 1967. *The Wolof of Senegambia,* 2nd ed. London: International African Institute.

Geertz, Clifford. 1960. *The Religion of Java.* Chicago: University of Chicago Press.

Gumperz, John. 1968. The Speech Community. *International Encyclopedia of the Social Sciences.* New York: Macmillan.

Halliday, Michael A. K. 1964. The Users and Uses of Language. In M. A. K. Halliday, A. McIntosh, and P. Strevens, eds., *The Linguistic Sciences and Language Teaching.* London: Longmans, pp. 75–110.

1978. *Language as Social Semiotic.* London: Edward Arnold.

Henry, Jules. 1936. The Linguistic Expression of Emotion. *American Anthropologist* 38:250–6.

Hill, Jane. 1985. The Grammar of Consciousness and the Consciousness of Grammar. *American Ethnologist* 12:725–37.

Irvine, Judith T. 1974. Strategies of Status Manipulation in the Wolof Greeting. In R. Bauman and J. Sherzer, eds., *Explorations in the Ethnography of Speaking.* London: Cambridge University Press, pp. 167–91.

1978. Wolof Noun Classification: The Social Setting of Divergent Change. *Language in Society* 7:37–64.

1979. Formality and Informality in Communicative Events. *American Anthropologist* 81:773–90.

1980. How Not to Ask a Favor in Wolof. *Papers in Linguistics* 13:3–50.

1982. Language and Affect: Some Cross-Cultural Issues. In H. Byrnes, ed., *Contemporary Perceptions of Language: Interdisciplinary Dimensions.* Georgetown University Round Table on Languages and Linguistics. Washington, DC: Georgetown University Press, pp. 31–47.

Jakobson, Roman. 1960. Linguistics and Poetics. In T. Sebeok, ed., *Style in Language.* Cambridge, MA: MIT Press, pp. 350–77.

Lutz, Catherine. 1982. The Domain of Emotion Words on Ifaluk. *American Ethnologist* 9:113–28.

1986. Emotion, Thought, and Estrangement: Emotion as a Cultural Category. *Cultural Anthropology* 1:287–309.

Lutz, Catherine, and Geoffrey White. 1986. The Anthropology of Emotions. *Annual Review of Anthropology* 15:405–36.

Marone, Oumar. 1969. Essai sur les fondements de l'éducation sénégalaise à la lumière des métaphores aqueuses de la langue wolof. *Bulletin de l'Institut Fondamental d'Afrique Noire* 31, sér. B:787–852.

Myers, Fred. 1979. Emotions and the Self: A Theory of Personhood and Political Order Among Pintupi Aborigines. *Ethos* 7:343–70.

Ochs, Elinor. 1988. *Culture and Language Development.* Cambridge: Cambridge University Press.

Riesman, Paul. 1983. On the Irrelevance of Child Rearing Practices for the Formation of Personality. *Culture, Medicine, and Psychiatry* 7:103–29.

Sapir, Edward. 1921. *Language.* New York: Harcourt Brace.

1927. Speech as a Personality Trait. *American Journal of Sociology* 32:892–905.

1930. The Cultural Approach to the Study of Personality. Paper delivered at the Hanover Conference, Social Science Research Council. To be published in *The Collected Works of Edward Sapir.* Berlin: de Gruyter.

Shweder, Richard. 1984. Anthropology's Romantic Rebellion Against the Enlightenment; or, There's More to Thinking Than Reason and Evidence. In R. Schweder and R. LeVine, eds., *Culture Theory: Essays on Mind, Self, and Emotion.* Cambridge: Cambridge University Press, pp. 27–66.

Silla, Ousmane. 1966. La persistance des castes dans la société Wolof contemporaine. *Bulletin de l'Institut Fondamental d'Afrique Noire* 28, sér. B:731–69.

Stankiewicz, Edward. 1964. Problems of Emotive Language. In T. Sebeok, A. S. Hayes, and M. C. Bateson, eds., *Approaches to Semiotics.* Transactions of the Indiana University Conference on Paralinguistics and Kinesics. The Hague: Mouton, pp. 239–64.

Wolff, John U., and S. Poedjosoedarmo. 1982. *Communicative Codes in Central Java.* Ithaca, NY: Cornell University Department of Asian Studies, Southeast Asia Program, Data Paper 116.

8. Language in the discourse of the emotions

DANIEL V. ROSENBERG

"Discourse" and "the emotions"

"The emotions" are a lexical domain in our Anglophone consciousness of the person, a higher status label for that family of objects known in the folk ethnopsychology as "feelings." "Discourse" is the consensus best name for what the human sciences today make of their perennially most reliable object – human symbolic behavior, especially as encoded in language – when this is conceived not as a fixed superstructure of collective meaning and order but as a fluid field of interested, indeed contentious and factious, social activity. In this chapter I consider what anthropologists have discerned and might be able to discern at the intersection of "discourse" and "[the] emotions."

A conception of culture that anthropologists came about a decade and a half ago to reconsider, and then largely to reject, had its foundations in a much-distilled inheritance of certain Genevan and Praguean understandings of linguistic structure, especially as that structure might be understood to emerge in the parallel segmentations of language's sensible medium – sound – and of meaning. In turning from that conception, anthropologists ceased to render culture as a set of freeze-dried crystallizations of symbols and meanings, and went on to reconstitute it as a field of oblique communicative vectors – discourses – truer to life, it seemed, even if threatening to undermine the neat order that the earlier ethnographic practice had been able to impute. These anthropologists intended a rediscovery of interested human agency, as a feature of willful individuals and as a feature of social segments – genders, classes, castes, and so on – or of corporate institutions, such as the state, the men's house, or the women's domestic group.

The period during which anthropologists have settled on "the emotions" as a domain of analysis, as virtually the domain of choice in psychological anthropology, is also a period in which they have championed a revamped picture of culture, not silently univocal but audibly multivocal. Accordingly, the contributors to this volume assign "the emotions," or a particular rhetorical construal of self and emotion, to one or another class of speakers in particular discursive contexts. All of them, more or less explicitly, locate their efforts on a certain trajectory, in which a transformation is said to be under way in the role language must play as foundation and datum for cultural accounts.

In what follows, I look at some claims made for and uses made of language on the part of those who seek a "discourse of the emotions." In examining some signal contributions of the last decade, I argue that the turn to "discourse" risks preserving much of what it aims to supersede. I claim that these contributions represent cooperative native and ethnographic reflections of lexical reference, and that such reflections are linguistic data, to be sure, but not discourse. I suggest that referential ideologies of these kinds must be located in a field in which sharper distinctions are made among *semantics, reference, pragmatics,* and *ideology.*

Knowledge and Passion

Michelle Z. Rosaldo's *Knowledge and Passion* (1980) prefigured the kind of account of "the emotions" in terms of "discourse" that characterizes many of today's efforts. In that text, Rosaldo offered a sustained metacommentary on the kind of ethnographic datum language must be. Language, she claimed, does something more than just "demarcate" the world into "classificatory grids"; "meaning," she insisted, "is bound up with use." She urged us to rely instead on "sentences and style," "common discourse," "habitual ways of talking," "daily life and talk," and the like. In taking what she called this Wittgensteinian turn, Rosaldo intended to find "the emotions" in the language of ordinary life and not in their famously problematic ritual embodiments. In addition, she argued that "the emotions" could not be encompassed by the methods of the so-called ethnographic semantics, and its successor cognitive anthropology, of the American anthropology of the 1960s and 1970s.[1] The practitioners of these methods, as many have noted, reasoned that a culture could most parsimoniously be captured by selecting from its language, in grammar-free and context-free fashion, classes of nouns (occasionally, adjectives), which in turn represented object-classes that corresponded with domains in the experiential world. The promotion of such a lexical glossary from datum to culture was effected by passage through an intermediate step, a cognitive "model" or "representation," which typically took the form of a spatial arrangement of the lexical items.

When *Knowledge and Passion* was published, that style of analysis was falling from favor under several influences, including the turn to pragmatics and context on the part of linguistic anthropology, the discipline that ostensibly had bred it; cultural anthropology's passage from ordered, timeless knowledge to disorderly macro- and microhistorical process; and cognitive psychology's (lately, "cognitive science" 's) replacement of nodal treelike representations of passively held knowledge (again, also largely lexical and spatial) with real-time processual schemata for quotidian engagement.

Knowledge and Passion finds "the emotions" embedded in ordinary process.[2] In place of the rigorous methodological abstraction from the ordinary on the part of ethnographic semantics, Rosaldo practiced "interpretation," which amounted in this case to a rich narrative about how certain Ilongot "emotional terms" – especially *'liget'*, loosely translatable as 'anger', also as the titular 'passion' – were instanced in discourse about the self and its orientation to important institutions, particularly kin relations, labor and economy, politics, and headhunting.

But in spite of the claims for a focus on everyday talk, for the discourse of daily life, Rosaldo returns repeatedly to a family of "emotional terms," "affective terms," or "focal analytical terms." These are mainly nouns. Her abstraction of such nominal foci from everyday talk is no less radical than the earlier ethnographic semantics abstraction, however much it may be less mechanical and conspicuous. And, despite a number of claims for a focus on functions of language beyond the referential, the purpose of the abstracted lexical foci is to stand for things. 'LIGET' and 'BEYA' are the essences of which *'liget'* and *'beya'* ('knowledge') are the names or labels. To be sure, the kinds of things to which *'liget'* and *'beya'* seem to refer are not the denotata demarcated in the earlier picture. One of the challenges in reading Rosaldo's work is to reconcile one's sense of *'liget'* and *'beya'* as quiddities with the author's arguments against our conceiving of them as denoted objects.

Rosaldo's reasons for wanting to reject the notion that meaning is an ostensive relation between word and object are fine. Yet *'liget'*, *'beya'*, and their kin seem to come to life, first as essences and then as seeming psychological forces, in a species of bilingual ethnographic writing in which the "focal terms," having been glossed early in the text, become so familiar to the reader that they can be used throughout the remainder of the account (in the form of the indigenous word in italics, with or without single quotation marks; or of an English gloss, with or without single quotation marks) in sentences in English grammar. There is, in my view, more than the usual ethnographic ambiguity about whether each sentence is to be understood as a kind of quotative, with an implied "Ilongot say that . . ." at its beginning, or whether some kind of authorial abstraction has been made.

The preponderance, grammatically and lexically, of English carries with it a radical infiltration not just of the world view encoded in the ethnographer's language, but of the ethnopsychology of the ethnographer's culture. In Rosaldo's account of Ilongot emotional life, *'liget'* and its Ilongot fellows inhabit the same world and the same grammar inhabited by "fury," "distraction," "courage," "irritation," "confusion," "separation," and "joy." What is more, the Ilongot names/things accept the same range of predicates and modifiers that the English terms do. Some of these modifiers follow the inherent tendency of English to spatialize, quantify, and generally 'physicalize' all nouns. Others seem to derive more directly from the tenets of American ethnopsychology, with its idioms of causation and motivation nested in near-animate forces subject to hydraulic pressures. Thus, *'liget'* and its kind have "weight"; their "energy" can be "diffused" or "concentrated"; if they are weighty enough, or if their "wildness" can be "controlled" and "focused," they are "loosed"; they may otherwise be suppressed; "derived" from or "bred" by other inner states or public circumstances, they may in turn be "creative" and "transcendant," "bearing fruits" and "stirring," "breeding," and "spurring" their own outcomes; capable of being "intense" and "disruptive," they need to be "dealt with"; and so on. Distinctions between use and mention, between the native's 'energy' and the ethnographer's energy, are suspended. *'Liget'* is embedded in a web of social-scientific idioms: It is "labor and reproductive" force marshaled in the "interest of collective life"; it can be "bred" by "inequality"; and so on. Finally, there is a stunning breadth of consequences brought about by *'liget'*, a vast range of contexts in which it is "expressed" and "displayed."[3]

Rosaldo's announced foundation is language in context, but *Knowledge and Passion* is an effort that abstracts from language and then *recon*-textualizes the abstracted product, an effort we must see as distinct from an understanding of language in context. In *Knowledge and Passion*, language is a symbolic medium from which certain things – words – are abstracted and made to stand for certain other things. What separates Rosaldo's work from that of her cognitive anthropological contemporaries is the status of these other things. The abstracted product, the "focal terms," achieve the status of leitmotifs, or master metaphors, in terms of which the author can interpret – this being the recontextualization – a vast range of beliefs and practices.

Rosaldo makes it clear that headhunting, the life cycle, marriage, and so on among the Ilongot can be described in sentences in which 'liget' figures as master metaphor. As such, the account echoes a very old Western tradition in which certain congeries of nouns/things, usually "passions" or "sentiments" (but compare also "virtues" and "vices"), are seen to be in collusion or competition with each other, with all of these, in turn, in more or less of an equilibrium with "reason." The Ilongot rendered in terms of 'liget' is a story that is resonant with an old genre in which all the peculiarities that seemed to characterize the French could be woven together under the slogan "vanity," and just so the Spaniards under "pride," the Zuni under "Apollonian," and the Kwakiutl under "Dionysian."

The idea that "the emotions" for a given people amount to a glossary of nouns/essences continues this old tradition. Most modern approaches to "the emotions" in alien settings make this glossary assumption; Rosaldo's is the position most faithful to the tradition, since it accounts for a vast range of practices in terms of one or two enshrined entries from such a glossary. The move from enshrined noun/essence to narrative leitmotif, and the further move from motif to culture, fosters a kind of cultural naturalism in which a small set of Ur-principles lurk behind everything as first causes. 'Liget' and its kind assume the status of natural, even animate, forces: ideals toward which any Ilongot behavior can be seen as striving, principles of which any practice becomes an expression. To that extent, the roles that 'liget' and its kind play belie the author's many claims against the mentalism and functionalism of the old-style culture and personality: They function as internal(ized), motivational forces, encoded and expressed in the grammar and idioms of English ascriptive talk.

Ethnographic metasemantics

In the anthropology of "the emotions," our arrival today at "discourse" in no small way rests on Rosaldo's articulation of an intellectual generation's discontent with its predecessors' understandings of language. By the mid-1980s, most anthropological commentaries on "the emotions" echoed Rosaldo's attack on denotation, reference, and classification.

"Ethnopsychological vocabulary," according to Kirkpatrick and White (1985:16), "is used to talk about personal and social experience, not to identify or classify 'objects' separable from their cultural contexts." The contributors to their volume (White and Kirkpatrick 1985)

> generally agree that the vocabulary in question does not function primarily to "classify" social reality in terms of taxonomic schemata consisting of categories related through contrast and inclusion. Rather, by focusing on frequently used words that point to salient cultural notions, such as Bimin-Kuskusmin *finiik* . . . , Marquesan *ka'oha* . . . , or Baining *akambain* . . . , the ethnographer is able to track inferential pathways through webs of associative knowledge which underly [sic] the terms' various meanings and uses. (1985:19)

It is not hard to see in this dismissal of an earlier picture the survival of many of that view's foundations. The analysis is anchored by a small selection of items from a vocabulary; those items stand for, and in the ethnographic account just are, locally important notions or concepts; the concepts or notions hang together in some structured way; the structure of concepts is something that natives know and share; as such, that structure "underlies" everyday practice, in particular the practice of using words to talk about things, with meaning-to-use understood as an instance of the relation of knowledge-to-action generally.

To be sure, the "net of senses" or "web of meanings" discerned by Rosaldo, in which words (concepts, images, symbols) "suggest," "hint at," "evoke," are "associated with" or "related to" each other, had for her no such internal location. The "senses" and "meanings" were intended as just public symbols. Many contributions of the mid-1980s, in which Rosaldo's influence nonetheless is evident, do locate these structures internally and mentally. They render them in a harder form, in the process very nearly resurrecting (even when disavowing) the earlier picture, as "associative knowledge," "organized knowledge structures," "inferential pathways," and the like. The focus has shifted away from the mechanics of constructing the arrays, but the elements of the array (lexemes), its form (quasi-spatial), and its status (cognitive) are the same.

Consider, by way of example, John Kirkpatrick's "Some Marquesan Understandings of Action and Identity" (1985). Kirkpatrick (1985:85) notes that Marquesan "ethnopsychology . . . is realized in everyday discourse, not in specialists' accounts of the world or strongly demarcated speech situations." He takes up three "terms," *'ka'oha'*, *'haka'ika'*, and *'keitani'*, which he glosses as 'concern,' 'shame,' and 'envy', respectively. Each is (in his words) a "term" and, at the same time, a "state" or "capability."

Situations in which the terms are (again in his words) "mentioned" and "used" are identified, and informants' "accounts of " the "terms"/ "states" are cited. We see, for example,

> how the sense of ka'oha as 'gift' and *mea ka'oha* as 'object of concern, compassion' can be closely linked to a view of ka'oha as a process integrating perception, emotion, and action:
>
> "I'm poor. I don't come to your place. You recognize [this]; you come to my place, bringing money [and] say, 'Take. You, your wife, your children will eat'. You just give, I didn't ask. That's ka'oha." (1985:88; brackets and quoting as in the original)

From a glossary uncovered in this way, Kirkpatrick (1985:88) moves outward to exemplify how all three "terms"/"states" "involve complex attitudes toward life in a social world."

Kirkpatrick takes the "terms"/"states" to be exemplary (as "tokens") of "types" of "general modes of engagement" or "personal processes" among Marquesans. The model of Marquesan ethnopsychology is an "array" of four "process"-types, representing all four permutations ($+/+$, $+/0$, $0/+$, and $0/0$) of the distinctive features "boundary" and "self-concept." The model "maps the assumptions Marquesans draw on to define 'concern', 'lust', and the like" (1985:98). Kirkpatrick shows that the four "process"-types, and their key (as well as lesser) lexical-categorical "tokens," can serve to describe Marquesan expectations about events and predicaments in everyday life, especially as these expectations change through the life cycle.

Note that the analysis depends on the ethnographer and the native focusing their attention on the same segments of speech. The informant's expression translated as "That's ka'oha" requires that Marquesan speakers be able to provide the equivalent of the English glossing routine

$$S[1] + \ldots S[n] +$$
$$S[n+1] \text{ (Demonstrative} + \text{[to be]} + \text{NP)}$$

in which the Demonstrative in $S[n+1]$ is a discourse anaphor for all of $S[1] + \ldots S[n]$, the verb 'to be' in $S[n+1]$ has a metasemantic sense, and the NP in $S[n+1]$ is what is being glossed. The formula must devolve on a salient linguistic focus, typically lexical and nominal, that can be reflected on by both native and ethnographer. Further, the glossing routine rests on a transitivity of reference, such that the routine works when S[1] + . . . S[n] provide a concrete referent – ideally approximating what we might dub an "ostension-cartoon," since the nearer it comes to something we could draw a picture of, the better it works – with 'that' referring as anaphor to the picture, and finally, with the lexical focus as equivalent (via 'to be') to 'that'. By such procedures, an initial glossary that maps words to scenes can be uncovered; as Kirkpatrick says, the "terms are treated as mapping realities," and the analysis rests on the native and the ethnographer sharing the assumption that this is how a metasemantic exercise should proceed.

If the ethnographic semantic strategy – words (now "key vernacular terms") as labels for things – persists, where in the turn to "natural discourse" (Kirkpatrick and White 1985:23) does the innovation lie? It lies, first, in the nature of the referents. In part because "the emotions" famously fail as tangible objects for ostensive reference, "emotion words" instead are said to refer to or "point to" "emotion concepts," which in turn are said to encode knowledge about social action. Thus:

> The authors in this volume repeatedly analyze emotion words . . .
> for what they say, implicitly or explicitly, about interactive situations. . . . We view emotion words . . . as guideposts to cultural knowledge about social and affective experience. . . . '[L]oneliness', *vivi'io*, and *awumbuk* differ largely in the ways the situation of an isolated person is understood to be problematic in American, Marquesan, and Baining culture.[4]

The "key [emotion] terms" serve as labels for chunks of native theory – "webs of associative knowledge" – about the individual as social actor, as evaluator of the moral propriety, and so on of surrounding events. They help the native describe social interaction; they provide the ethnographer with a name for part of the native theory about social interaction. As "terms" they name, and as "concepts" they are, "prototypical event scenarios," "schema-" or "script-"like microsocial guidelines.

Such a word-to-concept-to-scene mapping, however, is just reference of a different kind, with such "prototypical scenarios" replacing plants and animals. But in the rendering of such maps of models, we find as well a commentary about how the "key terms" may be "used." The microsocial scenario turns out to be, for a "key term," both its referent and the arena for its appropriate instancing. So, the second innovation seems to lie in an account of usage; an understanding of "natural discourse" takes the form of a menu that tells you when a term may be pulled out of its glossary and deployed. For "key emotion words," this kind of account aims to capture the native calculus about the conditions that must be met before a certain interpersonal state of affairs – an insult or a death, for example – warrants the "use" of certain words. The analysis then shows how a plurality of these calculi is a local model of and for interpersonal life.

Certainly, we find in this view a richer account of reference than the one provided by the earlier ethnographic semantics. Because the conditions for the use of "emotion words" engage the most intricate local presuppositions about the person as social (e.g., moral, political) actor, those words may be the best, or at least the most parsimonious, metaphors of native provenance for any "person-centered ethnography," and perhaps for ethnography generally.

Yet, for all the benefits that accrue to our specifying the conditions for the use of "key [ascriptive] terms," our doing so does not amount to a proper account of "natural discourse." For all the counsel that we attend to "everyday talk," the anthropology of "the emotions" in the mid-1980s has provided too little exemplification of how actual conversations proceed. The "key terms" are seldom contextualized in the grammar or in the speech situation. They are, as many things informants say are, metasemantic acts of revelation; they reveal a "concept" or "category," and they exemplify the correct usage of the word that names that "concept" or "category," thereby telling us something about the native theory of the word's contextual appropriateness in instances of reference. Such a metasemantics of appropriate lexical usage contains a commentary about everyday life of a sort that yesterday's ethnographic semantics did not provide. It appears to be an account of "natural discourse" because it tells us how words refer to everyday life and tells us when they might be useful in that life. As such, it is a familiar species of metapragmatics: a reflection on what you can do with words.

Once again, a metasemantics of this sort is not a contextualization but a recontextualization of the linguistic datum. From the relatively safe terrain on which native and ethnographer cooperate in a lexical metasemantics, the ethnographer imposes on the glossary so obtained the demand that it serve at once as a description of situated discourse and as the native theory about persons in social interaction. The first demand is met when words that refer to scenes are shown to be instanced in discourse. The second is met when a collocation of the conceptual essences of a family of terms is said to be a model of social life. This dual recontextualization reduces situated discourse to discourse about situations, and discourse about situations to word reference only. Interested human interaction appears as one of the mapped realities. Instead of exemplifying contextualized language use, investigators take word reference to be what language can be used for.

In recontextualizing language, ethnographers attribute agency to words. Words "say" things: Recall Kirkpatrick and White's observation that emotion words are analyzed "for what they say, implicitly or explicitly, about interactive situations."[5] The ethnographer gives the native ethnopsychology the shape of one of his or her own metapragmatic metaphors: An ethnopsychology is a list of words, each of which possesses an agentive power to refer, to "tell a story." The theory is packaged in words, and the words describe social life.

Alongside the many expressions in our current literature in which the key terms are the subjects for verbs of speaking such as 'to tell', 'to say', and 'to talk (about)' are expressions in which the terms/concepts take English psychological predicates. Kirkpatrick's claims that *'haka'ika'* "impels" and "inhibits" (1985:89), and that *'ka'oha'* can be "experienced" and "enacted" (1985:89), are among many examples.[6] On occasion, local notions about motivation are appealed to, but this appeal seldom takes the most reasonable tack, which would be to examine the verbal predicates that the nouns take in the original language, among other facts about their grammatical contexts. Most often these ethnographic predications slide ambiguously between that sense in which they would figure in any anthropological account about the enactment of an "underlying model" and that sense in which emotion "states" would manifest themselves in a local ethnopsychology about the enactment of internal states.

Just as our historical practice of enshrining noun families is well established in the domain of "the emotions," thus making our metalinguistic habits especially tenacious there, so there is another fact about "the emotions" *chez nous* that infiltrates our accounts. When we ask that the metasemantic glossary not only refer to the social world but also embody native cognition about it, we risk smuggling into the account what we elsewhere assert is peculiar to our own local ethnopsychology.

In the current picture, the key words have unique conceptual qualities, and these in turn constitute, or at least populate, the native ethnopsychological theory. So transfigured, they become the contents of an "underlying model." Our ethnopsychology intrudes when the underlying cognitive status of the ethnopsychology-as-model – recall Kirkpatrick's claim that "the model maps the assumptions Marquesans draw on to define 'concern', 'lust', and the like" – is confounded with our own ethnopsychological understanding of "the emotions" as underlying forces. The special risk of an "underlying model" account of "the emotions" is that we already conceive of "the emotions" as "underlying" our lives; we have trouble sustaining the distinction between the model's governance of life, as a scientific abstraction, and "the emotions' " governance, which as a local theory is ours and may or may not be theirs.

Grammar and indexical pragmatics, minimally

To the question that is the title of their 1982 essay, "Does the Concept of the Person Vary Cross-Culturally?," R. A. Shweder and E. J. Bourne answer, emphatically, "yes." Their concern is "with other people's conceptions of the person and ideas about the self." They aim to "interpret an alien mode of social thought," bearing the global description "concrete, undifferentiated, context-specific, or occasion-bound thinking," and

> culminating in the view that specific situations determine the moral character of a particular action, that the individual person *per se* is neither an object of importance nor inherently worthy of respect, that the individual as moral agent ought not be distinguished from the social status s(he) occupies; a view that, indeed, the individual as an abstract *ethical* and *normative* category is not to be acknowledged. (1982:97; emphases in the original)

Although the authors' focus is "the concept of the context-dependent person," I take the issues they raise about ascriptions of personality and character broadly speaking to be essentially the same as the ones we might raise about affect more narrowly.

The authors conducted interviews with seventeen American and seventy Indian (Orissan) informants. The American informants came from three groups, in each of which informants were acquainted with one another; each informant was asked, with reference to another member of the group, "How would you characterize so-and-so's personality?" Indian informants described "up to three friends, neighbors, or workmates" in response to the request translated as "Tell me in depth about so-and-so's character, nature, and behavior."

The responses of Shweder and Bourne's informants to these queries were coded along two dimensions: "context-dependent reference" versus "context-free reference" and "action reference" versus "abstract trait reference," with the latter glossed also as "does" versus "is" "reference." The result about differences in "modes of thinking" rests on statistical differences between Oriyas and Americans along these two dimensions. The dimensions, in turn, represent aggregate sums of judges' more specific ratings of fragments of informants' responses.

Shweder and Bourne's coding scheme captures a number of overt linguistic features of their informants' responses, but these coded features do not stand convincingly for nontrivial kinds of cultural differences in ascriptive practices. The coding categories capture the presence versus absence of some simple English grammatical categories, but these are at best oblique indices of the cultural construction of person concepts. To see how this might be the case, we need to retrace the journey from linguistic data to cultural account.

Oriyas are said to have a "context-dependent person concept"; their "attention is directed towards the behavioral context in which particular behavioral instances occurred." Oriya "context dependence" is a gloss on the statistical preponderance among Oriyas' responses of five kinds of "contextual qualifications." The units of informants' responses coded as either "qualified" or not were "clauses," each of which "contained no more than one subject-predicate-object sequence" (1982:112). When we examine "clauses" coded as "qualified,"[7] we can see that "context dependence" is a conclusion based on the presence of what are standardly called (a) prepositional phrases or (b) time and place adverbials. By contrast, the "context-independence" of Americans rests on the paucity of these constituents. So, among these examples that the authors provide,

(a(i)) 'He is honest with others'
(b(i)) 'Last year he did favors frequently'
(c(i)) 'She is stubborn'
(d(i)) 'He is verbally abusive'

the first two are "context dependent" and the latter two are "context independent."

Consider these sentences semantically, leaving (b(i)) to the side for now. As speakers of English, we will intuit that

(a(ii)) 'He is honest'
(c(ii)) 'She is stubborn with others'
(d(ii)) 'He is verbally abusive with others'

hardly differ from the members of the first set. The complement phrases that the constructions in (a), (c), and (d), namely

(e) (Personal Pronoun) + (to be [present]) +
(Adjective of ascription) . . .

allow are all of the form

(f) . . . + (Preposition) + (Object NP)

where all such Object NPs must be animate and sentient,[8] that is, *mini-mally* capable of perceiving the ascribed quality. '[W]ith others' makes overt the unmarked case of such Object NPs, as animate, sentient, and *human*, in distinction to the marked

(g) 'He is verbally abusive towards his dog'

and, additionally, makes overt the unmarked case of Subject NPs, as animate, intentional (or at least responsible), and human, ruling out the marked

(h(i)) 'He's ('She's'?) stubborn'

where 'he' is anaphoric for a lawn mower that will not start, and the like, since

(h(ii)) 'He's stubborn with others'

cannot be used with inanimate or nonresponsible antecedent subjects.

At least in this sample of sentences, then, the distributional facts, the facts about the contribution of structure to meaning, concerning 'with others' tell us so far that its overt instancing picks out referentially the unmarked case of human Subject and Object for sentences in which certain adjectives of ascription appear. We ought to expect a similar pattern for constructions that contain other ascriptive adjectives that require the referential disambiguation of human versus nonhuman subjects and objects.

'[To be] 'honest' [with]', of course, seems to require human subject. In addition, for most speakers, who find

(a(iii)) (?) 'He's honest with his dog'

unacceptable, it requires human object as well. In this case, the referential contribution of 'with others' rests only on its contrast with such constructions as

(a(iv)) 'He's honest with me'

for just those discourse contexts in which the speaker has already established a contrast between 'others' and 'me'. In the absence of such a context, 'with others' once again merely makes overt the unmarked case of human complement objects. On such grounds, we can conclude that for certain ascriptive adjectives, 'with others' just makes lexically overt what is *entailed*, semantically, by the adjective.

When considering (a(i)) against (a(ii)), we might ask questions about the discourse contexts in which they occur. In doing so, we will probably want to consider how such contrast pairs index the greater versus lesser authority of the speaker to ascribe character to the third party, and in particular how the speaker's access to the relevant evidence imparts that authority. To see how messy, and at the same time how important, these questions are, let us return to (b(i)), 'Last year he did favors frequently'.

What do speakers of English need to know in order to know whether (b(i)) is a "contextually qualified" attribution? In particular, what do they need to know in order to judge it "more qualified" than either of the following?

 (b(ii)) 'He does favors'
 (b(iii)) 'He did favors'[9]

Minimally, they need to know three things: (1) the kind of stress the sentence received when uttered; (2) the ratio between last year as a unit of time and the period of time that the speaker and addressee can presuppose the speaker's access to evidence about the third party's behavior; and (3) the length of time from the end of last year to the moment of speaking.[10]

Let us consider a simplified example,

 (b(iv)) 'Last year he did favors'

which by all accounts is also codable as "contextually qualified" in the Shweder and Bourne study. The adverbial 'last year' in (b(iv)) is unstressed when it merely contributes to what is indexed by the selection of the past tense of 'to do', namely, the location of the referent of the verb phrase in time vis-à-vis the moment of speaking. We can imagine a context in which an interlocutor just asks when the favors were done. But 'to do' in (b(iv)) can have a relatively aspectual sense, as (a kind of insinuation of) nondurative and completive aspect, in certain contexts, such as in response to 'Has he *ever* done favors (. . . in his *life*)?' Presumably this sense will be signaled in the speaker's response by stress on the adverbial 'last year'. With stress so placed, the speaker indexes something about the scope of his or her claims to having evidence for the predication. By delimiting the evidentiary claims at the same time that he or she asserts that the third party does indeed do favors, the speaker falsifies the interlocutor's implicit 'He has never done favors' while at the same time cooperates with the addressee by suggesting that the speaker has not witnessed the third party doing many favors. In other words, the speaker licenses the addressee to take the speaker's delimited exposure to the relevant evidence as evidence for a delimited ascription – the one the addressee seems to want – without the speaker's having to make such a predication referentially. The adverbial stress forces a pragmatic pun that rests on the sustained ambiguity between an (indexical) evidentiary delimitation (of how much the speaker claims to know) and a referential one (of how many favors there have been and of how durative, or completive, or iterative is the third party's tendency to perform them). Discursively, the former delimitation insinuates the latter.

Fortunately, there are facts about the speech situation that the addressee can invoke in disambiguating the stressed-adverbial pun form of (b(iv)). These are the facts I noted earlier in (2) and (3). Where the ratio in (2) approaches 1 (the speaker and addressee presuppose that the speaker knew the third party for one year, and that year was last year), and where the conversation takes place in January (or in the early summer, in U.S. academic contexts), there the adverbial imparts a maximally durative and noncompletive sense to the verb phrase. In this case, the pun can be disambiguated confidently in the direction of what, if we have to, we can call a "contextually nonqualified" attribution or reference. There is no reason for the addressee to interpret the speaker as wanting to delimit the scope of his or her claims to the evidence; equivalently, we can say that the indexical contribution of adverbial stress is minimal in this case.

At another extreme, in cases where the ratio in (2) approaches zero (participants presuppose the speaker's many years of knowledge about the third party) and where the speech situation occurs in December (April, say, in the academy), the addressee's appeal to such facts yields a different kind of disambiguation. Here the addressee will know that a certain kind of speech event has taken place, one bearing the folk label 'damning with faint praise'. In this case as well, stress on the time adverbial cannot be taken to index an evidentiary delimitation. It has instead the curious indexical function of signaling to addressee that the action referred to in the verb phrase is, in fact, the opposite of what it appears to be; that it is nondurative, noniterative, or completive – in short, rare.[11]

The two extreme cases I have pointed to seem to be the only safe grounds on which the addressee can manage a *purely referential* delimitation of the verb phrase; one of these cases we could gloss as "contextually nonqualified" and the other as "contextually qualified." These also happen to be, with good reason, the cases in which adverbial stress does not matter. In the vast terrain between the two extremes, the addressee must locate the expression in some cell of a matrix that maps (1) stress, against the ratio in (2), against the length of time in (3). The addressee does so just because the utterance in every one of these cells sustains an ambiguity between the evidentiary and the referential senses of the ascription in its verb phrase.

A proper analysis of the relations among tense, aspect, and explicit adverbial phrases, as grammatical phenomena the distribution of which both contributes to reference and indexes a variety of speech situations, lies beyond the purposes of this chapter.[12] To simplify, let us return to the particular context defined by the queries Shweder and Bourne put to their informants. There is every reason to think that informants' responses are simultaneously evidentiary and more strictly referential, with certain important constructions – indeed, many of the ones coded as "qualifications" – seeming to foreground the former function. In particular (and leaving translation issues to the side for the moment), the request to the Oriyas, "Tell me in depth about so-and-so's character, nature, and behavior," would seem to enjoin a maximal expansion for evidentiary purposes of every kind of predication, from complements that merely spell out what is referentially redundant (' . . . honest with others'), to complements that are simply required by the verb (consider 'he makes fun . . . ', which is awkward in English without some explicitly named object), to adverbials of time and place.

By giving 'with others' and other prepositional phrases and 'frequently' and other adverbials the notation "contextual qualification," and then taking the latter to be "context dependence," Shweder and Bourne rename a grammatical phenomenon a cognitive one, and this in turn an anthropological one. The renaming results on our metapragmatic intuition that any overt expansion of a minimal subject-verb-object string must be in the service of "better" or "more precise" reference, of a sharper picking out of objects in the world. We intuit this even when, by virtue of our lexical (in relations of entailment) and grammatical (in the governance of complement phrases) semantics, we can be said already safely to "know" much of what our overt expansion will seem to specify.

If the Shweder and Bourne coding scheme cannot distinguish a verb phrase expanded for pure referential delimitation from one expanded just because the grammar governs its expansion, from one expanded to index informants' evidentiary authority, from one expanded for other indexical reasons – having to do, for example, with the etiquette of disclosure (it being in certain contexts proper and in others improper to let on that you have seen the evidence) – and cannot unpackage analytically the standard case in which these functions coexist, then the ascriptive utterances they have collected cannot support the set of conclusions about "world view" and "mode of thought" that the authors propose. In particular, because overtly minimal ascriptive phrases can be expanded on grammatical and/or indexical grounds, and because such expansions are in many cases less referentially delimiting than unexpanded phrases, the statistical prevalence of these expansions among Oriyas cannot set us on a path that leads to "occasion-bound thinking" or to the "ethical and normative" irrelevance of the "abstract" "individual."

Conversation, minimally

In the foregoing, I have looked at Shweder and Bourne's analysis of what they call "descriptive phrases." Now I argue that this abstraction from language is as radical as the ethnographic semantic abstraction of lexemes and the ethnographic metasemantic abstraction of "key terms."

If the semantic and referential (and then cultural) consequences of the surface expansion of clause constituents may be trivial, so too can the fact of a clause's *non*expansion (what we might call the "nonqualified" American model, in the context of this study) be trivial. The reason is that referential delimitations can be made across clause boundaries, and as well across sentence and turn-at-speech boundaries. The subtleties of distinguishing referential from evidentiary and other indexical delimitations remain. Consider:

I. A: 'He is very loving toward his children.'
II. A: 'He is very loving, the kind of guy who's always showing affection, you know, like for his children.'
III. A: 'He is very loving. You should see the things he does for his children.'
IV. A: 'He is very loving.'
    B: 'I've never felt that way about him.'
    A: 'Have you ever seen him with his children on weekends?'

For Shweder and Bourne, I. must be a "qualified" clause, II is two clauses, one "qualified" and the other "nonqualified," III gets the same analysis as II, and IV has just one ascriptive clause, which must be "nonquali-fied."

Yet, our native speaker intuition that 'A' has predicated essentially the same thing(s) of 'him' in all of I–IV is sound. With a view to the kinds of conversations people actually have when they ascribe things to persons, our analysis ought to be able to capture all of these cross-clause, cross-sentence, and cross-turn-at-speech continuities. These will ex-ploit the structural facts of anaphora and ellipsis (among others); these, in turn, will interact with such features of conversational pragmatics as the structure of query-and-response routines, especially as these engage local expectations about the proper relations between abstraction and evidence; and these latter relations will have a specific shape for specific kinds of ascription, against the background of what the speaker and addressee presuppose of each other's knowledge of the object of ascrip-tion.

None of this can be discerned in the Shweder and Bourne abstraction of "descriptive phrases." Note that IV must, by any account, be seen as the maximally referentially delimiting ascription. Supposing such a con-versation to be coded in the current study, you would not know this fact. Its first turn would be analyzed as "nonqualified," and its last two turns could not be analyzed.[13]

The Shweder and Bourne study not only abstracts from connected discourse in its analysis but also forecloses it in its initial task design. American informants provided twenty written "descriptive phrases or sentences"; Oriyas responded orally "in as many or as few ways as they chose."[14] So, a two-sentence string such as III is possible for Oriyas as an answer in connected oral discourse to "Tell me in depth about . . . ," but would seem not to be possible for Americans: The second sentence is a poor candidate for a list of twenty distinct written answers to "How would you characterize so-and-so's personality?" If in utterances $n + \ldots$ in natural discourse the speaker will adduce "concrete" evidence for an "abstraction" in n (or if the speaker concludes "abstractly" in n what was predicated "concretely" in $m, m + \ldots$), the current study would seem to be able to capture such sequences for Oriyas but not for Amer-icans.

Semantics, reference, pragmatics, and ideology

By 1980, it seemed that if an abstract, ahistorical, and desiccated picture of such objects as "culture," "knowledge," and "text," along with an understanding of such objects as "person," "self," "author," and "reader" as nonagentive, disinterested, and unwitting, had been founded on a certain semiotic of "reference," "signification," and "classification," then it stood to reason that a human science of the concrete, processual, and interested would require a new semiotic. In "discourse" we found both a reconfigured object, a real, palpable manifestation of "culture," and so on, and a new semiotic, "discourse" seeming in the first instance to name some kind of linguistic object.

Yet, the advantages for the human sciences that might lie in the apparent nearness of "discourse" as situated activity to "discourse" as (semiotic foundation for) analytic abstraction have rarely been realized. For outside of linguistics proper, "discourse" has scarcely been conceived of as a semiotic datum at all. It has served as a metalinguistic metaphor whose use indexes its author's commitment to the idea that what is cultural is not timeless and disembodied artifact, but instead is like something you might say to me, on a certain day for a certain reason. But when everything cultural is *like* everyday speech, then everyday speech itself is a datum of uncertain status.

In this chapter, I have argued that in the first generation of anthropological approaches to ascriptive discourse, a passage was made from abstracted parts of speech to ideation and culture at large that bypassed the scene that is their true intersection – everyday discourse – and that this scene was bypassed even by investigators who named it as their place of work. I have argued that the ordinary context of everyday life emerged not in contextualized speech but in two kinds of recontextualization: one in which abstracted nouns were glossed in such a way as to establish that they referred to, and hence could be instanced in, everyday life (Rosaldo, Kirkpatrick); and another in which the statistical distribution of abstracted phenomena of surface grammar was said to establish the distribution across cultures of theories of the person as more versus less embedded in everyday predicament, with these theories corresponding to the literal propositional content of the abstracted phenomena (Shweder and Bourne). I have said that such recontextualizations are metasemantic and metapragmatic exercises, with a long history not least in the ascriptive domain, and against whose potential for fostering rich ethnographic description we must counterpose the risks of infiltration by the ethnographer's ethnopsychology.

The risks arise for two reasons. First, when we discover only isolable, nominal foci in our ethnographic metasemantic practices, we commit ourselves in our ethnographic writing to embedding these foci in our own grammar, and that grammar encodes an ethnopsychology in some measure. Second, a pervasive metalinguistic metaphor of our own ascriptive practices – indeed, of our own culture of "concepts," "emotional" and not – maps unique nouns to unique mental or underlying quiddities; much of our own ethnopsychology emerges in reflection on the referential power and appropriateness of isolable foci.

It was Whorf who proposed that facts of these two kinds are analytically distinct but not independent. In grammar, analogy of distribution entails analogy of meaning; the *semantics* of any distributional class, such as a class of nouns, emerges in the scope of its possible locations in a grammar of sentences. Equivalently, any class is a class only by virtue of its equivalency of distribution. By contrast, an *ideology* of reference is an oblique reflection on the semantics of apparent classes of salient segments of speech, understood not as it emerges in grammar but as it might denote objects in the world.

For the "emotions" or any other proposed class, then, we need to see that it is only in an *ideology* of reference that "key terms" will select unique quiddities or concepts. A mapping of this kind will be a true ethnopsychological datum for those cultures, such as the culture of speakers of American English, in which it is an attested practice. Where ethnopsychological utterances take the form of metalinguistic ideologies of referential function – everywhere, according to the Whorfian hypothesis – we need to examine them in their local forms.

It is not possible that the "key" segments on which natives reflect will everywhere be nouns. Nor is it possible that, to the extent that the grammatical segmentations are similar, the content of native reflection on those segments will be similar. This is so in part because the glosses of those segments will be unique, as the work of the past decade has established, but more centrally because the grammar that surrounds those segments is also unique, and it is in that grammar that meaning (equivalently, the possibility of glossing) is to be found. This *semantic* level of analysis must be seen as distinct from local (and transcultural) practices of lexical glossing; it is foundational of the latter, meaningful in its own right, and only obliquely accessible to native reflection.

As Silverstein (1984) has established, the (Whorfian) analogies or (Jakobsonian) equivalencies that inhere in a grammar emerge in the real time of conversation in the maintenance of topic–comment cohesion – of *reference* we can say. One of the curiosities of the discourse functionalism of the last decade is that it has seen itself as finding functions that would replace or overrule "reference," an impossible task should everyday speech be our object. But instead of recovering "reference" in ideologies of lexical appropriateness, we need to look more closely at actual conversations, from which we will be able to uncover foci of native interest in the parallelisms of referential cohesion.

Why do this? The contributors to this volume have discovered, in the turn to "discourse," that persons in other cultural settings provide multiplex homes for "the emotions" and many neighbors – such as somatics, characterology, behavioral predilection, belief, cognition, and rights – and their investigations have uncovered important forms of neighborly engagement. But as with other anthropological domains – consider "kinship" – so with "the emotions" has the excitement of expanding the domain (into "morality," "politics," "the body," and elsewhere) been accompanied by debates and worries over its continuing integrity. Moreover, the tension between a focal and an expanding domain is mirrored in a tension between "the emotions" as anthropological construct and "the 'emotions' " as Euro-American quotative, again a customary anthropological tension, and an issue on which I have taken a side typographically in this chapter. One way to resolve these tensions is to examine how the requirements of referential maintenance in conversation foster, but at the same time for any language delimit, the scope of the neighboring semantic terrain into which a speaker may turn the conversation. For an introduced topic, the *semantics* of grammar not only allows but circumscribes and even unifies what counts as coherent comment. Although such language- and culture-specific considerations may not everywhere yield "emotions," they should yield true local domains.

At the same time, the turn to "discourse" and especially to instead-of-"denotational" functions of speech risks an unprincipled expansion of "the emotions" (and any other) domain by the lights of the ethnographer's so-called speech-act theoretical classification by intents and purposes. There can be, I submit, no tactical use of the "speech-act" sort (judging, negotiating, complimenting, ostracizing, sympathizing, excusing, assuaging, pleading, flirting, self-presenting, and so on) that the passions will not be found to subserve, anywhere. To locate a *pragmatics* of ascriptive discourse, the most we can do is (1) investigate indexicals of a sort that we define typologically as "emotive";[15] (2) examine how the conversational deployment of shifting topic–comment foci not only maintains reference but also shifts the evidentiary requirements and expectations of ascriptions, at the same time turning the conversation in a direction that is locally construed as more versus less polite/rude, knowable/ineffable, sufficient/insufficient, and so on, compared with where it hitherto had been; and (3) take the local articulation of rationales for speaking ascriptively as a datum in its own right. For this last, we will need to keep in mind that the native metapragmatics of nonreferential functions is as expandable as ours is, and hence will not map uniquely onto "discourses" of unique kinds.

Notes

1. White (1978) and Lutz (1982) are two efforts to apprehend the language of ascription that have roots in ethnographic semantics, although the object of Rosaldo's criticism is the wider ethnographic semantics–cognitive anthropological zeitgeist.
2. But certainly not in cognitive models about ordinary process: Rosaldo's "emotional terms" are intended as public symbols, by appeal to (Rylean-cum-) Geertzian and Wittgensteinian defenses of the public. Aside from cognitive anthropology, another object of Rosaldo's criticisms is structuralism, seen also as a lifeless and too orderly abstraction of mental objects from public life. Although the entire history of Saussurean structuralism must be understood as an effort to isolate a public semiotic from a private mentalism, the coincidence in the 1960s and 1970s of American anthropology's cognitive turn and a decided mentalist turn in Levi-Strauss's structuralism, coupled with the iconic likenesses on paper between cognitive anthropology's trees and the like and Levi-Strauss's structures, made it possible by 1980 to attack the supposed mentalisms, with attendant methodologies, of both schools with the same stroke of the pen.
3. All of the quoted terms in the foregoing paragraph come from Rosaldo (1980:47, 49, 56–7, 161, 188, 217).
4. All three citations are from Kirkpatrick and White (1985:17).
5. See also N. Quinn, quoted in Kirkpatrick and White (1985:20): "In sum, the word 'commitment' tells a complex story about American marriage."
6. "Impels" and like terms are predicates typically assigned to "the emotions," but see also "Haka'ika involves a recognition that others may disapprove of . . . one's state or activity" (loc. cit.), which assumes that the term must be not only "state" but also conceptual microcosm.
7. Although several other kinds of coders' "qualification" categories are given, these are not included in the aggregate category, as defined on p. 116, which includes these: (a) "reference to a specific individual, often denoted by a proper or common noun (e.g., 'he gets angry with his father')"; (b) "reference to a specific group of others (e.g., 'he makes fun of his family')"; (c) "reference to people or others in general (e.g., 'he is honest with others')"; (d) "temporal [qualification]: statement of when or how frequently the attribute occurs (e.g., 'last year he did favors frequently')"; and (e) "[qualification by] locale: statement of where or in what location the attribute occurs (e.g., 'At school he puts on a front')" (1982:113).

   Among Oriyas, clauses rated as "contextually qualified" outnumber those rated "no qualification" by 2.53 to 1 (given as 3 to 1 in the text); Americans display a 1 to 1 ratio on this measure.
8. Although ['about' + (Object NP)], e.g., 'He is honest about financial mat-

ters', and relative clauses, e.g., 'He is honest where money is concerned', present exceptions.

9. Shweder and Bourne's (b(i)) appears to be "contextually qualified" by contrast with either (b(ii)) or (b(iii)), one or the other of which is the "subject-predicate-object" string coders presumably have access to, as speakers of English, as the "nonqualified" referential minimum that lies behind (b(i)). On the basis of the examples provided, it seems that either would do; no example is given in which mere specification of tense counts as "contextual qualification."

10. A fourth fact, the ratio of (2) to (3), is also relevant but makes things too complicated for our purposes here.

11. At the greatest extreme, adverbial stress becomes redundant for these ends; consider 'In December of his first term in office he frequently did good work', where stress on the time adverbials (along with winks, arched eyebrows, etc.) can only be interpreted as indexing the speaker's low estimation of the addressee's pragmatic competence.

12. By now, linguistically astute readers will have recognized that my discussion of examples has been a native grammarian's ad hoc intentionalist caricature of what are, strictly speaking, structural facts about derivation and distribution.

13. I leave aside here the classic statistician's problem about the independence of cases, the shoals on which so many attempts, including the current one, to draw psychological, sociological, and cultural conclusions from summed occurrences of abstracted language segments founder. Grammar, and anything we would want to call "discourse," conspire, if they do anything, to make speech segments nonindependent cases. Readers probably will have recognized already that what is wrong with the analysis of, say, I. versus III is not only that III is less "qualified" than I., but also that it sums to twice as many cases as I.

14. Shweder and Bourne are forthcoming about the nontandem design of their Indian and American studies, although I think they underestimate the importance of the differences between the two. They deal fully with the question of whether differences in education or caste would account for differences among subgroups of Indian informants, but they dismiss too easily the possibility that education, and especially the American within-the-academy discourse setting – the American informants were counseling psychologists, University of Chicago undergraduates, and nursery school teachers, all three of which groups we ought to expect to traffic in "abstract" and "context-free" ascriptions, especially when responding to queries from University of Chicago researchers – might account for the differences across cultures.

15. I have said little about two convergent traditions (with Hymes 1962 establishing their convergence) that do not take lexical discovery to be the key to the "language of emotion." One is modeled on Sapir's work (1927 especially), and the other is Praguean; both identify largely nonlexical indexicals of speech, usually called "expressive devices," that subserve an "emotive function." It is important to see that such efforts rest explicitly on universal-typological assumptions as defined in advance by the observer. They analyze indexicals but not semantics and reference as local phenomena; they are a different species of analysis from the one I have taken up in this chapter. Irvine draws a similar distinction between "the way people report or describe emotion" and "what they actually rely upon to impute

the emotion" (1982:34), and offers an interesting analysis in the Sapir–Prague tradition of the latter as "modes of affective expression" in Wolof. But there is no reason to presume that the "emotion[s]" on both sides of this distinction are conspecific beasts, and that expressive indexicals are to the lexicon and native reflections thereon as one "channel" or "means" to another of "expressing" the same underlying quality (Irvine 1982:32; although Irvine predicts that the two levels of analysis are only obliquely related, I argue that we should start with the working assumption that they are not related at all, executing the two levels of analysis at once only for what turn out to be duplex indexical-cum-semantic phenomena).

References

Hymes, Dell H. 1962. Linguistic Aspects of Cross-Cultural Personality Study. In B. Kaplan, ed., *Studying Personality Cross-Culturally.* Evanston, IL: Row, Peterson, pp. 313–59.

Irvine, Judith T. 1982. Language and Affect: Some Cross-Cultural Issues. In H. Byrnes, ed., *Contemporary Perceptions of Language: Interdisciplinary Dimensions.* Washington, DC: Georgetown University Press, pp. 31–47.

Kirkpatrick, John. 1985. Some Marquesan Understandings of Action and Identity. In G. M. White and J. Kirkpatrick, eds., *Person, Self, and Experience: Exploring Pacific Ethnopsychologies.* Berkeley: University of California Press, pp. 80–120.

Kirkpatrick, John, and Geoffrey M. White. 1985. Exploring Ethnopsychologies. In G. M. White and J. Kirkpatrick, eds., *Person, Self, and Experience: Exploring Pacific Ethnopsychologies.* Berkeley: University of California Press, pp. 3–32.

Lutz, Catherine. 1982. The Domain of Emotion Words on Ifaluk. *American Ethnologist* 9:113–28.

Lutz, Catherine, and Geoffrey M. White. 1986. The Anthropology of Emotions. *Annual Review of Anthropology* 15:405–36.

Rosaldo, Michelle Z. 1980. *Knowledge and Passion: Ilongot Notions of Self and Social Life.* Cambridge: Cambridge University Press.

Sapir, Edward. 1927. Speech as a Personality Trait. *American Journal of Sociology* 32:892–905.

Shweder, Richard A., and Edmund J. Bourne. 1982. Does the Concept of the Person Vary Cross-Culturally? In A. J. Marsella and G. M. White, eds., *Cultural Conceptions of Mental Health and Therapy.* Dordrecht: D. Reidel, pp. 97–137.

Silverstein, Michael. 1984. On the Pragmatic 'Poetry' of Prose: Parallelism, Repetition, and Cohesive Structure in the Time Course of Dyadic Conversation. In D. Schiffrin, ed., *Meaning, Form, and Use in Context: Linguistic Applications.* Washington, DC: Georgetown University Press, pp. 181–99.

White, Geoffrey M. 1978. Ambiguity and Ambivalence in A'ara Personality Descriptors. *American Ethnologist* 5:334–60.

White, Geoffrey M., and John Kirkpatrick, eds. 1985. *Person, Self, and Experience: Exploring Pacific Ethnopsychologies.* Berkeley: University of California Press.

9. Untouchability and the fear of death in a Tamil song

MARGARET TRAWICK

Introduction

This is a chapter about a song sung by Cēvi, a landless agricultural laborer living in the northern part of Madurai District in Tamil Nadu. Cēvi belongs to the Paṟaiyar jāti, one of the largest of the untouchable castes in South India. Paṟaiyars are untouchable (*tīṇḍā*) to higher castes because their traditional duties, still performed by them in this part of Tamil Nadu, include the handling and processing of human and animal feces and corpses. The Paṟaiyars of Cēvi's village perform these duties matter-of-factly and conscientiously, and in general are firm in their adherence to the established social values of Tamil villagers, even as they sometimes militantly seek to improve their rank and their economic situation vis-à-vis higher castes and landowners.[1] Cēvi is a young married woman of twenty-five and is the mother of four children, all sons.[2] She is also considered to be one of the best singers in the large village where she lives, although she is not a professional performer. She is one of the many thousands who contribute to, and draw from, the vast and variegated corpus of unwritten verbal art in Tamil Nadu.

The work of Cēvi's to be considered here is a hymn sung by her to and for the local Kuṟavar goddess Singammāḷ. Kuṟavars are another untouchable caste in Tamil Nadu, lower than the Paṟaiyars and untouchable even to them.[3] Kuṟavars live as migrant scavengers, claim Marathi ancestry, and distinguish themselves from the Tamil people surrounding them by noticeable features of dress, speech, and way of life. I shall say more about them presently.

Cēvi's performance of the hymn to Singammāḷ was recorded by my assistant, Kuppucāmi, a twenty-year-old male kinsman of Cēvi's, in the spring of 1984.[4] Kuppucāmi had explained to Cēvi that I was interested in "nonmovie, nonwritten" songs that were sung by people of that village, and had asked her in advance if she would agree to be recorded. She had obviously given some thought to the proposal, and perhaps had even rehearsed the song in advance, when Kuppucāmi returned to her house some weeks later with my portable cassette tape recorder. The recording session was quite formal, including a brief, audience-directed introductory dialogue between the performer and the "MC," as though for a radio program. Cēvi chose in particular this song as one she would sing to a Western audience.

Cēvi sang the hymn in a strong, clear voice. Her performance took nearly an hour. The name "Singammā" formed a constant refrain, repeated at the end of every line in the song. The name as Cēvi sang it was murmured, quiet, low in pitch, persistent, like a moan. Sometimes the "-mā" in "Singammā" quavered heavily, ending in a fall to a hanging tone, like a sob. It was as though Cēvi were feeling for Singammā. But Cēvi's voice never broke. Her performance was highly expressive but also strongly controlled – between the abandonment of wept singing and the expressionlessness of chant. In its precisely measured, trembling passion, it somewhat resembled classical South Indian music.

The story told by the song

The story of Singammā, as recounted in Cēvi's song, is stark and elliptical.[5] As it opens, we learn that Singammā is kept confined in the house by her brothers' wives. But one day, as she sees her brothers' wives coming, she "puts on different clothes" and slips off to the market to sell trinkets (a traditional occupation of Kuṟavars). Her brothers weep when they come home and find her missing. They go to the market, where Singammā is playing cymbals (*ciṅkipōḍḍu*) and selling songs at the dried-fish store. Her lame older brother (*noṇḍi aṇṇan*) meets her there but does not recognize her. Still in town at dusk, Singammā goes to a wedding feast, gathers up the leftover rice from discarded leaves there, and brings it back home in jars (Kuṟavars traditionally get the polluted, leftover food discarded at weddings). For punishment, her brothers send her to a house in the forest and make her stay there, "grinding and pounding with a mortar." All four brothers go into the house, pull the doors shut and lock them, and the mortar stone pounds. Then Singammā says: "The sun has set on our good caste; we are excluded from caste (*jātilēyum taḷḷuvaḍi*)."

The lame older brother's wedding day arrives. Singammā is to cook and serve at the wedding feast, but the pots of rice and milk won't boil for her – the sun will not allow it. (The Tamil festival of the sun, cele-brated around winter solstice time, is marked by the boiling of a rice-milk dish called *poṅkal*. If the pot boils over, it means that the sun will bless that family with abundance in the coming year. If the pot fails to boil over, it is an evil sign.)

Singammā is again locked in the house, "weeping in her heart." But at dusk she declares, "If my honor (*paṭṭi*) is destroyed, let the doors of the house stay shut, but if my honor is undestroyed, let them open." The doors open, and Singammā flees. Her brothers come home and ask where Singammā is, and their wives say, "A husband has married her and taken her away." The brothers then dig holes in the floor inside the house. The holes are to be Singammā's grave.

Singammā lies down to sleep, with her head on her mother's lap. Her mother tells her that because she is excluded from the caste and pots will not boil for her, her brothers are going to kill her. As she lies with her head in her mother's lap, she takes a louse comb in her hand and assumes the form of louse eggs. While she is in this form, her brothers pound rice for her mouth (rice is put in the mouth of a corpse before burial) and drop chicken and crow meat in the holes in which she is to be entombed. While the lame older brother weeps, they kill and dis-member (*kulaicukum*) her human body and bury it in the holes. Only the heart of the mother (*attā*) is not pleased by this act, says the song.

From Singammā's grave, a poisonous red oleander plant (*cevvaraḷi*) springs up. The lame older brother comes to the place where the olean-der has grown. A poisonous earthworm (*pūṉākam*) emerges from the oleander and tells the brother to build a palace there for Singammā. The brothers crumble the house and build a foundation on that site; when they do so, an oleander bud blossoms for Singammā. Then the lame older brother touches (*tīṇḍu*) the earthworm, which, in return, tells him a story. It says that it once lived in the house. It says that Singammā's brothers' wives saw it and told Singammā to catch it and take it away; both it and Singammā left the house, "weeping and sobbing." The earthworm concludes its story by saying, "Even if you build palaces, you may not stay. Only the lame older brother may stay."

All the brothers and their wives then come to that place to burn lime for mortar. As soon as they have burned and moistened the lime, build-ings grow up in that spot. A woman comes to live there, and when she does so, the building in which she lives "leans over with its founda-tion." Singammā then appears to the woman. The woman asks her where she comes from. Singammā replies, "I came from within the house itself." Then, as the song goes, Singammā, having emerged from within the house, "rising up high, speaking with unsheathed energy, wearing pearls," addresses her lame older brother, telling him, "You are the one who killed me, who saw my sin, who undid me. That which entered the house truly was. Tell me to rise up outside. Now I will stand up straight and show you." She leaves the house and goes outside; they raise her up. And the final stanza of the song says, "As soon as they raised you up, Singammā, your building, too, stood up tall."

Pollution and fear

A multitude of questions might be asked of this song. Here I will be asking three general categories of question. First, what is Cēvi *doing* when she sings this song to my tape recorder? If the song is, among other things, an act of self-expression, what is being expressed? In what does this self-expression consist? Why does it have to be done?

Second, of all the songs that Cēvi might have chosen to put on the tape recorder, why does she choose this one?

Third, given that the song is by an untouchable woman about a woman who is untouchable to her, and since it is a song about death, about being defiled and polluted, can the song tell us anything about the meaning of such pollution in South India, about how it feels to be beyond the pale?

Much has been written on the topic of "ritual pollution" in South Asia. The entire caste system, as well as the internal organization of castes, is said by some to be founded on this concept.[6] The pollution avoidance that separates caste from caste is often described by ethnographers as though it were a mechanical process with little affective content. A Brahman is said to cleanse himself of "ritual pollution" (after a death in the family, for instance, or after having touched a polluted person) by pouring water over his head; he does not really scrub himself, as he would if he were sprayed by a skunk or fell into a sewer. And yet, compulsive cleanliness often does go along with extreme orthopraxy among Hindus. Similarly, one searches in vain through the ethnographic literature for testimonies on the part of high-caste people concerning the gut revulsion they feel toward low-caste people. And yet if one asks, one finds that revulsion is there. It is much stronger in some individuals than in others, for no two people even in the same family have the same emotional makeup, but for all its variability, revulsion toward pollution and the polluted is a well-articulated, culturally sanctioned feeling in Tamil Nadu.

A response of revulsion to someone or something is called in Tamil *payam*, a word that we often translate into English as 'fear', for it means that, too. An ugly person is said to be 'fearsome', *payaṅkaramāka*, even by friends who know that the person is harmless. I have heard one woman say of another that she possesses 'fearsome beauty' (*payaṅkaramāna aṟaku*) – a statement that perhaps harks back to the ancient Tamil idea that a beautiful woman is dangerous; she may literally take a man's breath away. Beauty and death are closely associated in Tamil thought. Extreme attractiveness and extreme repulsiveness have the same dangerous emotional power and are often treated as transforms of each other. Both are to be avoided.

Anything that a person avoids may be said to be the object of *payam*. A man concerned for his reputation says that he fears (*payppaḍuvēn*) nothing but shame (*paṟi*). Thieving little boys are said to be fear inducing (*payaṅkaramāka*). A vegetarian man looking down on a plate of meat calls the sight that he sees and his feeling when he sees it fearsome (*payamāka*). Of a timid child, it is said that fear (*payam*) is part of its nature. A child afflicted with the evil eye is said to experience *payam*. A woman suffering chronic anxiety after the death of a child refers to her feeling as *payam*. If a person is suddenly frightened, he may become sick afterward as a consequence of *payam*. Demons lurking in the dark forest may kill their unwary victims by suddenly surprising them and inducing *payam* in them. This *payam*, the feeling of fear itself, is said to be what kills the demon afflicted.

Tamil *payam*, like English "fear," is a complex term whose meanings are varied and diffuse. To attempt to define it precisely would be a mistake. However, one can go so far as to say that Tamil *payam*, much more than English "fear," is a thing itself to be avoided. In the eyes of most Tamil people, *payam* appears to be not so much a healthy, life-preserving instinct as a dangerous, life-corroding disease.

If there is one feeling that goes with pollution, that feeling is surely *payam*. To submit to *payam* is to lose control, to come under another's power, to let part or all of one's life flow away. *Payam* is the feeling evoked by death, and it can cause more death to happen. To survive in the face of it, one must put some kind of fence around it or around oneself.

Paṟaiyars and Kuṟavars

Tamil Paṟaiyars are in a difficult situation, for in many South Indian village communities, they *are* this fence. They are untouchable to others because they deal with the substances of death, all those substances that are shunned by others in order that they may feel live and whole. According to the overwhelming consensus of the society of which they are part, Paṟaiyars' own living bodies *belong* among those substances of death. They *are* filth, merged with what is excreted and left behind. Hence they are avoided, feared, and despised.

One effective way that Paṟaiyars have found of dealing with this abject status is to deny it by passing it on to others, placing these others between themselves and death. Traditionally, the scapegoats for the Paṟaiyars have been Kuṟavars, who, because of their way of life, admirably fill this symbolic role. Although most Paṟaiyars are landless, hence impoverished and symbolically disembodied, Kuṟavars are even more conspicuously without a place. They have no fixed homes, no mud huts, but only rag tents and a territory through which they wander, a territory that in no sense belongs to them. Their regular haunts are train stations, bus stops, markets, and festivals – crossroads of every kind. The women in their daily rounds pick through garbage bins and gather rice off the *eccil-ilai*, the 'spittle leaves', thrown away by others after meals and feasts. This is not the desperate strategy of a starving few but the normal and highly visible way of life of the Kuṟavar community.

The word *kuṟavar*, 'hill dweller', is in modern times a polite name for a foraging community elsewhere called *kuruvikkāraṅka*. The latter name derives from the word for small fowl (*kuruvi*), which men of that community hunt. The commonest *kuruvi* of present-day Tamil Nadu is the aggressively greedy, noisy, and messy English sparrow. I have heard one Tamil woman say, on observing two English sparrows copulating, "You shameless thing; you will do it even to your own daughter." One implication of the name *kuruvikkārar* is that its bearers, like the birds they hunt, are lawless, dirty, and of no consequence.

In particular, however, Kuṟavars are known for hunting and eating scavenging beasts and birds, such as jackals and crows. In modern times, Kuṟavar men may still be seen wandering with their rifles through fields and wastelands, with crows their principal quarry. Kuṟavars are also known for keeping pigs, which feed on human excrement. Other castes also keep pigs, but Kuṟavars are the only people who will eat crows, for crows are, above all others, the birds of death. Crows, like some other birds, eat carrion. In ancient times, human corpses used to be offered by Tamils specifically to crows (*Tirumantiram* verse 191), and crows are still treated as the embodiment of dead ancestors and given offerings of rice on the festival day of *poṅkal*, which marks the end of winter, the season of the crow, and the return of the lifegiving sun. In Tamil the cry of the crow, *kā kā*, is a cry for protection (*kāppu*) and evokes images of feces (*kakka*), darkness, and the wandering wind (*kāṭṭu*).

Paṟaiyars are despised by other castes for eating the meat of cattle, the purest, most lifegiving of animals, whose destruction, therefore, is the gravest of sins. But as eaters of crows, Kuṟavars eat the eaters of death.

Finally, Kuṟavars also are thought to be sexually lawless. The term *ciṅki* in Tamil means both 'Kuṟavar woman' and 'whore' (the name Singammā, or *ciṅkammā* according to the system of transcription used in this paper, would be synonymous in Tamil with 'Kuṟavar woman'. *Singh* is a North Indian surname meaning 'lion', whence the Tamil word for lion, *ciṅkam*). The notion that Kuṟavar women sell their bodies in the market together with their trinkets is helped along by their different style of dress; they wear a kind of skirt and blouse instead of a sari. In songs sung by Paṟaiyars, Kuṟavars are stereotypically and mockingly accused of brother–sister incest.

For this reason, Cēvi's song came as a surprise to me. Rather than mocking or rejecting the Kuṟavar heroine, Cēvi's song shows deep sympathy for her. Rather than pushing the Singammā song to the margins of her repertory or giving it short shrift, Cēvi places it at center stage and honors it with a style of performance both formal and moving. Why?

An approach to the study of fear and pollution

In seeking an answer to this question, I have turned to a recent book by the French literary critic Julia Kristeva, entitled *Powers of Horror: An Essay on Abjection*, which discusses Indian thought (as represented by French ethnographers) at some length.[7] Kristeva's approach to literature, language, and culture is feminist, psychoanalytic, and semiotic.[8] In particular, she argues that language is, before all else, a sexual act: The formation of the speaking subject and its entry into the symbolic world are founded upon the division between masculine and feminine. I would not claim that the psychoanalytic-cum-semiotic approach elaborated by Kristeva is the only one that might throw light on the significance(s) of Cēvi's song, but I would suggest that this approach may be of great value to ethnographers interested in the relations between gender, language, and the construction of the self.

The basic premises of Kristeva's work might be summarized as follows:

Any human language consists of a set of conventions encoding ontology – how the world is, how it is supposed to be. These conventions are largely (in Saussure's terms) arbitrary and (in Peirce's terms) legislated. Such conventions join together to form a whole, a coherent system; at least they present the appearance of doing so. This seemingly whole and coherent system may be called the "symbolic world." It is the world of meaning and relations, of totality and law. It is also called (by Jacques Lacan) the "Law of the Father" (Le Nom du Père) because it is legislated, so it seems, by a distant and inaccessible authority. It is already there before one is born. The individual self has no say in its decrees.

Entry into this phallic, totalizing, symbolic world, the world of meaning created by the ancestors, begins with the subject–object distinction. The self, in order to exist and have meaning, must be delimited and defined. Self and not-self, subject and object, are defined against each other, as each other's opposites, each other's negations. Inasmuch as "there exist only differences" (Saussure), the self, the subject, can only be defined negatively, as *not* this or that. I am Jane; I am not Joan or John. I am little; I am not big. I am child, not mother or father. I am part of the world; I am not the world. I follow the rules; I do not make them.

The speaking subject, therefore, the self that knows language and its own name, is by its very inception not whole. It feels itself to be incomplete and fragmented. In this sense, it is castrated. It desires its opposite to make it whole again. It desires to embrace, to own and to be the symbolic-system-as-totality. It desires to become the father, to appropriate the code in its perfect wholeness. But it never achieves this end, because the perfect wholeness of the symbolic world is only an illusion and, just for this reason, stays always out of reach.

Prior, however, to the subject–object distinction, prior to the relation between self as part and the Law of the Father as whole, one dwells in another state, in a relation between what might be called the "proto-self" and the body of the mother from which one has not yet been fully separated. The body of the mother is different from the Law of the Father. The Law of the Father is an abstract code that governs the self through definition. The mother's body is a physical presence that controls the child through physical pressures.

In the presymbolic state, before the Law of the Father takes over, one has just been born. One has just been through "the immemorial violence with which a body becomes separated from another body in order to be" (Kristeva 1982:10). From here on out, one will keep oneself intact only by constantly repeating such extrications. Birth is the first abjection, the first casting out. What has been abjected and left behind is the body of the mother, which, however, will still threaten, as long as one has not fully separated from it, not just to take away a part of one's being (castration) but to engulf one's whole being entirely.

The body of the mother, therefore, is prior to and more powerful than the Law of the Father. The encompassing precondition of meaning, it threatens meaning itself.[9] If meaning is the totality composed of arbitrary, legislated distinctions, there is still this presymbolic state that points to the void upon which meaning is founded. Hence the detotalizing effect of the outcast, of that which has been expelled from the self at birth, but not quite completely. "The jettisoned object . . . lies outside, beyond the set, and does not seem to agree to the rules of the game. And yet, from its place of banishment, the abject does not cease challenging its master" (1982:2).

The abject is that which is lost; the object is that which is not yet obtained. The object is the Law of the Father. The abject, which precedes, encompasses, and threatens to overthrow the object, and with it all of significance, is first of all the body of the mother. At the other end of life, taking the place of the mother's body, is the corpse, from which also one is incompletely separated and which also defies meaning:

> The corpse does not *signify* death. . . . Without make-up or masks, refuse and corpses *show me* what I permanently thrust aside in order to live. These body fluids, this defilement, this shit is what life withstands, hardly and with difficulty, on the part of death. There, I am at the border of my condition as a living being. My body extricates itself, as being alive, from that border. Such wastes drop so that I might live until, from loss to loss, nothing remains in me and my entire body falls beyond the limit – *cadere*, cadaver.
>
> If dung signifies the other side of the border, the place where I am not and which permits me to be, the corpse, the most sickening of wastes, is a border that has encroached upon everything. It is no longer "I" who expel. "I" is expelled.
>
> . . . The corpse is the utmost of abjection. It is death infecting life. It is something rejected from which one does not part. (1982:3–4)

There are, perhaps, some people who live their whole lives in this twilight, presymbolic state, a state not of radical, once-and-for-all separation of self from other, but rather a graded continuum of always partial separations. In South Asian society, argues Kristeva, an absolute separation of self from other, self from *mother*, is never established. Instead of this single, radical separation, there occurs a series of multiple, graded, and partial separations – rituals of purification, acts of defilement, the caste hierarchy. The feminine is not foreign, alien, and other: It remains part of one's own. Marriage is endogamous; the boundary between incestuous and proper unions is shifting; and the horror of incest, of being swallowed up again by the mother, is great. Self is divided from other, not absolutely, as subject from object, but relatively, as inside from outside. Self dwelling in the world of nontotal separation is defined in terms of *place* (the physical pressures against the body) more than in terms of *name* (the words used to define the person). It wanders over a territory, never fully detached from this territory, the soil that nurtures it, the earth from which it sprung. The Law of the Father – all totalizing social codes and conventions, all arrangements of the superego, above all, language – never quite displaces the authority of the mother. Language gives a form to and encloses the horror of death, as speech replaces the mother's breast in the mouth – but never quite completely.

The abject is what is left over, what is remaindered. It is what each self leaves behind in order to be whole and live. But in South Asian thought the remainder is also, often enough, the source of new life.

"Here is perhaps the essential point," Kristeva concludes:

> The remainder appears to be co-extensive with the entire architecture of non-totalizing thought. In its view there is nothing that is everything; nothing is exhaustive, there is a residue in every system – in cosmogony, food ritual, and even sacrifice, which deposits, through ashes, for instance, ambivalent remains. A challenge to our monotheistic and monological universes, such a mode of thinking apparently needs the ambivalence of remainder if it is not to become enclosed within *one* single-level symbolics, and thus always posits a non-object as polluting as it is reviving – defilement and genesis. That is why the poet of the *Atharva Veda* extols the defiling and rejuvenating remainder (*uchista*) as precondition for all forms. "Upon remainder the name and the form are founded, upon remainder the world is founded. . . . Being and non-being, both are in the remainder, death, vigor." (1982:76)

My analysis of Cēvi's song is built on the thoughts of Kristeva just outlined. One of the things I wish to show is that Cēvi, being *always* close both to the corpse (because she is a Paṟaiyar) and to the body of the mother (because she is female and Indian),[10] is not fully governed by Language or the Father in the way that we are: She breaks their rules, she makes her own, and she does so systematically. I would suggest that many aspects of Cēvi's style point to an actively detotalizing artistic technique. By calling this technique "detotalizing," I mean that it not only refuses to be bound by any single, internally consistent, authoritatively legislated, holistic set of rules for linguistic behavior, but that it actively sabotages those rules, like a bomber selecting key structures to explode.

Cēvi as an untouchable, a handler of feces and corpses, is more threatened than others by those very powers of horror, the engulfing powers of death and the fear of death, that have been thrust upon her by those others in order that they might live, in order that they might be whole, clean, and intact. She must face this darkness directly and somehow give form to it if she is to give form to herself. But in order to do this, she must shatter the perfect image of the other that the other has created for himself. She must shatter the code. Her voice is not a revolutionary voice, for it does not seek to replace one order with another. Rather, her voice upholds the twilight world, the world of no one order, of no one clear way of seeing, the world of *māya*, of multiplicity, of relative rather than absolute differences, of countless gradations, of remainders.

In performing her hymn to Singammā, Cēvi confronts her own abjection, and as she does so, her voice becomes the voice of abjection that Kristeva describes, "from its place of banishment . . . challenging its master." Singammā is to Cēvi the horror that threatens to swallow her, the corpse from which she, even more than others, cannot part. The goddess of this hymn is, like so many Indian goddesses, the mother of death as well as of birth. In Cēvi's song, her being as corpse is especially strongly emphasized. She is also the excluded, cast out, abject in that sense. She is to Cēvi what Cēvi is to the rest of Indian society, and she is at the same time what all people must exclude from themselves in order to be whole. The terrible dilemma of the untouchable: self-definition. She is not whole, she is fragmented. She is defined in terms of place, above all in terms of within and without, and she is also without a place, wandering. In inscribing the song of Singammā on the tape recorder, Cēvi may give a place to her fears – not only name and form, but an objective locality to her abjection. Like the scription of the author, and (I mean no disrespect here) like that portion of himself that a baby first learns to part with, Cēvi's tape-recorded song is her loving gift to the world beyond her ken.[11] Cēvi's song expresses the state of incomplete separation, the remaindered state, that engenders antitotalizing visions. As she sings she becomes, like the goddess she sings of, a flagrant rule breaker, rejecting and reconstructing languages, making room for something new to grow.

Detotalizing strategies in Cēvi's art

We may speak of events on at least two levels here. On one level are the various themes and events of the story, what the story is *about*. We might call this the "level of the explicit." On another level is the way the story is told, what the story *expresses*. We might call this the "level of the implicit."

On the level of what the story is about, there are numerous discomforting reminders of the nonwholeness of existence, as the song dwells on the themes of death, exile, twilight times, leftover food, and remainders. These themes are mingled with a whole series of violations of Tamil social code: Singammā breaks out of the house against the will of her brothers; she sells her songs at the dried-fish store (fish being a conventional symbol for female genitals); she gathers up polluted rice to take back home; her brothers rape, murder, and dismember her; they bury her in the floor of the house; they build one house on the remains of another.

But I would like to consider here not so much the "what" of Cēvi's story as the "how," precisely those aspects of a tale that we do *not* focus on when we hear it, because they point away from themselves – those aspects that we call "style," that are all the more powerful *because* they are not always subject to the full light of consciousness.

Anomalies of inclusion and exclusion

In Cēvi's performance, on the level of explicit content, the level of focus, a preoccupation with problems of inclusion and exclusion is manifest in the repeated themes of confinement and exile. Simultaneously on the level of nonfocus, on the level of *means* of expression, states of exclusion and inclusion are repeatedly remarked, stumbled over, defied, and commingled.

A key example of this scrambling of the categories of exclusion and inclusion comes in the section describing the caste exclusion of Kuṟa-vars. At the beginning of this section, the song tells how Singammā is punished by her brothers for leaving the house and going to the market. They lock her in the house alone in the forest (stanzas 33–6):

Leaving you within the house, Singammā
All four doors, Singammā, Singammā
They closed and locked and came, Singammā, Singammā.
All four men, Singammā,
All four men, Singammā, Singammā,
Went inside the house, Singammā, Singammā.
And as they went inside the house, Singammā,
The mortar stone pounds, doesn't it, Singammā, Singammā,
The mortar stone pounds, doesn't it, Singammā.
And as the mortar stone pounds, Singammā,
All four doors, Singammā, Singammā,
They pulled shut and locked, Singammā, Singammā.
To them, to all four of them, Singammā,
Singammā could give an answer, couldn't she, Singammā.
In our (excl.) good jāti, Singammā,
In our (excl.) good jāti, Singammā, Singammā,
The sun (sg.) has fallen and gone (pl.),
                              Singammā, Singammā, we (excl.)
In the tāli . . . in the jāti are excluded,
                              Singammā, Singammā.

The first part of this passage, although indirect, strongly implies gang rape of Singammā by her four brothers. The image of incestuous multiple rape is linked to ambiguities concerning inside and outside (are the brothers inside the house where Singammā is confined, or outside it?), concerning coming and going (are the brothers approaching Singammā, or are they withdrawing from her?), concerning desire and repulsion (do the brothers act out of love or hatred?), and concerning open and closed (what is happening to Singammā's body?).

As a whole, the passage seems to point to the link between questions of incest and questions of caste inclusion. (*Jāti* literally means "birth group." It is generally glossed in English as "caste.") The dilemma is simple: To stay within the caste (as well as to abide by the rules of the caste system as a whole), we must marry within our group. But if we marry too closely within our group – or in other words, if we stress *inclusion* too heavily – we will be radically *excluded*: Either we will be driven from our caste, or our caste will be driven from among the body of castes.

Most interesting are the details of person and case in the last few lines. The sun sets *"in* the jāti"; the brothers and their sister are "excluded *in* the jāti." There are ways to express "out of" and "away from" in Tamil, but Cēvi chooses not to use them here. And in the phrases "in *our* good jāti" and *"we* are excluded," the *exclusive* (excluding the listener) rather than the *inclusive* forms of the first person plural are used. If a sister is addressing her brothers regarding "our" caste, it would only make sense for her to use the inclusive form. Although the *topic* of the passage is *exclusion,* the *pronoun* "we" should be *inclusive.* As though to underline this anomaly, two stanzas later, the brothers speaking to the sister use the *inclusive* form of "we" to refer to precisely that body from which the sister has now been *excluded* (stanza 40):

> Because you acted wrongly, Singammā,
> Excluded from our (incl.) jāti, Singammā, Singammā,
> Excluded from the jāti, Singammā, Singammā.

Here it seems as though the ingroup–outgroup ambiguity is striking at the heart of grammar.

One more deviation from the code deserves mention here, for it also points to the link between ambiguities of inclusion and ambiguities of marriage rules. The deviation is actually a slip – a Freudian slip in the strictest sense. Having taken a breath, Cēvi begins a line, "tālilēyum . . ." She then stops abruptly, returns to the beginning of the melodic phrase, and sings, "jātilēyum taḷḷuvaḍi Singammā Singammā." Evidently she has said *tāli* where she meant to say *jāti.* The *tāli* is the marriage necklace that a husband ties around his wife's neck on their wedding day. It is a powerful symbol for Tamils of the bound and confined state of married womanhood. The term *jāti* means 'caste'. The whole line could be translated, "We are excluded from the tāli, (I mean) from the jāti, Singammā." However, in this line, both *tāli* and *jāti* are in the locative case, so that a more literal translation would be, "We are excluded *in* the tāli, *in* the jāti, Singammā." As I have mentioned, there are precise ways of expressing the concept "out of" in Tamil. But in the preceding stanza, Cēvi, for whatever reasons, chooses not to use them, to say "in" when she means "out of." All such evidence considered together suggests that questions of inclusion and exclusion, problems defining what is inside and what is outside, run deep in Cēvi's mind.

On this same level, the level of nonfocus, there is also a scrambling of the categories of singular and plural. This is yet another way in which the concept of totality may be subtly fragmented or, conversely, the concept of fragmentation may be expressed. So Singammā's body becomes plural – plural louse eggs and then plural pieces buried in plural graves. The sun – by whose masculine authority (referred to as such in the song) Singammā is expelled from the caste – also receives a plural marker. The plurality of Singammā's brothers is pluralized; throughout the song, their numbers keep inexplicably changing: sometimes they are four, sometimes five, sometimes seven. And finally, the truth that Singammā speaks when she emerges from her grave is called not *the* truth but "truths," plural.

Remainders and incomplete separations

The detotalizing vision of the person who is subject to abjection, argues Kristeva, is founded upon incomplete separations of all kinds. It is founded upon remainders. No matter how much you try to separate thing A from thing B, other from self, there is always a little bit left over, that sticks on. No system, especially no living system, is hermetically sealed. No single vision can account for everything. Every paradigm has anomalies. All grammars leak.

Cēvi's song expresses, above all else, this state of incomplete separation between self and other, of fertile remainders proliferating new visions and (we would hope) new cultures. The stumbling over the inclusive versus the exclusive "we" is a case in point. "Are you and I separate, or are we together?" this stumbling asks. "Are brother and sister one, or are they not?" A similar relation mediates Cēvi, the singer, the untouchable, and Singammā, the goddess, the mother, the corpse, untouchable to the untouchable, other to a self who is herself other. These two, also, are partly but not fully separated.

In the song, Singammā is "you," Cēvi is "I." Cēvi is the singer, Singammā the topic of her song. But this topic and this singer, this "you" and this "I," are never very far apart. A sense of immediacy runs through every line. This feeling of closeness is produced, first of all, by Cēvi's preferential use of the present tense. In this song of 101 stanzas, 41 are in the present tense, 31 are indefinite or unspecified as to tense, and 29 are in the past tense. The tenses are all mingled. Sometimes we are present, other times inexplicably past.

This feeling of partial presence, of *relative nonseparation* between the singer and the subject of the song, is further strengthened by the singer's directly addressing the subject, calling out the name "Singammā" in every line; by the frequent use of the second person (e.g., stanza 9, "You are going to the Mēlūr Market to sell baubles, Singammā"); and by the equally frequent use of tag questions (e.g., stanza 24, "On the stony ground of Mēlūr, a wedding is taking place, isn't it, Singammā?"). But these are intermingled with references to Singammā in the third person, as though she were absent.

Then there is the device we call "enjambement," which frequently occurs in all varieties of Tamil verbal art and which Cēvi employs very heavily in the hymn to Singammā. Enjambement appears when a metric line (or musical phrase, or set of words uttered in a breath) does not correspond with a grammatical sentence or phrase, so that the first word of a new sentence appears at the end of a metric line and the sentence is completed on the next line. What results is a kind of verbal "remaindering." In the hymn to Singammā, almost always the word that is so remaindered is *nī*, 'you', so that many lines end *Singammā nī . . .* , "Singammā, you . . ." What is predicated of "Singammā you" is left to the next line. Meanwhile this "you" hangs in limbo.

The way the name "Singammā" wanders

However, this detotalizing vision, the principle of the remainder, manifests most strongly not through poetic devices like enjambement, which themselves by now have become almost like grammatical rules, patterned and predictable, but rather through a more troubling, though seemingly simple, thing: the repeated refrain "Singammā," the name cried out once, twice, three or four times at the end of each of the more than 300 lines of the song. The hymn is to and about Singammā; the name cried out is always the same and always (or *almost* always) in the same place – the end of the line. For she is the mother of death. Her musical presence is constant. And yet, from the point of view of *grammar*, Singammā's place in the song is ill-defined. The cry of her name floats through the song like a ghost, its place in the total order of each stanza, its relation to the whole of each sentence, shifting, inconstant, and therefore from point to point difficult to determine. This indeterminacy of the grammatical status of the name "Singammā" affects the narrative structure at crucial spots and fills it with doubt.

As we follow the journey of Singammā, of the *name* "Singammā," through the song, we become lost – *I* became lost – because the degree to which this name is bound to the narrative, and the ways in which it is bound, both vary widely. In the first two stanzas it is clear: Singammā is being addressed by the singer, who is going to narrate to Singammā her own story. "I am going to tell the story of your birth, Singammā," Cēvi sings. But this clear division between singer, topic, and addressee, or more generally between narrative and narrative context, very soon becomes blurred. For instance, when one of the characters speaks in the song, that is, when there is embedded speech, then the refrain "Singammā" becomes ambiguously incorporated into that embedded speech. Then it is no longer direct address, no longer the singer's own word to the goddess, but something removed from both of them.

In other places, Singammā herself speaks, and then the cry of her name seems not, as when Singammā is addressed, embedded in the narrative and thus distanced from the context, but rather the reverse – dislocated from the narrative, an intrusion from the context. For example, consider stanzas 43–44:

> Six o'clock has come, Singammā.
> Six o'clock has come, Singammā, Singammā.
> If my honor is destroyed, Singammā, I too,
> If my honor is destroyed, Singammā, I too
> Must stay inside the house, Singammā, Singammā, I am
> A woman of perfect honor, Singammā, Singammā,
> A woman of perfect honor, Singammā, Singammā, these
> Four doors must open up, Singammā, Singammā.

Here it sounds at first as though the singer is addressing Singammā directly in her own voice, the voice of Cēvi. She seems to be saying, "I, too, must stay confined, Singammā. I, too, am a woman of perfect honor. I, too, am like you." Later it seems that the singer must have intended the words "I, too," to be attributed to Singammā herself, the "I" to refer to her, whereas the cry "Singammā, Singammā" is not included in the speech "I am a woman of perfect honor" but is simply the song's refrain, put there to keep time. Yet this echo of identification between the singer and the heroine of the song remains strong on the level of music, that is, on the level of what one is made to feel, if not on the level of what makes logical sense, throughout the performance. The words "Singammā, I too," are stressed in the song; they *sound* as though they are part of the same pronouncement, uttered by the same voice; and they linger that way in the mind of the hearer.

Elsewhere, Singammā is speaking, addressing her mother, and with the refrain, it seems that she addresses her as "mother, Singammā" – the same pair of terms by which she herself is addressed by her own mother subsequently.

In yet another place (stanza 94), Singammā addresses her lame elder brother and accuses him, saying:

> You are the one who killed me, Singammā,
> The one who saw my sin, Singammā, Singammā,
> The one who undid me, Singammā . . .

In stanzas containing dialogue between two characters, neither of whom is Singammā, the refrain appears completely free-floating, as when the brothers' wives say to the brothers (stanza 51):

> "Your younger sister has been taken away
>   by a husband, Singammā, Singammā . . .

Finally, there are stanzas in which the name "Singammā" becomes split into two forms, one of them tightly bound to the syntax of that particular stanza, the other either attached as a vocative or divorced from the text and free-floating, in stanza 51. For instance (stanzas 33 and 37):

> All four brothers having spoken, Singammā,
> They sent Singammā away, Singammā, Singammā . . .

> To them, to all four of them Singammā,
> Singammā could give an answer, couldn't she, Singammā?

In sum, as one listens to stanza after stanza of the hymn to Singammā, one hears the name "Singammā" sometimes closely incorporated into the syntactic and narrative structure of the song, sometimes loosely incorporated, sometimes unincorporated, and sometimes split into two forms, one incorporated and the other not. In the in-between, loosely incorporated areas, there occur faint, ambiguous, partial identifications between Singammā and others, notably her mother, her brother, and the singer. I would suggest that this way of handling the name in the refrain is not just the consequence of random fluctuations in *parole*, but that it bears meaning. I think that it may say something about the indistinct boundaries between persons in Cēvi's world, about the absence of total separation between self and the substrate of self. It gives us a view from the far side of wholeness, from one who is placeless and always remaindered.

Conclusion

I have tried to show in this chapter how the Tamil untouchable singer Cēvi, not only in her choice of a song to sing but in the very way that she sings it, fragments visions of wholeness, which, like the one brightly burning and unchallenged sun in the hot South Indian sky, govern the world Cēvi lives in, but never quite completely. Cēvi's share of her world is part of that never-quite-completely, the in-between space of defiling though fertile remainders, the substrate from which the soul seeking freedom and purity tries to extract itself, but never quite can. Cēvi speaks from that place of defilement, reminding us in her own way that our wholeness is partial, being bought, as it is, at her expense.

But this is not the end. To do us the service of humbling us is not Cēvi's only aim in singing this song, surely. She also is seeking her own wholeness, I would surmise, for who wants to stay forever in the shit? If she defies the code that excludes her from the best portion of life, this is partly, perhaps, in order that she may create a more happy place for herself.

Cēvi also wants wholeness, we might guess, and so in this song she tries to create it for herself. But she creates her wholeness in a different way from the way prescribed in ancient Indian law books – not by excluding the other, but by embracing her. Singammā the Kuṟatti, abject beyond Cēvi's own abjection, is this other whom Cēvi embraces.

So the song is completed, not in the death and disembodiment that have been its themes throughout, but in the new and fully embodied life of this embrace. It ends with Singammā resurrected and having a place, a palace, a home of her own. It ends with her standing up straight and beautiful in the daylight.

To form a word around death is to get a hold on it. To cry out "mā" is to put the lost mother back in the mouth. I think that for Cēvi, to give Singammā a song and to put this song on the tape recorder is rather like giving her a building, giving her a shrine, giving her a sound and strong body, so that she is not a corpse or a shade any longer. And singing this song for her, making her story public, is rather like setting her free, letting her stand up straight again in the light and the open air, where everyone can see and admire her.

Notes

1. There is an unresolved debate concerning the degree to which South In-
    dian untouchables accept the principle of caste hierarchy. Berreman (1971),
    Mencher (1974), and Gough (1973) argue that untouchables subscribe to an
    essentially egalitarian ideology. Moffatt (1979) points out that Tamil un-
    touchables replicate the caste hierarchy among themselves; therefore, they
    must subscribe to its principles. In previous publications (1986, 1988), I
    have tried to show that the verbal art of Tamil untouchables does covertly
    challenge some of the principles of caste hierarchy. Many of the songs of
    untouchables show strong ambivalence both toward the singers' status in
    the community and toward their own status as persons.
2. For want of space, I am not able to include in this chapter the details of
    Cēvi's autobiography, which she provided some time after she performed
    the song of Singammā for me. In another publication (Trawick in press), I
    discuss this autobiography, which manifests many of the same preoccu-
    pations that are expressed in the song.
3. See Moffatt (1979) and McGilvray (1983) on the relationship between Ku-
    ṟavars, Kuruvikkāraṅka, and Paṟaiyars in Tamil and Sri Lankan society.
4. Cēvi's song was recorded as part of a project on Tamil articulations of love
    (*anpu*) and related sentiments. The project included open-ended, tape-
    recorded interviews with about 100 people in Cēvi's village, together with
    recordings of songs sung by those same people.
5. The absence of any obvious figurative language in the hymn to Singammā
    is notable, since most Tamil poetry, both oral and written, is florid with
    metaphor, internal parallelism, and other forms of ornamentation.
6. For example, Dumont (1970), Harper (1964), Khare (1976).
7. Kristeva cites as her ethnological and Indological sources Georges Bataille,
    Mary Douglas, V. S. Naipaul, Louis Dumont, Charles Malamoud, K. Mad-
    dock, Kathleen Gough, Murray Emeneau, S. Lindenbaum, and Célestin
    Bouglé. In her discussion of purity and pollution in India, she relies most
    heavily on Dumont (1970), Bouglé (1969), and Douglas (1969).
8. As a feminist, Kristeva is in the school of Simone de Beauvoir; her psycho-
    analytic training comes from Jacques Lacan; she was trained in semiotic
    and literary studies by Roland Barthes.
9. Ashis Nandy (1983) makes a very similar point concerning the relation be-
    tween colonizer and colonized.
10. Much has been written about how Indian *men* feel (or might be surmised
    to feel) about their mothers, but not much has been written about how
    Indian *women* feel about their mothers. So it is hard to cite authorities on
    this matter. Regarding the great stress in South Asia on the body of the
    mother (or woman in general) as the origin of life and death, we may cite
    the work of Carstairs (1957), Kakar (1981), Yalman (1963), and Hart (1973).
    Regarding the sense of connectedness between mother and daughter in
    India, some information is given by Beck (1982), Shulman (1980), and Tra-
    wick (1986, 1990).
11. See Derrida (1974) on scription as spoor.

References

Beck, Brenda. 1982. *The Three Twins: The Telling of a South Indian Folk Epic*. Bloomington: Indiana University Press.

Berreman, Gerald. 1971. The Brahmanical View of Caste. *Contributions to Indian Sociology* (n.s.) 5:16–23.

Bouglé, Célestin. 1969. *Essai sur le regime des castes*. Paris: Presses Universitaires de France.

Carstairs, G. Morris. 1957. *The Twice-Born*. London: Hogarth Press.

Derrida, Jacques. 1974. *Of Grammatology*. Gayatri Spivak, trans. Baltimore: Johns Hopkins University Press.

Douglas, Mary. 1969. *Purity and Danger*. London: Routledge & Kegan Paul.

Dumont, Louis. 1970. *Homo Hierarchicus: An Essay on the Caste System*. Chicago: University of Chicago Press.

Gough, Kathleen. 1973. Harijans in Thanjavur. In K. Gough and H. P. Sharma, eds., *Imperialism and Revolution in South Asia*. New York: Monthly Review Press, pp. 222–45.

Harper, Edward. 1964. Ritual Pollution as an Integrator of Caste and Religion. *Journal of Asian Studies* 2:151–97.

Hart, George. 1973. Women and the Sacred in Ancient Tamilnad. *Journal of Asian Studies* 32:233–50.

Kakar, Sudhir. 1981. *The Inner World: A Psycho-Analytic Study of Childhood and Society in India*. Delhi: Oxford University Press.

Khare, Ravindra S. 1976. *The Hindu Hearth and Home*. New Delhi: Vikas Publishing House.

Kristeva, Julia. 1982. *Powers of Horror: An Essay on Abjection*. Leon Roudiez, trans. New York: Columbia University Press.

McGilvray, Dennis. 1983. Paraiyar Drummers of Sri Lanka: Consensus and Constraint in an Untouchable Caste. *American Ethnologist* 10:97–115.

Mencher, Joan. 1974. The Caste System Upside Down, or the Not-So-Mysterious East. *Current Anthropology* 15:469–93.

Moffatt, Michael. 1979. *An Untouchable Community in South India: Structure and Consensus*. Princeton: Princeton University Press.

Nandy, Ashis. 1983. *The Intimate Enemy: Loss and Recovery of Self Under Colonialism*. Delhi: Oxford University Press.

Shulman, David. 1980. *Tamil Temple Myths: Sacrifice and Divine Marriage in the South Indian Saiva Tradition*. Princeton: Princeton University Press.

Trawick (Egnor), Margaret. 1982. The Changed Mother. *Contributions to Asian Studies* 18:24–45.

    1986. Iconicity in Paraiyar Crying Songs. In A. K. Ramanujan and S. Blackburn, eds., *Another Harmony: New Essays on the Folklore of India*. Berkeley: University of California Press, pp. 294–344.

    1988. Spirits and Voices in Tamil Songs. *American Ethnologist* 15:193–215.

    1990. Desire in Kinship. In *Notes on Love in a Tamil Family*. Berkeley and Los Angeles: University of California Press.

    In press. Wandering Lost: A Landless Laborer's Sense of Place and Self. In Arjun Appadurai, Frank Korom, Margaret Mills, eds., *Tale, Text and Time: Interpreting South Asian Expressive Traditions*. Philadelphia: University of Pennsylvania Press.

Yalman, Nur. 1963. On the Purity and Sexuality of Women in the Castes of Ceylon and Malabar. *Journal of the Royal Anthropological Institute* 93:25–58.

Index

Attachment, 2, 81–2
Attribution of emotion, 47–8, 60,
154–5
and personalization, 85
of "sadness" and "shame" among
A'ara, 56–66
see also Language; Personality
Audiences
for emotion talk, 71, 73–7, 87–9,
105–10
for emotional performance, 114–17
as interpreters, 115
and rank and register, 138–9
Authenticity, 107, 114, 155–6
and creation of shared emotions,
106–7
of emotional expression, 105–
10
see also Sincerity
Awlad 'Ali Bedouins, 15, 24, 28–44
and discourses on "love," (*hasham*),
30–7
and gender relations, 30–2
and good person (*tahashams*), 32
and institution of *mijla's*, 43
and love poetry (*ghinnawa*), 28–44
political economy of, 38
and sentiment, cultural construction of, 30
and sexual propriety, 33–5
social order of, 33–4
weddings of, 39

Babb, L., 94
Babchuk, W., 80
Bailey, F., 49
Baining (New Britain)
emotional discourse of, 14
Bakhtin, M., 19, 128
Bales, R., 75–82
Bali, 3
Barthes, R., 205
Basso, E., 10
Bataille, G., 205
Bauman, R., 116, 118
Beach, K., 88
Beauvoir, S. de, 203
Beck, B., 205
Beebe-Center, J., 5
Beeman, W., 126, 127
Begging in India, 100–2, 108–9
Bellah, R., 78

Berreman, G., 205
Besnier, N., 114, 120
Bharati, A., 96
Bhatgaon, Fiji, 14, 17, 113, 116–24,
152
Bienenfeld, P., 88
Birnbaum, D. A., 81
Bloomfield, L., 126
Body
disorders of, and emotion, 87
in emotion, 12–13, 26, 87, 92–3
of mother and abjection, 193–5
and "three bodies" of emotion, 20
of women and labor pain, 89
and women's emotion, 79–81
"Body hexis," 12–13
Bougle, C., 205
Bourdieu, P., 12, 92
Bourne, E., 172–5, 177–9, 180, 184
Bowlby, J., 81–2
Breckenridge, C., 104
Brenneis, D., 10, 17, 56, 73, 106, 116,
122–3, 127, 130, 152
Briggs, J., 3, 48
Burrow, T., 96

Camara, S., 159
Cancian, F., 5, 74
Carroll, A., 88
Carstairs, G., 205
Caste hierarchy
Hindu, 191, 205
and principle of exclusion/inclu-
sion, 197–8
and principle of pollution and rit-
ual avoidance, 189
Wolof, and register differences,
131–59
Chewong (Malaysia), 4
Chodorow, N., 75, 82
Chomsky, N., 126
Cognitive anthropology, 19, 25, 88,
162–83
critique of, 162–85
Cohen, R., 96
Collier, J., 34
Colonialism
and fear, 14, 77
and self, 205
Comaroff, J., 19
Communication of emotion
nonverbal and paralinguistic, 127

Emotion (*cont.*)
  as embedded in social relations,
    27
  and evocation vs. expression, 117
  and experience, 113
  expression of, 49–50, 80, 114
  function of, in mediating social ac-
    tion, 47
  as gesture in Bhatgaon, 118
  Hindi terms for, 118
  "hypercognized" vs. "hypocog-
    nized," 120–1, 123
  as idiom, 4, 6, 11, 14–15, 51, 113,
    115
  as interactive phenomena, 10–11,
    115
  as judgment, 11
  linguists' preconceptions of, 126
  as performance, 47
  phenomenology of, 100
  as political statements, 43
  and power, 2, 5–6, 13–15, 28, 30,
    78, 88
  as psychic "energy," 3
  as rhetoric, 49, 60, 62, 115
  schemas of, 47–8
  shared and individualized, 119
  and social action, 27–8, 130–1
  social contexts of, 65
  and social relations, 27, 65
  and state, 5, 6
  theories of, 46
  and words, 65, 85, 114, 169–71,
    181–3, 185
  see also Discourse; Morality and
    emotions; West
Emotion talk
  as creation of social reality, 57
  evocative power of, 66
  and moral evaluation, 57–64
  see also Discourse; Language
Emotion words
  as agentive, 171
  glossary approach to, 166
  see also Focal emotion terms
Emotional communion, 109–10
Emotional control
  in American rhetoric, 16, 70–83,
    87–8
  in anger, 119
  in Wolof discourse, 133–5
Emotional expression, 105, 114

and conventions, 157
facial, 80
lexical vs. nonlexical approaches
  to, 184–5
in linguistic structure, 127
sex differences in recognition of facial, 78
Emotional idiom, 115
  indirect quality of, 51
Emotionality
  created by power, 87
  cultural construction of, 4
  expression and differences in, 153
  and female, 80
  of female as product of evolution,
    80
  and premenstrual syndrome, 79
  and sexuality, 6, 72, 87
  of Wolof griots, 133–5
  and women, 71, 77–8, 80–3
Enthusiasm among Wolof, 148–9
Epstein, A., 66
Errington, J., 129, 157
Ervin-Tripp, S., 129
Essentialism, 72, 74
  in emotion study, 1–3, 162–85
Ethnocentrism of scientific and ordinary discourses of emotion, 25
Ethnography of Communication, 41,
  114
Ethnopsychology, 26
  embedded in ethnographer's lin-
    guistic practice, 180
  and knowledge, 65
  as vocabulary of emotion, 167, 180
  see also West and discourses on
    self
Etiology of emotion, 85–6
Euro-American emotional life, 20, 25,
  41, 43, 182
  and the state, 5, 152
  see also West
Evil eye
  as culturally organized expression
    of envy, 100
  dangers of, 99, 100, 102, 107
Evolution
  and gender differences, 82
  and women and mother love,
    80
Explicit vs. implicit levels of meaning, 197

Morphology and syntax of register,
140
Motherhood
and emotions ascribed to maternal
virtue, 78, 81–2
Kristeva's view of, 194–5, 205
Myers, F., 3–4, 26, 27, 42, 48, 56,
113, 114, 130

Naipaul, V. S., 205
Nandy, A., 205
Narayan, K., 111
Negation and personality, 86
nervois, 14
Nietzsche, F., 27
Normalization, 19
Nosanchuk, T., 81
Nukulaelae (Micronesia), 120

Obeyesekere, G., 4
Ochs, E., 10, 120, 127, 152, 156
Oppositional uses of emotional rhet-
oric, 77, 89
Oriyas, 173, 177, 178–9
Orthopraxy, Hindu, 189
Osgood, C., 114

Pacific and emotion, 66, 113
Parsons, T., 75, 82
"Participation structure," 121
Patriarchy, 77
Peirce, C., 193
Performance
and coherence and force in emo-
tion, 63
see also Audience
Person, cultural images of, 128
Personality, 93
Orissan and American views of,
172
Personalization of emotion, 83–7
Peter, S., 32
Philips, S., 121
Phonology and differences in regis-
ter, 136–7
Pintupi, 4
Playfulness (*tamashabhaw*) in Bhat-
gaon, 118–19, 121
Pocock, D., 100
Poedjosoedarmo, S., 129
Poetics, and aesthetics and "ethno-
poetics," 106–10, 116–19, 196–
201

Poetry
Bedouin, 29, 36–7
as ethnic symbol in Indian aesthetics, 94, 106
"oppositional," as political, 36
Tamil oral, 186, 195
Wolof oral narrative, 134
Politics of emotion discourse, 15, 30,
78–81
Pollution
associated with "fear," 191–2, 195
avoidance of, 189–90
Poole, F., 48
Postmodernism and discourse, 8
Poststructuralism, 7–9, 65
Power
and creation of emotionality, 87
and emotion discourse, 10, 14, 28,
41, 70, 78
and emotional practice, 20
and status differences, 14
Pragmatics, 11, 41, 65
conversational, 179
of praise, 95, 106
and presumptions of emotion in
Indian poetics, 106–7
Praise
as adoration and appraisal, 102
in begging, 101–2
constraints on, 99–100
and creation of "communities of
sentiment," 94, 107
and cultural construction of reputation, 98
and dependence, 97–102
emotional authenticity of, 106
English etymology of, 111
and envy/anger, 110
as formulaic and hyperbolic, 94
functions of, 95
and hierarchy and dependence, 97
in Hindu India, 94–111
modes of, 94, 102, 103–5
and politics of everyday life, 110
as reputation building, 98
as ritual of worship, 94–9
and self, 106
and sexual modesty, 100
as strategy of circumlocution, 98
of things, 104–5
Vedic and everyday, 96
in Wolof, 144

Sexuality (*cont.*)
   and emotionality, 72
   and emotions, 34–5, 72, 143
   and language, 192
   Western discourses on, 6, 20, 72, 87
Shame
   A'ara, 50, 59–60, 63, 66
   attribution of, 60–1
   Fulani, 4
Sherzer, J., 8
Shibamoto, J., 87
Shields, S., 5, 74, 80–1
Shimanoff, S., 86, 89
Shulman, D., 205
Shweder, R., 126, 172, 175, 177, 179, 180, 184
Silla, O., 158
Silver, M., 10
Silverstein, M., 181
Sincerity
   of emotions, 114, 116
   and hypocrisy, 157
   see Authenticity
Singing style
   as detotalizing, 196
   and emotion, 187
Slavery, 155, 159
Smith-Rosenberg, C., 89
Sociability and emotion discourse, 13–14
Social aesthetics
   in Bhatgaon, 116, 117–19
   and link to ethnopsychology, 116
   see also Aesthetics; Poetics
Social change, 89
   among A'ara, 52
   among Bedouins, 28, 37
   and gender and emotions, 87
Social cohesion, 14
Social hierarchy
   and emotion, 4
   and styles of speaking, 131
   Wolof, 132–5
   See also Caste hierarchy; Power
Social structure and emotion
   among Bedouins, 33–4
   and emotion in Bhatgaon, 122
   and emotional control of rhetoric, 73
   among Swat Pukhtun (Pakistan), 2
   among Wolof, 132–5, 159

Socialization and models of emotion, 81, 88
Sociolinguistics, 41
   and discourse theory, 8, 11
   and emotion, 27
   and registers, 126–34, 152
Solomon, R., 11
Solomon Islands, 15, 46, 52
Song of South Indian woman, 18, 186–205
Sontag, S., 5
South India, 18, 95, 100, 186–7, 189, 204
   and music, 186–87
   and poetry, 94
Spiro, M., 3
Sri Lanka, 4, 205
Stankiewicz, E., 126
Stearns, C., 5
Stearns, P., 5
Stoler, A., 14, 77
Strathern M., 53, 77
Structuralism, 183
Structure and event: dialectic of, in emotion discourse, 64
   as emotion discourse, 47
Subjectivity and subjection, 19
Sullivan, W., 78
Syntactic analysis of emotion discourse, 70, 83–7
   see also Grammaticality

Tamil, 94, 96, 103, 186–206
   and oral poetry and song, 186, 201, 205
   social code of, 197
   and untouchables, 186, 204–5
   see also Authenticity; Caste hierarchy; Poetry; Pollution; South India
Taussig, M., 14, 77
Tedlock, D., 8
Temperament, 133
Tense and personalization, 85
Thompson, R., 80
Totality, symbolic concept of, in meaning system, 193, 200
Totalization and language, 193
Trawick, M., 15, 18, 89, 186–206
Trukese, 66

Unconscious, 87
   and emotion discourse, 64